Layered Urbanisms

Gregg Pasquarelli
Versioning—6.0

Galia Solomonoff
Brooklyn Civic Space

Mario Gooden
Global Topologies

Edited by Nina Rappaport and
Julia Stanat with Erin Carraher
and Christopher Yost

Louis I. Kahn Visiting
Assistant Professorship

Yale School of Architecture

Yale School of Architecture
180 York Street
New Haven, Connecticut 06520
www.architecture.yale.edu

Distributed by
W. W. Norton & Company Inc.
500 Fifth Avenue
New York, New York 10110
www.wwnorton.com

This book was made possible through an endowment
for the Louis I. Kahn Visiting Assistant Professorship
at the Yale School of Architecture. It is the first in a
series of publications of the Louis I. Kahn Assistant
Professorship published through the dean's office.

Editor: Nina Rappaport, with Julia Stanat

Design: mgmt. design

Library of Congress Cataloging-in-Publication Data

Layered Urbanisms / Gregg Pasquarelli, Galia
Solomonoff, Mario Gooden

p. cm. -- (Louis I. Kahn visiting assistant
professorship ; v. 1)

ISBN 978-0-393-73250-4 (pbk.)

1. City planning. I. Pasquarelli, Gregg.
II. Solomonoff, Galia. III. Gooden, Mario.
IV. Rappaport, Nina. V. Stanat, Julia.

NA9031.L345 2007
711'.4--dc22
2007041565

Contents

PREFACE

The Louis I. Kahn Visiting Assistant Professorship chair at the Yale School of Architecture was established in 2004 by a contribution to the school to bring the voices of younger, emerging architects into the advanced design studios and seminars. By exposing students to innovative views on architectural practice, design, and urbanism, they are inspired with new perspectives and approaches to design. This book, *Layered Urbanisms,* documents the work of this chairmanship's first three studios, led by Gregg Pasquarelli of SHoP Architects, Galia Solomonoff of Solomonoff Architecture Studio, and Mario Gooden of Huff + Gooden Architects, respectively.

Layered Urbanisms first profiles each visiting architect through an interview and descriptions of their own practice, and then it presents the studio problem in a short brief; the student work and excerpts from the studio discussions, that follow respond to and interpret that brief. Each studio investigated a specific issue involved in design and urban planning in New York City. This book is thematically organized around the design ideas that evolved from each studio. Some student projects occupy multiple themes, while others are more focused. The themes provide the reader with a window into the dialogue between the students and professors in their particular approaches to resolving the assigned problem.

The Pasquarelli studio, "Versioning— 6.0," examined New York City zoning laws, public spaces, techniques of construction with fabrication technology, and ideas of versioning. It focused on four themes: Code Evaluation and Rewriting, Formal Language and Mechanics, Reinterpreting Density, and Structure and Tectonics. These themes proved critical in improving the quality of privately owned public spaces, or PoPS, without sacrificing the needs of the developer's bottom line. Each team of students, either by using structural code revisions or formal means, devised a solution for the problem that redefined the design and use of PoPS.

The Solomonoff studio, "Brooklyn Civic Space," investigated the roles of the developer, architect, and the community in urban design at the Atlantic Yards site, in Brooklyn. The students were faced with a real site and project in New York that continues today to be contested on multiple platforms. In developing multifaceted projects, the students investigated the issues of scale, profitability, and community integration. The themes that were identified include Morphological Play, Publicness, Downtown Suburbia, and Beyond Now. The projects were as diverse as the problems themselves and showed ingenuity in balancing large program requirements with the need for green space in the community.

The Gooden studio, "Global Topologies," was concerned with the influence of globalization and the threat of terrorism on urban design, specifically at the United Nations complex, in New York. In dealing with issues of conflict and security, the studio projects were categorized into the themes Mediation, Subversion, Negotiation, and Observation, following the political processes that were used to solve the problems. The students, working on the United Nations Plaza site, addressed issues concerning edge conditions, the recontextualization of security equipment, and the integration of surveillance methods into the existing UN complex.

The work of these three practitioners, as represented by their Yale studios, exemplifies new directions in urban design from an architectural perspective, engaging many layers of the city and the insertions therein. Animating space with media, art, and multiple layers of activities, students dug into and around the city itself to find unexplored, unused areas of occupation and ways to provide public space and amenities. From the understanding of the developer's role and the use of the city-mandated floor-area ratio, or FAR, for the allocation of public space to the invasion of normally controlled and secured sites and the bridging over of infrastructures to create residential spaces, these architects pushed the students into uncharted territories. While functioning at both the global and local levels, the work goes beyond urban utopias to a pragmatism that uses regulations and programmatic requirements to make cities more livable.

Because of the breadth of the work and scope of ideas concentrated here, this book required the assistance of many people. The editors would like to thank Gregg Pasquarelli, Galia Solomonoff, and Mario Gooden, for their reviews of the text and images, as well as all the students who submitted their work. For the Pasquarelli studio, the editors would like to thank the student editors Sal Wilson and Erin Carraher, as well as participants Ezra Groskin, Ken Gowland, Brendan Lee, Spencer Luckey, Yong Mei, Edward Richardson, Brady Stone, Stephen Van Dyck, Yang Yang, Esin Yurekli, and Damian Zunino. For the Solomonoff studio, we would like to thank participants Mathew Ford, James Fullton, Matt Hutchinson, Aniket Shahane, Noah Shepherd, Brett Spearman, and Tracy Yu. For the Gooden studio, we would like to thank student editors Chris Yost and Yen-Rong Chen, as well as participants Ruth Gyuse, Diala Hanna, Derek Hoeferlin, Lee Lim, Aniket Shahane, Noah Shepherd, and Vanessa Ruff. We extend our utmost appreciation to mgmt. design; David Delp, copy editor; Nancy Green of W. W. Norton Press, our distributor, and Dean Robert A. M. Stern, for whose guidance we are grateful.

— Nina Rappaport and Julia Stanat, editors

INTRODUCTION

In 2004 the Yale School of Architecture inaugurated a new chairmanship, the Louis I. Kahn Visiting Assistant Professorship of Architecture. The Kahn endowment was the gift of an anonymous donor with the express purpose of bringing young practitioner-educators to the school to teach an advanced studio and seminar for a term. The Kahn Visiting Assistant Professorship beautifully compliments the school's other endowed visiting professorships, which have traditionally brought more established teacher-practitioners to the school. Included in the gift was the expectation that the work of the visitors and their students would be published so that others could benefit from the ideas exchanged. *Layered Urbanisms* is the inaugural volume of the book series fulfilling that promise.

Louis I. Kahn (1901–1974), perhaps the greatest American architect of the post-World War II era, was closely associated with Yale as a teacher and practicing architect. Yale is home to his first important building, the Art Gallery (1951–53), and his last, the Yale Center for British Art (1973–77). Kahn was fresh to teaching when he came to Yale in 1947 to begin what would be ten years as chief critic in the department of architecture. As a teacher he worked closely with students, pushing them to be unconventional and encouraging them to go beyond their initial ideas. He inspired a generation of architects, leading them to new solutions that became the basis of their independent work.

In 1999, with gifts from former Yale students and friends, the Louis I. Kahn Visiting Professorship was inaugurated. Daniel Libeskind was the first incumbent; Tod Williams, Billie Tsien, and Frank Gehry have subsequently been Kahn professors, and the current occupant of the chair is Peter D. Eisenman.

The Louis I. Kahn Visiting Assistant Professorship is Yale's second endowed chair to honor Kahn. As of this writing, seven architects have been chosen to occupy this chair.

The inaugural Louis I. Kahn Visiting Assistant Professor was Gregg Pasquarelli, who offered the studio "Versioning—6.0." I first got to know Gregg in the early 1990s when he was a student at Columbia, where he studied after receiving a bachelor's of science degree from the business school at Villanova University. From our first encounter, I realized he was a force to be reckoned with—a young talent with a sure sense of himself and of the new possibilities opening up in architecture, not only in its relationship to craft but also to commerce. After receiving the master's of architecture degree from Columbia in 1994, Gregg worked as a designer and a project and site architect in the office of Greg Lynn/FORM before co-founding the firm SHoP in 1996, a partnership that quickly established itself as a leader among the new generation of architects, exploring advanced digital fabrication techniques as a way to generate and realize bold designs.

In a few short years SHoP has grown to a seventy-person practice located in Lower Manhattan, with a varied repertoire that ranges from master plans to buildings for commercial and public clients. The firm's work has been exhibited internationally, including the 2004 and 2006 editions of the Venice Biennale of Architecture in the American Pavilion. As Louis I. Kahn Visiting Assistant Professor, Gregg proved himself to be an exceptional teacher and in fall 2006 he returned to Yale as the Eero Saarinen Visiting Professor.

Galia Solomonoff was the second person to be appointed to the Louis I. Kahn Visiting Assistant Professorship. Galia's studio, "Brooklyn Civic Spaces," very provocatively took on

the planning of the Atlantic Yards in Brooklyn. Galia attended the National University of Rosario School of Architecture in her native Argentina before coming to New York to complete undergraduate training, receiving her bachelor's of science in architecture from City College and then going on to graduate study at Columbia University, where I had the pleasure to meet her and where she made evident her capacity for bold, clear architectural thought. Galia received her master's of architecture from Columbia in 1994, where she received the McKim Prize and the William Kinne Fellows Traveling Prize.

After working for several different firms including OMA/Rem Koolhaas, Galia, then a teacher at Columbia, established in 1999 her partnership with Alan Koch, Lyn Rice, and Linda Taalman, practicing together as Open-Office. Selected as an "Emerging Voice" by the Architectural League in April 2002, OpenOffice was included in *Architectural Record's* "Design Vanguard" selection in September 2003. In 2004, Galia established her own firm, Solomonoff Architecture Studio, and continues to work in New York.

An outstanding talent as an architect and teacher, Mario Gooden, the third Louis I. Kahn Visiting Assistant Professor, offered a studio, "Global Topologies," which applied global security topologies to the requirements of the United Nations complex in New York. I first met Mario when he was a student at Columbia, where he received his master's of architecture in 1990. Mario was the top student in his class, garnering the McKim Prize, Columbia's highest award for design excellence.

After Columbia, Gooden joined the firm of Ray Huff, in Charleston, South Carolina, and in 1996 the firm was restructured as Huff + Gooden Architects. Mario is not only an active practitioner but also a widely sought-after teacher.

From 1993 to 2001 he was assistant professor at the University of Florida where, in 1996, he was recognized as Teacher of the Year. In 1998, he was the graduate thesis adviser at Southern California Institute of Architects; in 1999, he was distinguished visiting critic at the University of Arizona, Tucson; and beginning in 2001, he was visiting assistant professor at Columbia for three consecutive fall terms. In 2001, he was selected as an "Emerging Voice" by the Architectural League of New York. In fall 2006, after his highly successful term as the Louis I. Kahn Visiting Assistant Professor, Gooden joined the Yale faculty as critic in architecture.

In its brief history, the Louis I. Kahn Visiting Assistant Professorship has already proven invaluable to the culture of our school, invigorating our advanced studios and seminar rooms with fresh ideas on timely subjects. The measure of its contribution can be seen in the student work included in this book. As the program continues, the school is guaranteed a continuing flow of young practitioner-teachers who will bring to New Haven new concepts and techniques that address the complex issues and challenges of contemporary architecture. The work of these subsequent studios will be published in turn.

I would like to thank the first three Kahn Visiting Assistant Professors for their engagement with the School of Architecture and for helping to make this joint volume of their work possible. I would also like to thank the book's production team led by Nina Rappaport, publications director; Julia Stanat ('05) of the Solomonoff studio; Erin Carraher ('04) of the Pasquarelli studio; and Christopher Yost ('05) of the Gooden studio.

—Robert A. M. Stern, dean
J. M. Hoppin Professor of Architecture
December 2007

Gregg Pasquarelli

Galia Solomonoff

Mario Gooden

Gregg Pasquarelli is a partner at SHoP Architects with William Sharples, Chris Sharples, Corie Sharples, and Kimberly Holden, in New York. Pasquarelli received a bachelor's of science from The School of Business at Villanova University and a master's of architecture from Columbia University, where he graduated with honors for excellence in design. Following graduation, he was a designer, project manager, and site architect for the office of Greg Lynn FORM and worked on the Korean Presbyterian Church, in Queens. He serves on the board of directors of the Architectural League of New York and is a Young Leader Fellow of the National Committee of U.S.-China relations. In this discussion with Nina Rappaport about his firm's approach to design and development, he is joined by William Sharples.

Nina Rappaport: SHoP has become an architecture practice that not only designs and fabricates structures but also finances structures, which gives it more control over its work as well as involvement. How are you part of development projects as well as the design team?

Gregg Pasquarelli: Our interest in development is about having a certain amount of control. But it is even more about believing in your product and standing by the ideas behind the design, both conceptually and financially. I don't think we are interested in spending other people's money to create images; we are interested in developing new relationships of practice. Working with Jeff Brown as a client and partner on Porter House was the ideal situation. In the Porter House marketing brochure it says that we are architects who think like developers, and he is a developer who thinks like an architect. It is that kind of integration that gives you the opportunity to make better buildings.

We worked on it together from the beginning. We sat down and sketched an idea on a napkin at the corner diner. This is how we approached the building. We did the pro forma together, continually rethinking different financial and building structures and observed the impact each decision had on another.

NR: What drives your design ideas, especially for a project like this? Do you begin with a design concept, or is your work driven by technology, with an emphasis more on the process and the problem-solving than the aesthetics?

GP: As the designer we make a gesture with the big idea of how we want to solve the problem, but there is never an aesthetic or stylistic agenda. I believe one scripts one's own obsolescence by being stylistic. We never want to have a Blue Period; there should be blue buildings and other buildings. We are concerned with what a project demands at a point in time with the new, emergent technologies—that was what brought the five of us at SHoP together. It was never about, let's do deconstructivism or modernism or historicism. We really like problem-solving in new ways, but at the same time we respect space, light, materials, and construction.

In school we could never understand why architects were being reduced to producing what the latest image was rather than really thinking about how to problem-solve. On the one hand that not only included the design and aesthetics but also the way that buildings engaged the city, engaged in technology, engaged in culture. This led us toward performance-based design, looking at design that was really about understanding the kind of nuance between physical form and effect. We found the two places where that was really best achieved were the aerospace industry and the automotive industry. There, the computer became a really important tool not because it could make great-looking images, not because it could make double-curving surfaces with great textures on them, but because it

could help incorporate difference and begin to really get an understanding of what the differences meant as a kind of effect. The result was often a complex form—it was usually very expensive to build—but then we used the technology on a second level to look at how we could build with it so we could keep the construction costs at a standard level. It was never about the form; it was always about how a project was made and how it performed that really mattered to us the most.

NR: How does development of a project then contribute to the design process for a building in terms of constraints and freedoms?

GP: It is a theory of practice that relies on problem-solving, making, and having an effect. Porter House really changed the way we were thinking about things. We decided to try to exchange our design, technology, and marketing knowledge—and the ability to produce more architecture for the same price—for equity positions in our buildings. There are a few buildings that we are part owners in now, but it is about the ability to change the way of doing things, the ability to try and push the design, to try and push the kind of financial model architects work in—but more importantly it's about the change in the relationship between ourselves and our clients. As soon as our clients knew that we had skin in the game, they stopped questioning our designs. When we were just for hire, we would show many ideas and they would become suspect that we were trying to spend money to build an edifice for ourselves. When they realized we would lose if the design didn't work and that we would make more money if the design was good, they suddenly trusted us. We got a tremendous amount of freedom to design in return.

NR: How do your investigations into new technologies and uses of mass customization, for example, transform your work and the ability to use prefabricated elements for large-scale projects?

William Sharples: Prefabrication can be about understanding the parameters of a system in which we know what materials we need and how we can assemble them but use them for only one job. In the end we have less overhead to create standardization, and with mass customization we can do it differently on every project. Some people have asked if we are going to patent the procedures, but then you have to control the environment in which the product is built. We are not interested in that or in being a design-build firm.

GP: The construction process changes both the design and the financial model, which accomplishes three things: one, we are able to build the building for slightly less, so we can outbid our competitors for the property; two, it gives us a higher-quality product because we can use better materials and have a more customized, highly specific design.

WS: Three is the schedule, which is tied to the bank that is doing the financing. If we can reduce that schedule, we can save money on interest expenses, which have a larger downside risk than construction. Time is as important as details.

NR: How are your projects similar or different according to site and context? How do they perform aesthetically?

GP: Our work is not about traditional notions of street, wall, volume, setbacks, and aesthetics but about occupying a site and space, changing the rules of occupying the space, and thinking about the operative nature of the way architecture engages the city and negotiates a new building.

All techniques have a certain look. A soufflé has to be vertical and puffy, but it doesn't mean it is about image representation—that because it looks like a soufflé it must taste like a good

soufflé or that because you are eating a soufflé you must be in an expensive restaurant. It is not about image; it is about content and execution.

The aesthetic matters; we are designers, so we pick things that we like, but we don't have a catalog of elements that we compose on an elevation. The elevation is the most worthless drawing in architecture; it doesn't solve problems spatially. You need to think three-dimensionally and procedurally at the same time.

WS: We always refer back to Renaissance master-builders and the way they built models, which we do but with virtual problem-solving models. We are looking at the level of detail and tectonics in the three-dimensional realm. There is a false sense of security when you bring it into plan, section, and elevation that you have solved something, but you haven't solved anything.

GP: It really became about questioning the notion of plan, section, and elevation as the proper way to draw: were these the best methods architecture could use in order to deal with the issue that is a complicated three-dimensional idea? So we convert it into a two-dimensional abstract drawing system and hand it to somebody else to then re-create, not only into three dimensions but four dimensions, with time and process of assembly. For the several differentiated bricks of Brunelleschi's dome or three pieces of mass-customized zinc out of the 4,000 pieces that went into a building like the Porter House, we really started to see that this did not eliminate the architect from really being engaged but actually returned us closer to the period of the master-builder.

NR: How do you actually teach this technique, procedure, and problem-solving process?

GP: Students have to design and fabricate one model a week, and we don't care whether it is the ugliest project

when they are finished, as long as they have developed a consistent logic to argue and fabricate it simultaneously. It is a matter of being willing to learn a completely other way of thinking where there are ideas of simultaneity between concept and production. And like any good Newtonian, as far as you stretch in one direction, you must balance it in the other direction and hold on tighter. The more we experiment with a new kind of form and problem-solving, the more we need to hold on to how it gets puts together and what the financial parameters are. This is when we think architecture gets interesting.

NR: How have you worked with integrating sustainable issues and structural issues into more holistic buildings?

GP: The new building for the Fashion Institute of Technology, in New York, shows how the main idea for a public space incorporates sustainability in a holistic way. We didn't want to make clip-on gadgets. Think about bad stereos that have gadgets all over them compared with the great stereo that has just one button. If you make a really smart building that performs through really subtle spatial and engineering moves, it has one button. In thinking about the program and the site, we came up with a simple building, with the social-condenser space above the classrooms in a thickened façade that could hold the programs and respond to the nature of the design school.

NR: You are also working at a larger scale on the East River waterfront development project, in New York. How do you take concepts of mass customization and apply them to the urban scale within esplanade concepts?

GP: We put together a team with Richard Rogers for a new master plan, from Water Street up to 700 feet out into the East River to possibly extend the island of Manhattan and create new

SHoP, Porter House, showing the eight-foot cantilever of the 20,000-square-foot addition, New York City, 2003.

SHoP, Porter House, custom-fabricated zinc-panel system and vertical lighting, New York City, 2003.

SHoP, rendering of East River waterfront master-plan esplanade, with Rogers Stirk Harbour Architects, New York City, 2006.

space. It was a seamless think tank with a menu-driven, nonaesthetic design charrette. The East Side waterfront master plan is thinking about New York City within a new paradigm while being free of architectural history and using technology to generate new relationships of urban problem-solving. We are very excited about helping to give something back to a city that has given us so much.

NR: When you invest both money and design talent on a project, is that more of a risk than most architects are willing to take? Is that risk invigorating or precarious?

GP: If we are unwilling to take the risk, we will not get the reward. It is very simple, and this is how it works: Those who take the most risk get the biggest reward. Architecture is the last great generalist profession. We are the ones who can be out there and can really understand what all of these guys are doing, and we can use our understanding of culture and really make a difference, but we are really not ever getting off the risk thing. The next thing that we are trying to do in some of our projects is to just get rid of the client.

If we can do that and raise the funds to put the lenders at ease, we can actually really change the way architecture gets made. We want to prove the model works and prove good design can generate revenue; then we can get out of the cycle of mediocrity. To us, that is the most important thing we can contribute to the practice of architecture. It doesn't mean we are going to design all the buildings, but it is about all of us, together, trying to prove that what we do and what we have to offer culture is important and that we can make a difference.

NR: How can architects better control the variations in the cost and fluctuations of the market?

GP: I think if you design with a certain amount of flexibility, you can change the resolution of the architecture. If you go from a 72 dpi to a 1,440 dpi in the amount of detailing you can do, you can still get the design you are looking for in terms of the intention, but you can also dial up or down the level of detail to hit whatever the budget is. Instead of getting a project value-engineered, you just get it at a slightly smaller or larger dpi. Of course there is a point where the dpi is so bad that you are not really interested in it, and then you have to go to a new thing; but if you can start to build that flexibility into the way you are thinking about it from day one, then you have a much greater chance of getting your vision put forward. By embracing that aspect early in the process as you move forward, you are much more likely to get the buildings that you want built.

NR: How do you integrate the technology, financing, and programming to improve architecture and the urban environment?

GP: Any time there is a huge technological shift it means there is opportunity, and so what do we do as a profession with that opportunity? Do we just continue to work by the hour like attorney's? Do we continue to only produce images? Or do we really partake in the making of culture, making cities better places to live and really getting people excited? It is time to take ownership in what we do and make architecture more relevant than it has ever been.

SHoP, Camera Obscura, Mitchell Park, Greenport, New York, 2006. Two-thousand three hundred unique structural components were three-dimensionally modeled, laser-cut, and labeled as a kit of parts to be assembled on the site.

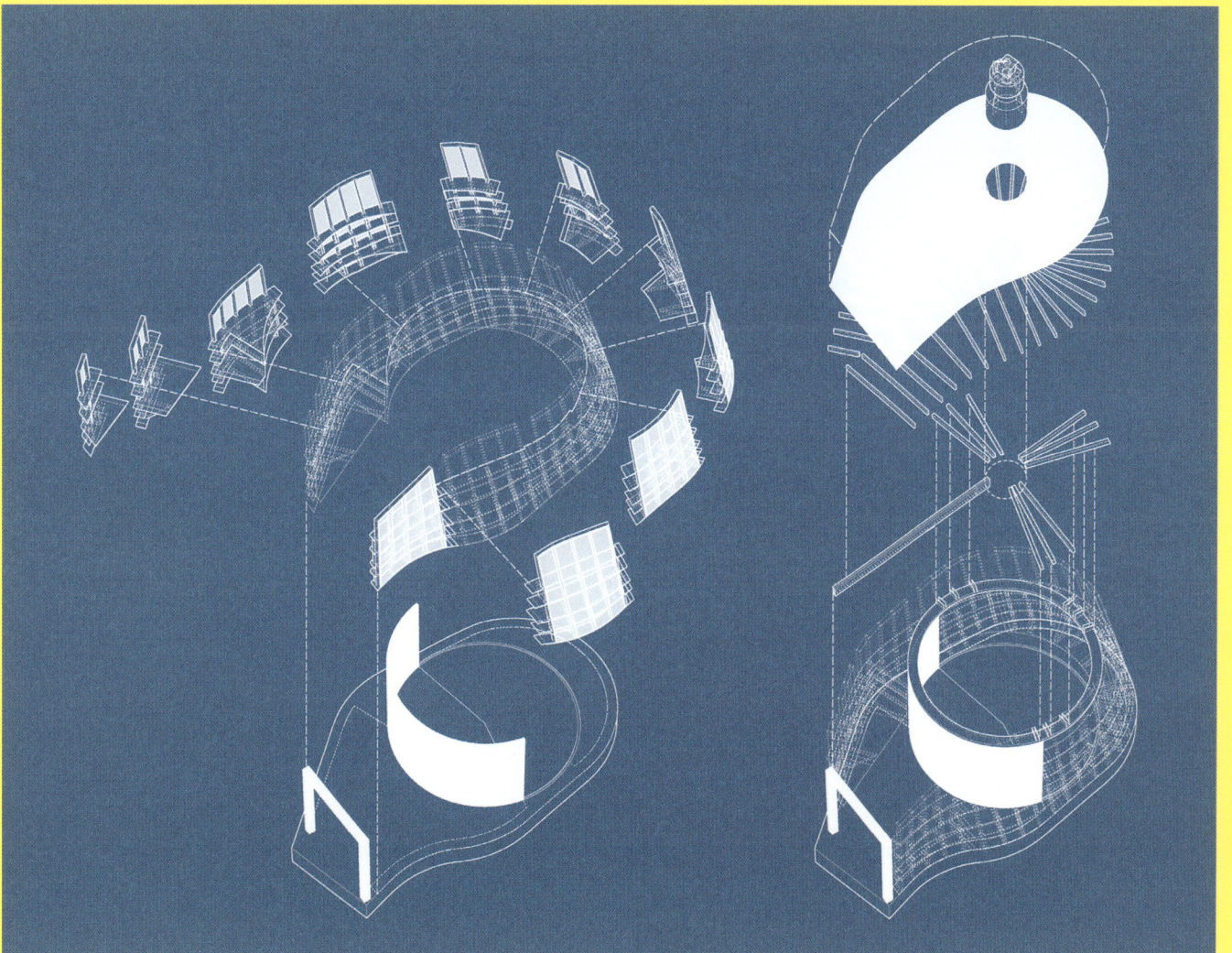

SHoP, Camera Obscura process, Mitchell Park, Greenport, New York, 2006.

VERSIO
—6.0

THE THICKNESS
OF PRIVATELY HELD
PUBLIC SPACE

"Versioning" is an operative term meant to describe a recent significant shift in the way architects are using technology to expand, in time as well as in territory, the potential effects of design on our world.

Versioning should be seen as an attitude rather than an ideology. It allows architects to think and practice across multiple disciplines, freely borrowing tactics from film, food, finance, fashion, economics, and politics for use in design or, by reversing the model, using architectural theory to participate in other fields. Digital technology has enabled architects to rethink the design process in terms of procedure and outcome in ways that common practice, the construction industry, and conventional design methodologies cannot conceive. This has had an equally profound impact on legal practices, insurance liabilities, and design/production partnerships, thereby initiating a restructuring of the traditional relations of power, responsibility, and accountability in design. Versioning implies design's shift away from a system of horizontal integration (designers as simply the generators of representational form) toward a system of vertical integration (designers driving how space is conceived and constructed and what its effects are culturally). Versioning is important to architects because it attempts to remove architecture from a stylistically driven cycle of consumption.

This studio's goal, as organized by Gregg Pasquarelli, the first Kahn Visiting Assistant Professor, was to put the idea of versioning to work within the complex physical, economic, and governmental constructs of Privately owned Public Spaces, or PoPS, in Lower Manhattan. Student teams of two each made careful examinations of the existing zoning code

as it pertains to PoPS, which include plazas, arcades, and parks. These spaces are the result of a clause introduced into the 1961 rewriting of the zoning code to provide more public space within the ever-densifying urban fabric of Manhattan by giving economic incentives to developers. Unfortunately, the majority of the resulting spaces exist as unprogrammed, barren, or even inaccessible areas that provide no public good.

New York City was the first in the country to develop a zoning code, the first of which was written in 1916 in an attempt to regulate building mass and bulk through a series of proportional relationships determined by street widths and theoretical building envelopes. In the first half of the twentieth century, as building and elevator technologies began to progress at rapid rates, building sizes also grew at exponential rates, turning the streets and avenues of Manhattan into vast urban canyons. The 1961 reworking attempted to address this issue with the establishment of certain setback requirements, the recognition of the use groups that determine the kinds of programs allowable within a site, and the development of the floor-area ratio, or FAR, which is a variable factor, defines the overall mass of a building based on its site's area. For example, a building on a 100-foot-by-100-foot site that has a FAR of five could contain a maximum of 50,000 square feet (100 feet by 100 feet by five feet). This equation translates to either a five-story building that covers the entire site, a ten-story building that covers half the site, a twenty-story building that covers a quarter of the site, or any combination of floor shapes and sizes that add up to less than the maximum FAR.

A legal construct introduced in the 1961 code, incentive-based zoning was an innovation that offered developers opportunities to gain FAR bonuses for providing spaces or amenities to the public. At the time the code was being

rewritten, such urban masterpieces as the Lever House and Seagram Building, both of which created new types of vibrant public spaces within their sites, had recently been completed. The authors of the code saw these buildings as benchmarks in urban planning and wanted to encourage other developers to similarly innovate. The result was the invention of PoPS; in exchange for creating spaces accessible to the public that met certain guidelines established in the code, developers received FAR bonuses, allowing them to have more than the previously allotted amount of space for their sites.

Since its inception, the PoPS bonus has resulted in private-office and residential developers in New York City receiving over 16 million square feet of bonused FAR, along with other zoning concessions, in return for which they have provided more than 500 plazas, arcades, covered pedestrian spaces, and other privately owned public spaces to greater or lesser effect.

Beginning with a careful consideration of the existing zoning code, the Pasquarelli studio quickly came to appreciate the law's power to shape and define space. Students investigated dynamic and performative modeling techniques that focus on understanding the external influences that shape a design strategy to find ways to work with or subvert the system from within.

Each team was asked to execute design strategies rooted in techniques of fabrication and assembly and was limited only by their ability to work within the existing PoPS code and an allowance given to change one part of the code. Each group developed a general proposal to affect the public on the urban scale while designing in parallel technological and architectural strategies to test their system by deploying it at a specific site within the city.

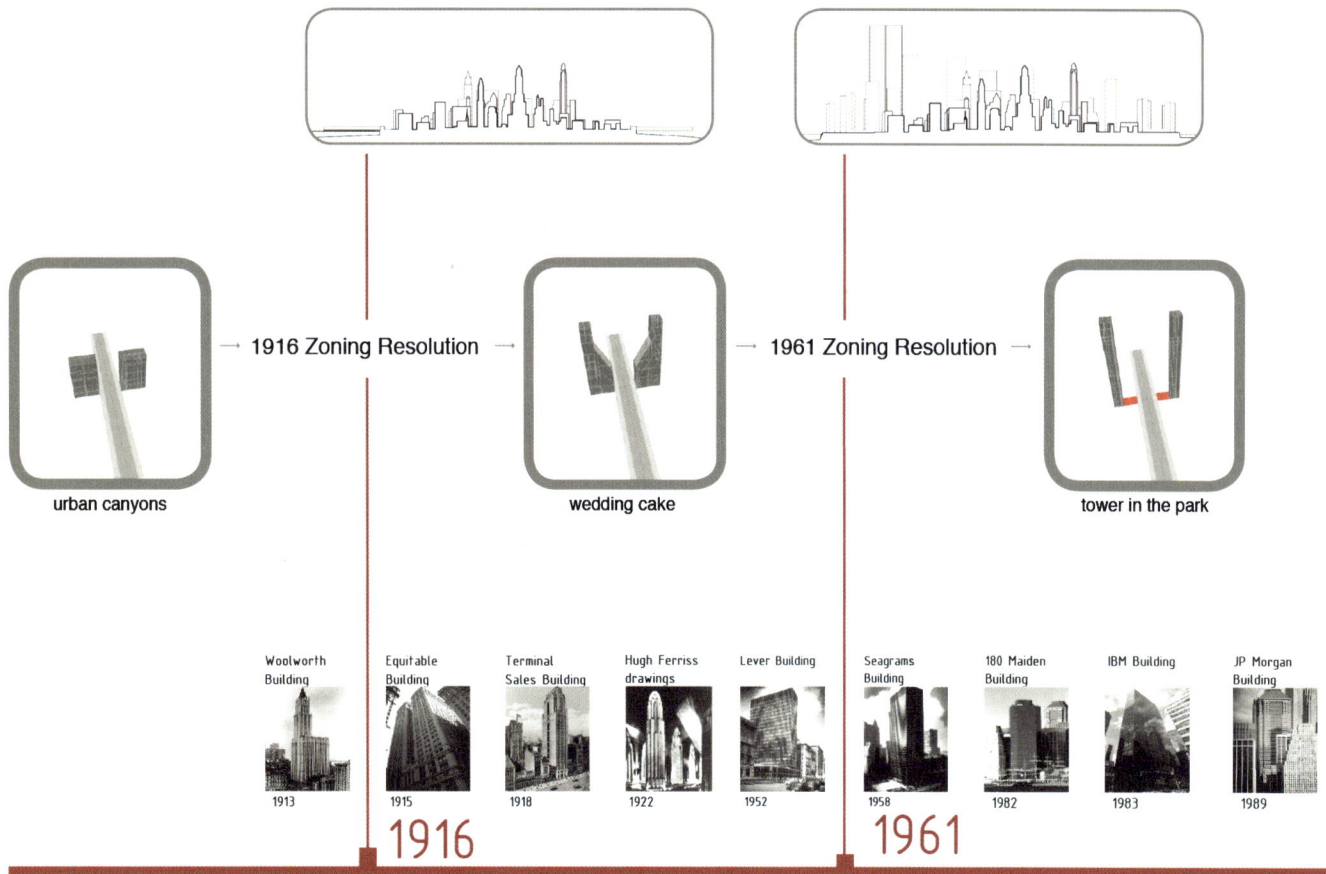

urban canyons → 1916 Zoning Resolution → wedding cake → 1961 Zoning Resolution → tower in the park

Woolworth Building	Equitable Building	Terminal Sales Building	Hugh Ferriss drawings	Lever Building	Seagrams Building	180 Maiden Building	IBM Building	JP Morgan Building
1913	1915	1918	1922	1952	1958	1982	1983	1989

1916   **1961**

1.01

Taking the attitude that there is a significant opportunity to improve New York City's existing inventory of more than 500 zoning-created, privately owned public spaces, the studio developed general concepts for recasting the islands of a randomly formed urban archipelago into vital parts of an integrated spatial network. To design, the studio used a composite organizational strategy meant to embody a comprehensive blending of program, structure, and skin into a fluid thickness capable of responding tactically to zoning, topography, and program, as well as configurability at multiple scales.

The studio at Yale was itself part of a larger-scale study, in part generated by the work of Jerold Kayden, who, in conjunction with the City Planning Commission and the Municipal Art Society, embarked on a study of the state of existing PoPS, the results of which were published in the 2000 book *Privately Owned Public Space.* Six architecture, urban design, and landscape design studios at the City University of New York, Columbia University, Harvard University, the University of Pennsylvania, Princeton University, and Yale University took on the redefinition of PoPS as their semester's study. Students from all the schools participated in meetings with leaders from the City Planning Commission and the Municipal Art Society, toured existing PoPS, and benefited from the ongoing critiques of Kayden and others who continue to be immersed in efforts to redefine PoPS. In addition to each studio's individual reviews, a group exhibition was hung at New York's Van Alen Institute, providing a public forum on the future of public space.

— Gregg Pasquarelli

1.01 Timeline of Zoning Resolution introductions and their impact on the urban landscape. (Erin Carraher and Stephen Van Dyck)

1.02 View of underside of armature and folded panel assembly in this group's final large-scale model. Components of this model were carved by a three-axis computerized mill, laser-cut, and assembled with pop rivets. (Ezra Groskin and Damian Zunino)

1.03 Early study model formalizing the complex relationships created by time-coded programs placed in adjacencies in such a way as to create 24-hour activity bars at the perimeter of the city. (Yang Yang and Yong Mei)

1.02

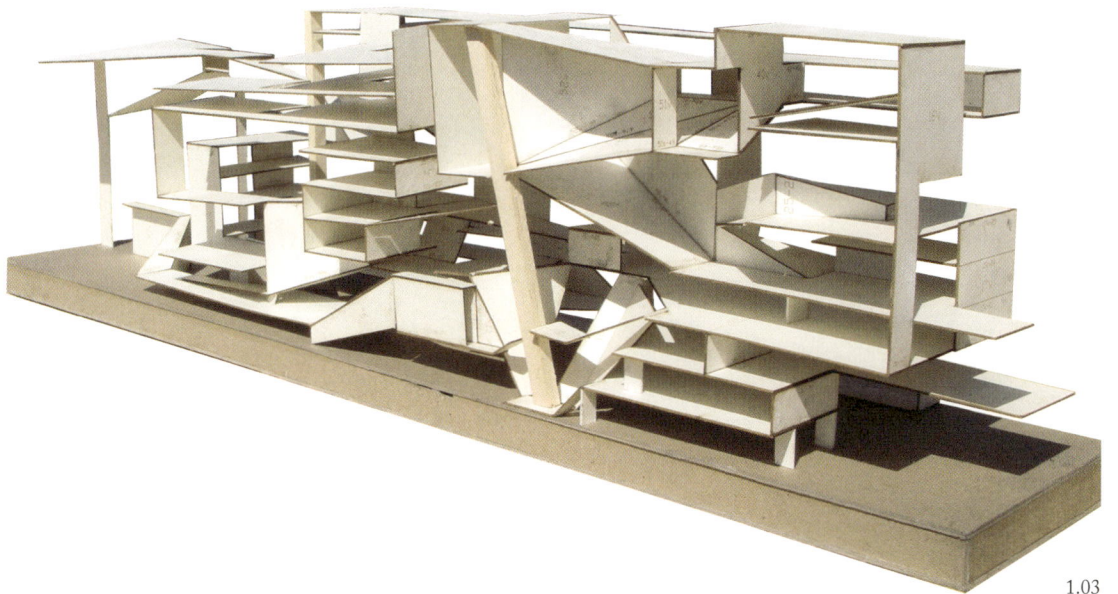

1.03

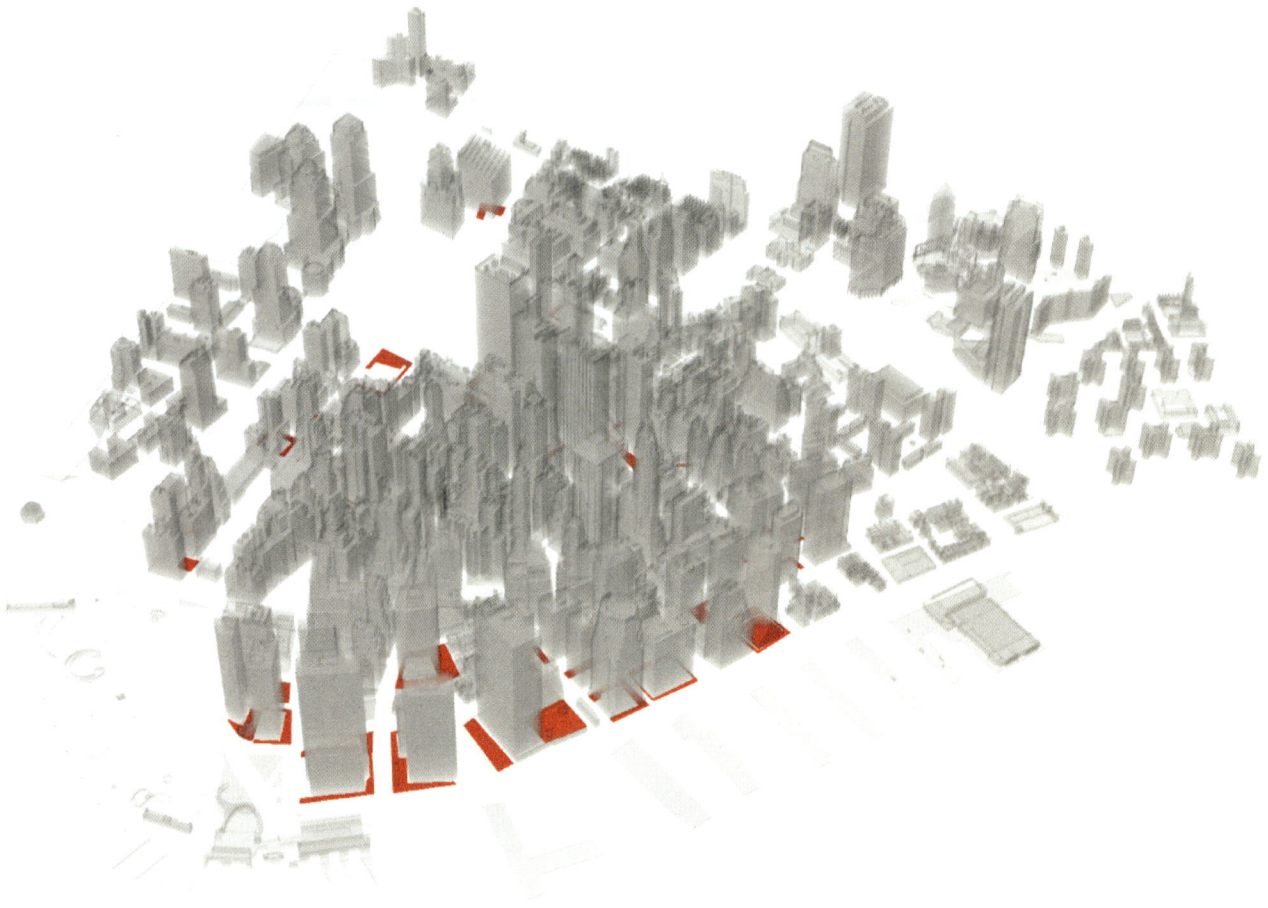

1.04

DEFINITIONS

PoPS

Privately owned public spaces (PoPS) were introduced into the New York City zoning code in 1961 as a type of incentive-based economic bonus to developers for providing public space within their site. The intent was to provide more "light and air" at street level for the public amid rapidly densifying street-walls during the first half of the twentieth century. Almost every building realistically eligible for the PoPS bonus has taken advantage of it in the ensuing time. Of the over 500 PoPS that have been built as a result of the 1961 code, many were poorly designed or have been poorly maintained, creating a gaping difference between the over 5.5 million square feet of space that has been gained by developers and the type and quality of space given to the public.

FAR

Floor-area ratio, or FAR, is a factor determined by use group and zone within a city that is employed to determine the maximum amount of square footage that can be used within a given site, or footprint. For example, a 100-foot-by-100-foot site in a zone with a FAR of five could have a total of 50,000 square feet of usable space built within it. This amount of space can theoretically be distributed over the site in any number of ways—a five-story building that covers the entire site, as a ten-story building that covers half the site, and so on—but the building is typically subject to certain rules as to how the space can be organized.

FAR Bonus, or Incentive Bonusing

A FAR bonus is a ratio or factor by which the base FAR of a site can be increased as the result of providing public amenities or spaces within the site. Often referred to as incentive bonusing, this practice was developed in the 1961 code as a way to encourage developers to create public spaces within their sites, rather than prescribing how they should do so. Though FAR bonuses increase the overall mass of a building on a site, the increase is justified by the increased amount of public space at the street level. The typical PoPS bonus in the existing code provides for three square feet of private space to be added for every square foot of public space built.

Use Group

A use group is a type of activity—residential, commercial, or manufacturing—that is acceptable within a particular zone. For example, in a zone that has been determined to be residential, buildings that contain manufacturing activities would not be permitted. These are typically related to FAR in that a manufacturing zone will most likely have a higher FAR than a commercial zone.

Height and Setback

Defined by the zoning code, height and setback regulations define the maximum height that a building can rise from street level before having to step back its façade a determined distance. Originally determined in the 1916 zoning code as a proportional relationship based on the width of a street on which a building, sometimes allowing buildings to rise 250 feet above the street at the property line, this requirement changed in the 1961 code to a height of 85 feet, or six stories.

Sky-Exposure Plane

The sky-exposure plane is an imaginary plane that begins at the setback height and extends at a predetermined angle away from the street, further limiting the envelope of the building and resulting in a ziggurat, or "wedding cake,"-shaped profile for buildings that wanted to build to the limits of the code. The 1916 code allowed for buildings or portions of buildings covering twenty-five percent or less of a site to rise to an infinite height with no setback requirements. Though more desirable for buildings in the International Style than the wedding-cake typology, the tower option was usually not feasible economically, as a developer would have to amass a very large site to be able to provide a building with the desired floor area within the tower limits. The 1961 code expanded this ratio to 40 percent to 55 percent in many areas.

Zoning

Zoning is a term used to describe the legal process of regulating height, size, use, and arrangement of buildings allowable in a particular location.

1.04 Illustration of existing PoPS in Lower Manhattan.

1.05 Examples of privately owned public spaces in Lower Manhattan that are most heavily used: One New York Plaza, 55 Water Street, 60 Wall Street, 77 Water Street, 110 Wall Street, 180 Maiden Lane, and Goldman Sachs.

1.05

METHODOLOGY

During the course of the studio, new processes of extraction were explored in an attempt to develop languages to transpose forces from the arenas of law, construction, theory, economics, and other related fields into the making of space. The project began with a study of dynamic and performative modeling focused on understanding the external influences that shape a design strategy. Students were asked to deploy design strategies rooted in techniques of fabrication and assembly to create a composite organizational strategy that embodied a comprehensive blending of program, structure, and skin into a fluid thickness capable of responding tactically to zoning, topographic, and programmatic criteria at multiple scales. Grounded in this approach was a set of tooling techniques that optimize commonality while being capable of accepting data that may form irregular, varied, and intricate relationships. Both normative and non-standardized approaches to building systems were investigated and led the projects to an array of heterogeneous manufacturing and assembly techniques. The studio considered the broader concepts of the nature of spatial networks and public space and focused on the generation of specific proto-logical design interventions for the specific plazas selected by the students.

It is traditionally assumed that the greater the variety of tasks ascribed to a performative object, the less capable it will be of handling any one well. The studio asked if it is possible to design a manufacturing process that is capable of multitasking, that is, of maneuvering between a number of disjunctive criteria. The goal of the studio was to then question the separation of performance data and its independent requirements by bringing together practices and techniques not necessarily common to the field of architecture. Thus, the ordering of space and form through the practice of design, fabrication, and construction could begin to create a performative bridging between different fields. The privileging of an assembly-based technique necessitated the development of newly invented drawing types that inform fabrication and construction processes, moving the designs away from image-based systems of representation and toward a vertical integration of making and effect.

Inspired by such contemporary technologies as shipbuilding, automotive design, and prefabricated housing —techniques in which intricate three-dimensional assemblages are fabricated from discrete components while being individually customizable—innovative systems of prefabricated construction were developed by the various teams. One group created a system of structural metal panels, corrugated with programmatic folds assembled on large armatures to create a public *piano nobile* over existing constructions and streets. Another group challenged themselves to work solely within the loopholes of the existing code to redefine the system performatively from within, while others chose to build up dense bars of program at the periphery of Lower Manhattan to activate the district as a whole. Still others chose to introduce sustainability as a generative force on the zoning code, creating a strategy for open-source zoning not unlike those currently in place in the LEED system, thus rewarding environmentally responsible design with economic benefits.

Each team design was based on the collapse of program, surface, and structure, making a new thickness of architectural devices and construction techniques to create an affect. It is within this thickness that the use of versioning was explored. Many different of techniques, materials, probabilities, and aesthetics were developed by the teams because there was no adherence to any architectural convention. Each project was required to reveal the rationale underlying its choices in ways that allowed others to understand the process of thinking, making, and creating. All students were expected to use dynamic modeling, animation, sketching, rendering, drawing, and physical model-building with equal emphasis. Unique models were required weekly, with the end goal being a large-scale model that would demonstrate both the architectonic system and construction techniques developed throughout the semester.

1.04 One of the results of creating a mass-customized building system is the necessity of keeping hundreds of similar model pieces organized. By instituting a complex numbering system, models comprising many discrete components could be assembled quickly.

1.05

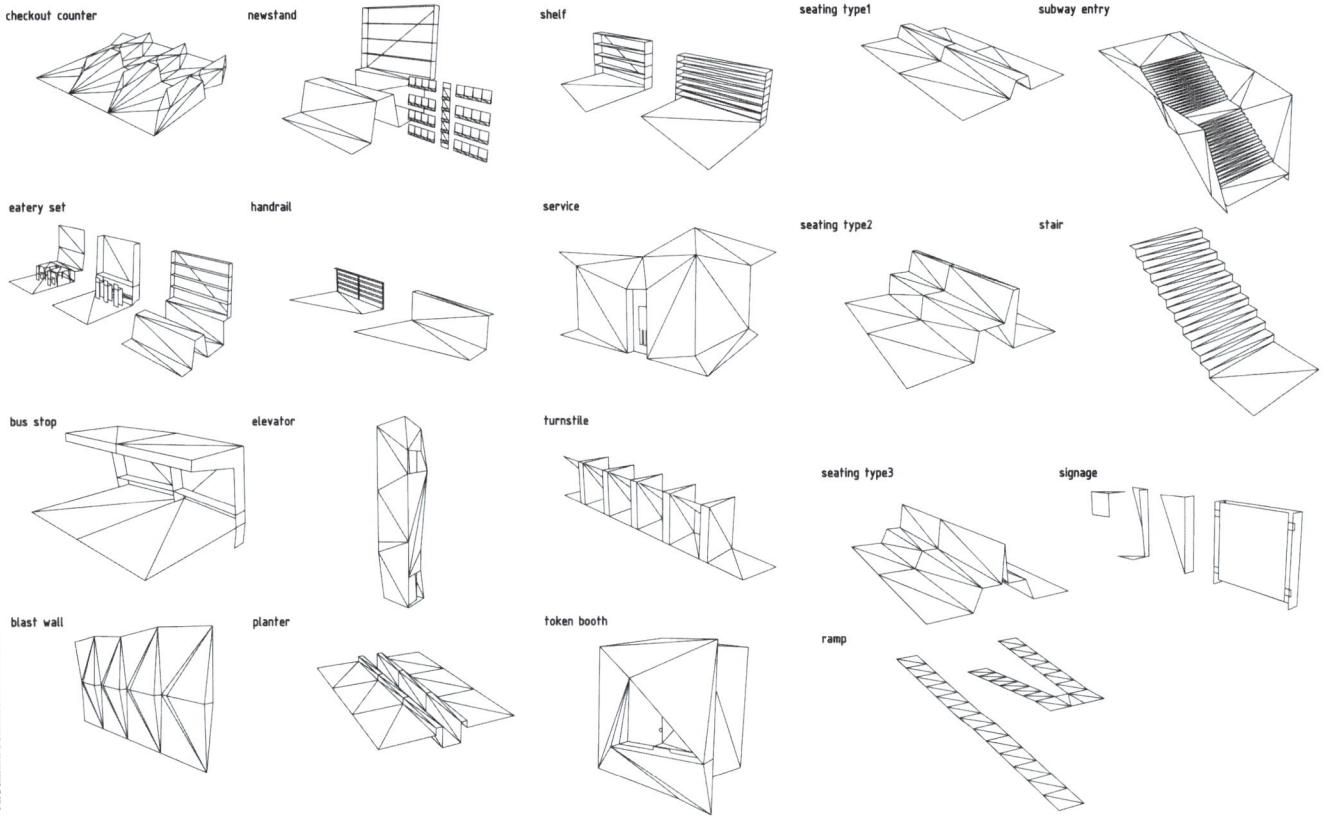

PROGRAM/SURFACE TYPOLOGIES

checkout counter　　newstand　　shelf　　seating type1　　subway entry

eatery set　　handrail　　service　　seating type2　　stair

bus stop　　elevator　　turnstile　　seating type3　　signage

blast wall　　planter　　token booth　　ramp

1.06

1.05 As with origami, the Japanese art of paper folding, architectural folds create structural elements within sheet materials along with opportunities for integrating programmatic elements. (Damian Zunino and Ezra Groskin)

1.06 Programmatic folds created within the existing definition of allowable obstructions in the seating clause of the 1961 Plaza Guidlines. (Ken Gowland and Esin Yurekli)

1.07–08 Views of the program bar from below and from the East River. (Yang Yang and Yong Mei)

1.07

1.08

PROJEC

CODE EVALUATION AND REWRITING: INCENTIVE-BASED DESIGN

Each project began with an examination of the existing zoning code as it pertains to PoPS, with the assumption that the code plays a powerful role in defining the urban fabric. Most of the spaces built as a result of the existing code were found to be barren, neglected, indistinct, unprogrammed, and not beneficial to the public. Each team was challenged to propose one change in the zoning code that would affect the PoPS system, creating both better spaces for the public and increased benefits for the developers. Each project identified key issues regarding the relationship of public and private, rethought the role and nature of PoPS, chose goals based on an analysis of historical models and contemporary building techniques, and defined new methods of FAR bonusing in order to integrate habitable, functional, and healthy public space into the urban landscape.

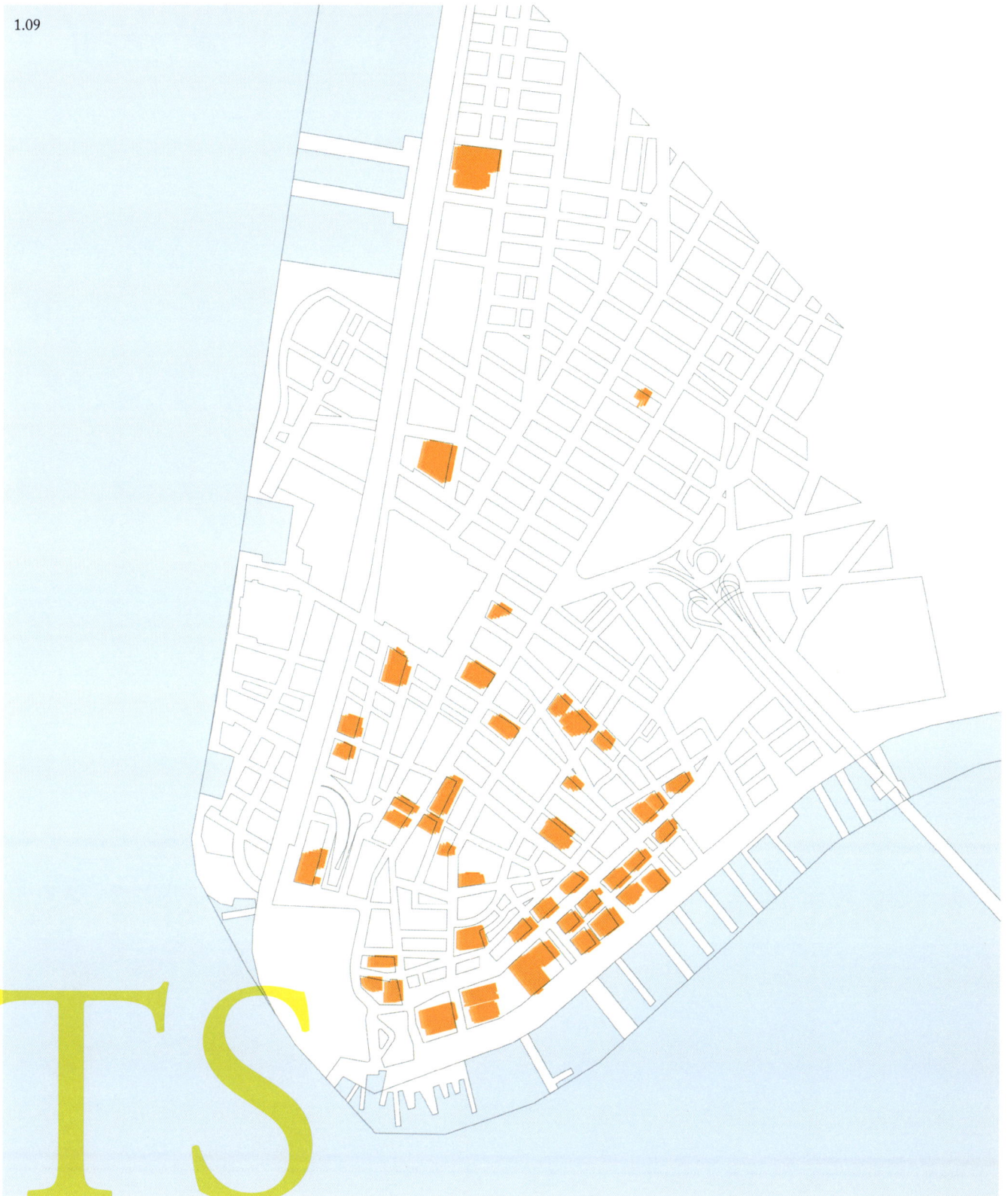

1.09

1.09 Map of Existing PoPS in Lower Manhattan

Damian Zunino and Ezra Groskin:
1.10 Illustration of the amount of area gained by
developers as a result of PoPS bonuses if it were to
be combined.

1.11 Park space illustrating the amount of PoPS
spaces if they were to be combined.

1.12 Illustration of additional FAR on buildings
that received PoPS bonuses.

In essence, the private sector has gained nine times
as much space as the public since the PoPS bonus
incentive began. Although the public has been
given 671,766 square feet of open space in Lower
Manhattan, the same size as the World Trade Center
site, developers have been able to add 5,356,463
square feet to their buildings, making a gigantic
addition and filling an entire 200-foot-by-400-foot
block, equal to a FAR rating/cumulative of 67. The
city started the PoPS bonus to bring light and air to
the streets amid rapidly rising and densifying blocks
in the early 1960s. Modeled after such urban masterpieces as the Seagram Building, the FAR bonus soon
became manipulated by developers to suit their own
needs. One can question whether the public has
gained any light, air, or benefit at all, as buildings
have essentially grown by 20 percent.

1.13–14 In our proposal, "Hyper PoPs," it is assumed
that a developer desires the maximum 20 percent
FAR bonus and that the bonus space designed for
the public exists on a single, predefined plane above
street level. By altering the code to require a fixed
ratio of public-to-bonus space, we establish that as
the building size increases, the bonus size increases.
At a certain point before the 20 percent maximum is
reached, the area of public space required to achieve
the FAR bonus surpasses the size of the building's
lot; the relationship then becomes imaginary and
must be accommodated in other ways. This surplus
space is the foundation of our project. The idea
behind our proposed code is that this extra space
must exist somewhere and thus is traded, negotiated,
and concentrated within districts, forming a network
of public space that connects from one developer's
site to the next developer's site, over streets, through
existing buildings, and around vertical obstructions.

Erin Carraher and Stephen Van Dyck:
1.15 With the requirement that new models be
generated on a weekly basis, methods for rapidly
exploring multiple scenarios of massing were
developed even at the early stages of the project.
When exploring options for code revisions, a 3D
printed site model and quickly generated minia-
ture models helped visualize possible outcomes to
proposed parameters.

Ken Gowland and Esin Yurekli:
1.16 Diagrams illustrating the transformation of
the Cartesian grid into a three-dimensional coordinate system that serves as the framework for multiple surfaces slipping above and below one another.

Edward Mitchell: It would be interesting to compare this scheme with a scan
of Central Park, where there are no flat
surfaces. Similarly, you have a multiplied
surface that does other things.

1.10

1.11

1.12

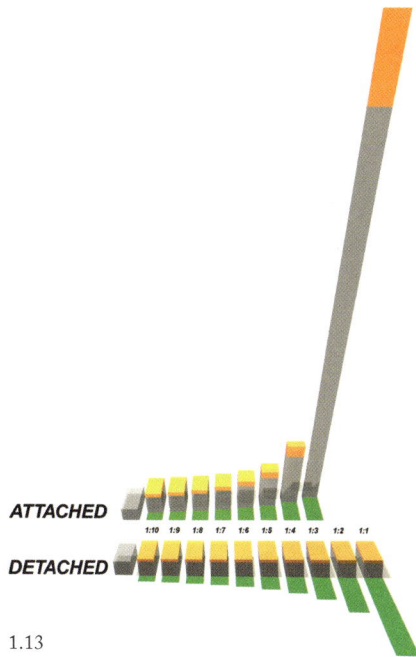

ATTACHED

1:10 1:9 1:8 1:7 1:6 1:5 1:4 1:3 1:2 1:1

DETACHED

1.13

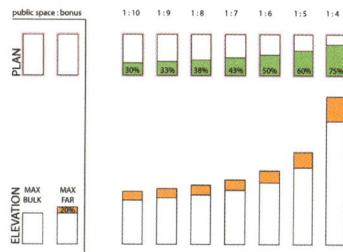

1.14

1.15

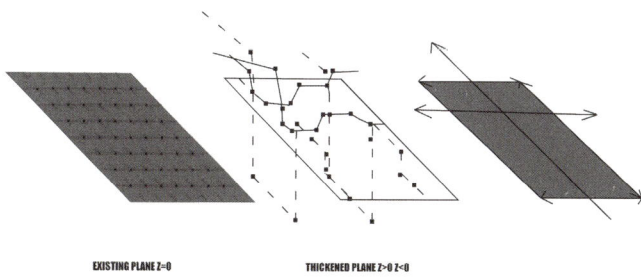

EXISTING PLANE Z=0   THICKENED PLANE Z>0 Z<0

1.16

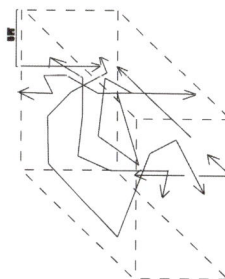

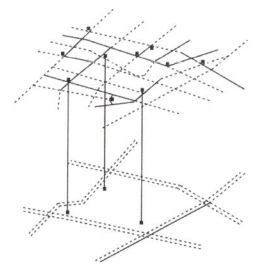

URBAN NETWORK NODES STREET-SUBWAY SYSTEM POPS

01 AUTOMOBILE ACCESS

INTEGRATION

02_PEDESTRIAN ACCESS

CONNECTION

STREET

02_POTENTIAL CULTURAL INTENSITIES

DESTINATION

FULTON STREET

WATER STREET

FDR

05   04   03   02   01

03

03

03

02

01

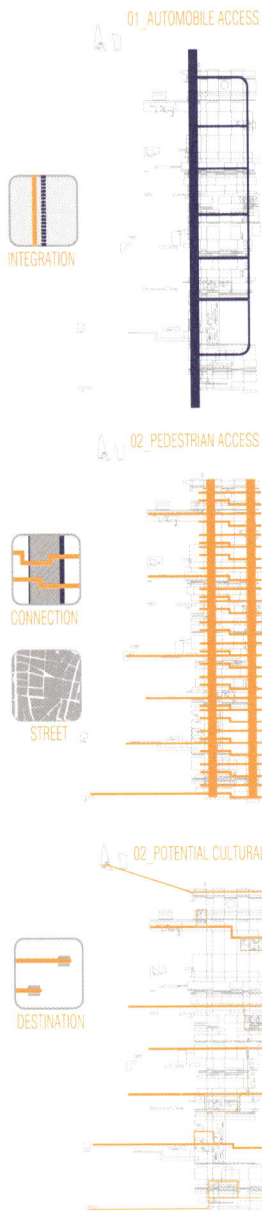

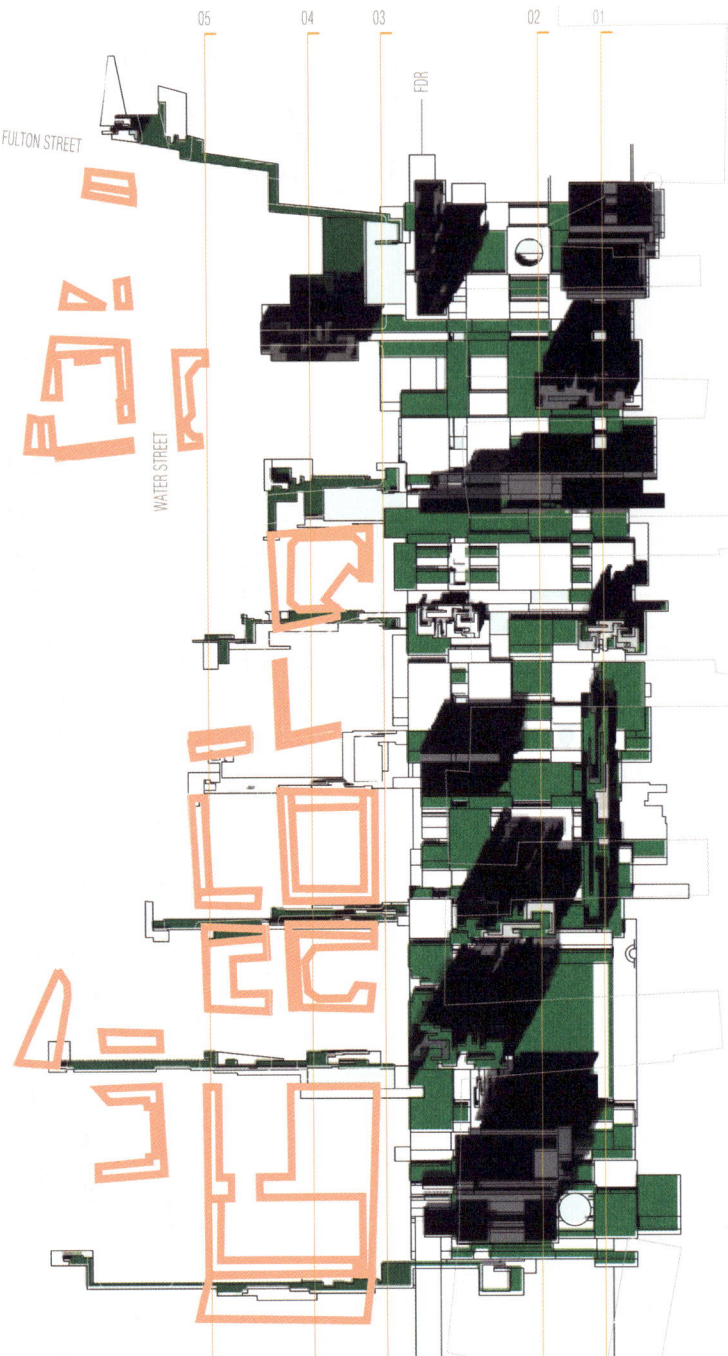

Gregg Pasquarelli: The only difference is that Olmsted was about separating three forms of infrastructure—the carriage, the horse, and the person—and this one is almost about blending them. When you're walking across the plaza there is a slipperiness of inside to outside, public or private, and after a while you wouldn't know which territory you're in.

Spencer Luckey and Edward Richardson:
1.17 The basic diagram is office space on the street side, housing on the water, and big box underneath. We developed a pixel called a pentomino, a shape made of five cubes, that has infinite spatial variations when manipulated and combined in directional fields. We then made extrusions in the cross grain. One set of extrusions was piled on top of the other, giving the plinth, or public ground plane,

a varying section. The PoPS aggregated through this process to increase the surface areas while maintaining the desired level of aeration within the ever-growing mass.

1.18 The Joy-to-Stuff Ratio is the time a person has to enjoy life versus the time a person spends accumulating material goods. Based on this principle, our idea was to build out the waterfront by encouraging development through FAR bonuses. The result is a hybrid model of housing and big-box retail that integrates itself into the highway and the street grid and is punctuated by pockets of public space.

Brady Stone and Brendan Lee:
1.19 We proposed an entity called the "PoPS Network." It takes on the model of the Business Improvement District (BID), wherein the BID would be an alliance of property owners who have an interest in improving their PoPS. An outside sponsor or a private organization would be approached to "theme" the whole space. Rather than create discrete PoPS with municipally legislated trees and benches,

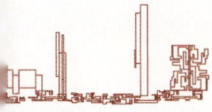

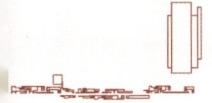

1.17

1.18

1 Wall Street Plaza
Special Permit Plaza
9,907 sf

(10) Trees

(98) Linear feet of Seating
(1) Circular Bench
(24) Movable Chairs

(1) Water Element

(2) Public Artworks

100 Wall Street
Arcade
2518 sf

Plaza
5933 sf

(No) Required Amenities

Active
Sports Field
Putting Green
Basketball Court
Climbing Wall
Running Trail
Adventure Playground
Skate Park

Passive
Sculpture Park
Dining Garden
Commuter Lounge
Winter Garden
Urban Beach
Viewing Platform
Smoking Lounge

Service
Newsstand
Public Restrooms
Food Kiosk
Bus Stop Shelter
Farmer's Market
Community Center
Flea Market Hall
Internet Kiosks
Childcare Center

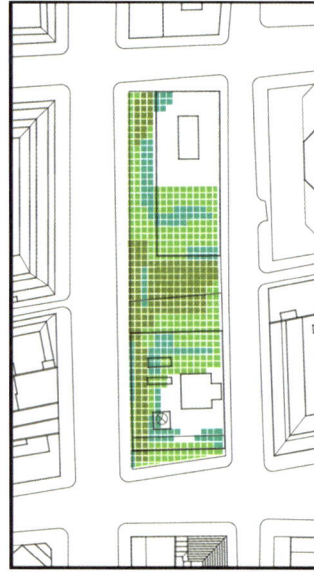

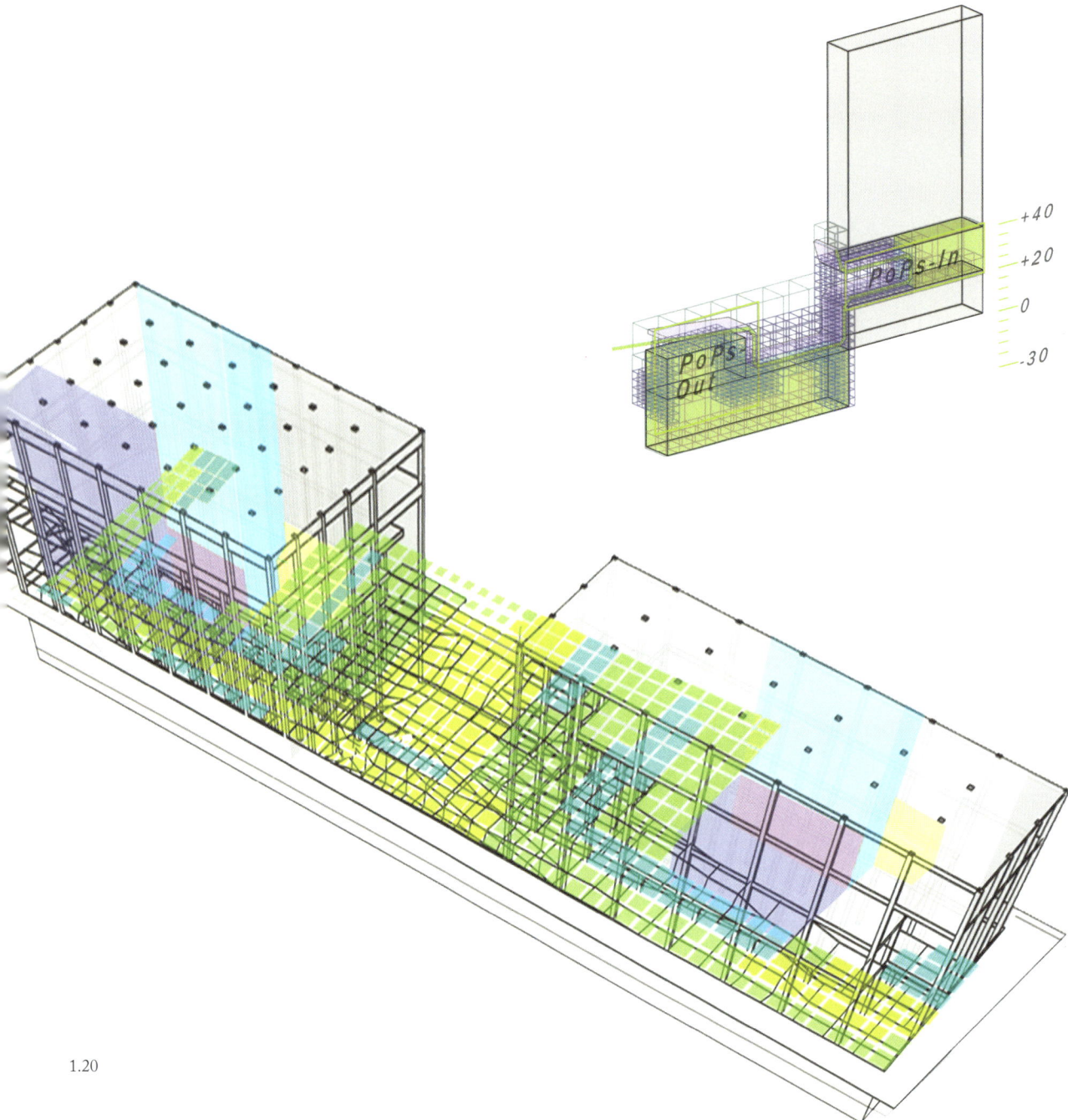

[Before]

[After]

1.19

PoPs-In

PoPs
Out

+40
+20
0
-30

1.20

1.21

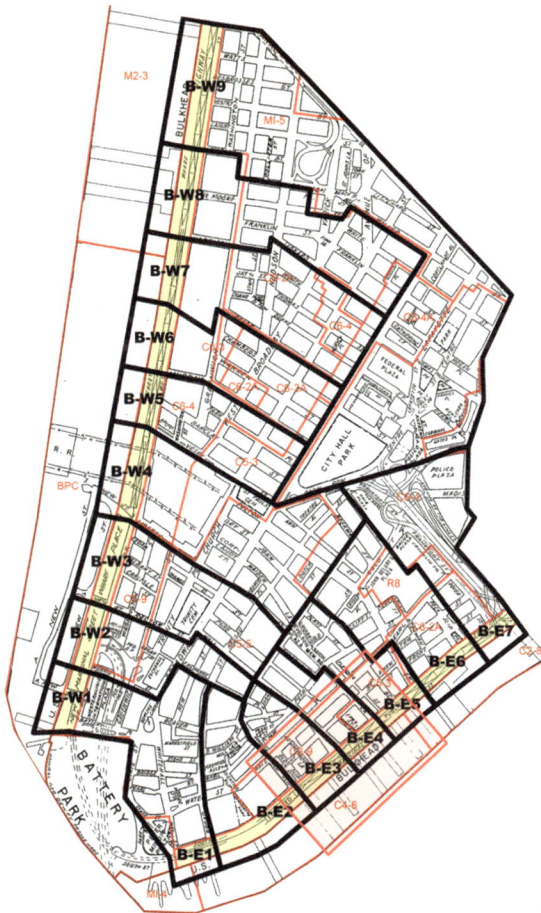

1.22

there would be an aggregation of programs with themes such as the "Guggenheim Art Park" or the "Six Flags Activity Park." To capitalize on the latent programmatic potential of the site, retail spaces would expand by making large, open spaces as destinations. A variable pixilation of public and private and the spatial results of such an exchange would define the programmatic distribution.

1.20 The diagram is one of simple exchange, of addition and subtraction. There is a multiplier applied: for every one square foot of privatized (retail) space occupied in the public realm, the public gets two square feet of space within the private building. Where the existing program is carved out of a building to introduce public space, the owner will be able to go back in and surround the newly activated public space with private retail space, thus making it an attractive trade for both parties.

Yang Yang and Yong Mei:
1.21–22 A critical zone was identified around the perimeter of Lower Manhattan; it was proposed that by activating the perimeter, adjacent spaces would feed into the system. The proposal, which used a four-dimensional logic to promote 24-hour activity by weaving together program based on time, is manifest in this early study in which a framework for various programs is built on top of the FDR Drive.

Edward Mitchell: You should have a generalized strategy about how you fill in the planometric logic with a time frame based on development, and that would give you the key to the financing and tell you who would need to plug in first, who would go in second, and so on. You need to insert those things and zone them and see how they feed back into the system to give you a link back into the rest of the city.

Spencer Luckey and Edward Richardson:
1.23 Diagrams showing the process developed for transferring square footage from buildings eligible for more FAR than their site will allow to areas along the perimeter of Lower Manhattan at Battery Park and the East River adding density and program.

William Sharples: The activation of that new perimeter is more than transferring square footage to the periphery, which raises a certain amount of money, but there is also the possibility of injecting the infrastructure that is needed for a 24-hour city because it aerates the situation and pulls you into the fabric.

Erin Carraher and Stephen Van Dyck:
1.24 This project developed performance-based, sustainable code requirements, taking the stance that "the public" is not only people on the street but also those who live and work in the buildings in question. We believe the careful incorporation of active and passive sustainable devices into the design of new buildings in Lower Manhattan would in essence bring with them light and air.

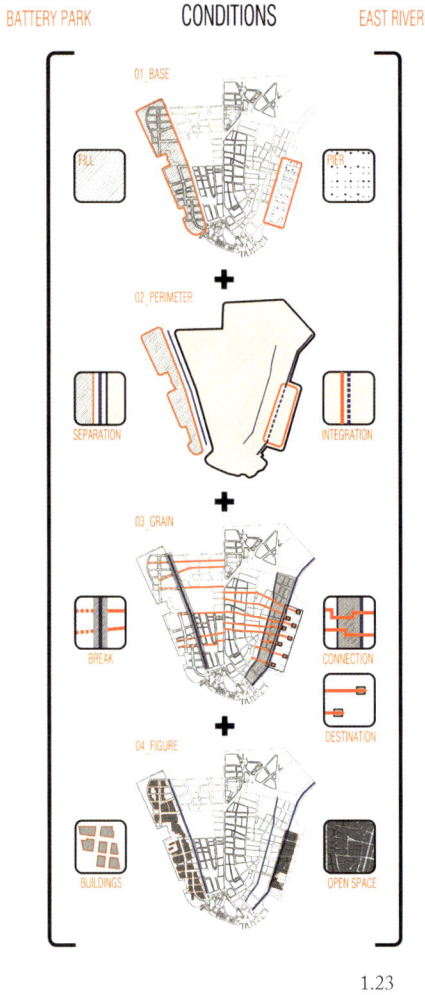

01 BASE

FILL   IDEA

+

02 PERIMETER

SEPARATION   INTEGRATION

+

03 GRAIN

BREAK   CONNECTION

DESTINATION

+

04 FIGURE

BUILDINGS   OPEN SPACE

1.23

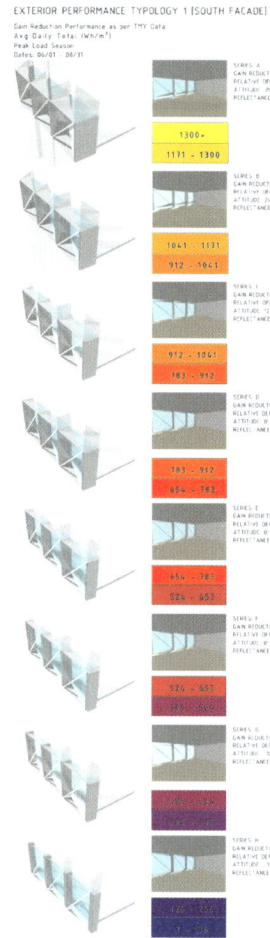

EXTERIOR PERFORMANCE TYPOLOGY 1 [SOUTH FACADE]

Gain Reduction Performance as per TMY Data
Avg Daily Total (Wh/m²)
Peak Load Season
Dates: 06/01 - 06/31

East Elevation

1.24

For example, radiation-gain studies completed in the performance-modeling program EcoTect provided site-specific information that helped tune the horizontal fins of the structural system, allowing them to serve as passive sustainable devices. Under the new sustainable code, the incorporation of this element, though not an actual public space, resulted in a FAR bonus due to the increased quality of space for those in the building.

Ken Gowland and Esin Yurekli:
1.25 View of the internal relationship of the slipping surfaces within the computer model. By modeling the complex relationships among three-dimensional components from the very beginning of the project, we were able to continually visualize spatial characteristics of our design from multiple scales and vantage points.

The existing PoPS are for the most part an urban no-man's lands, voids that occur in the middle of the city that have no value unto themselves; they actually highlight the schism between public and private they were designed to overcome. We see a delineation between that which is clearly public streetscape and that which is clearly private building. We want to elaborate an ideal relationship between the public and private in which they inform and feed off each other.

1.26 This project works within the framework of the 1961 Plaza Guidelines in order to create a reciprocal relationship between public and private desires through the bridging and integration of contextual urban features and the development of additional public and private areas. Public amenities (transportation/recreation space), private spaces (commercial office buildings), and new development opportunities (retail/entertainment programs) are bridged and combined in a thickened transitional zone that materializes a new type of space that is something between public and private.

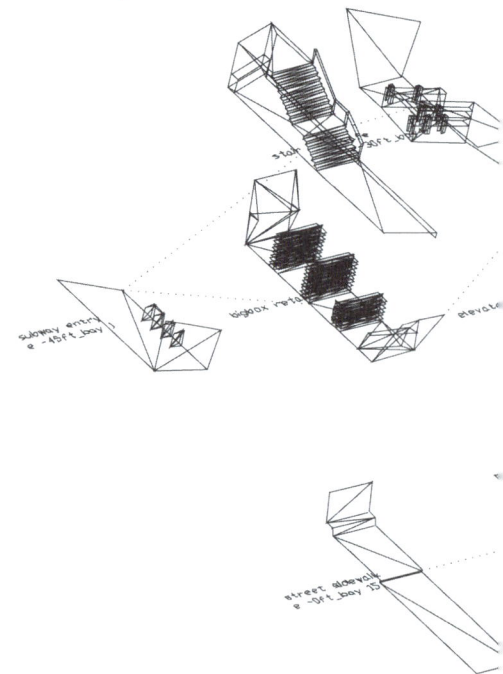

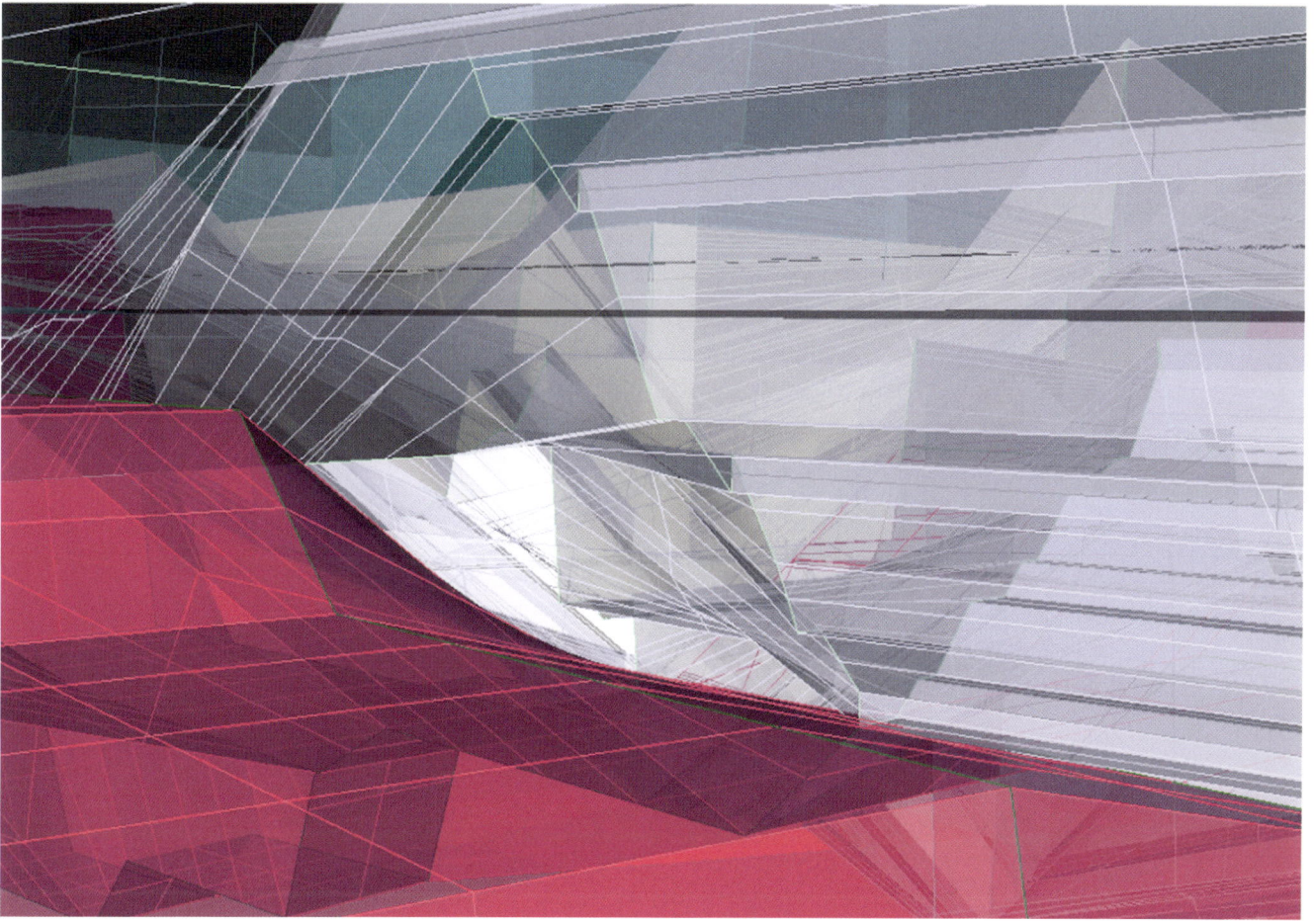

1.25

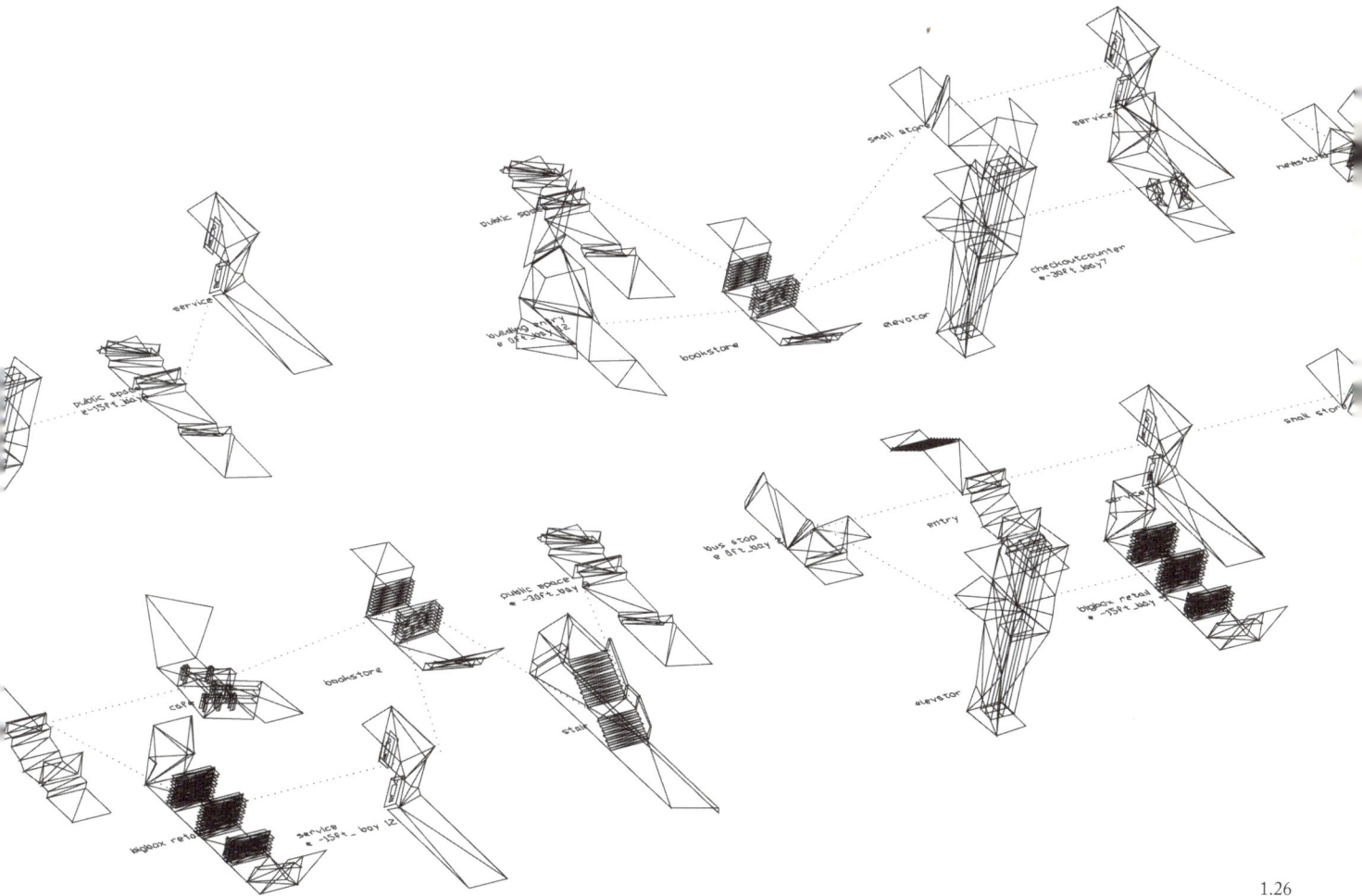

1.26

FORMAL LANGUAGE AND MECHANICS

Each team developed a zoning-based mechanism to implement their ideas at the urban scale: either a structural system, a reimagining of spatial and temporal adjacencies, or a way to retroactively incorporate public space into existing structures. Versioning was used to generate strategies for defining space and to reimagine existing construction methods using digital technologies. Each code mutation was manifest at both the urban scale and a test site, where actual localized conditions were plugged into the model and affected the implementation of the formal language. Emphasis was placed on developing urban techniques in the vein of open-source computer models, rather than static images, and by doing so created dynamic systems that reacted to the local conditions.

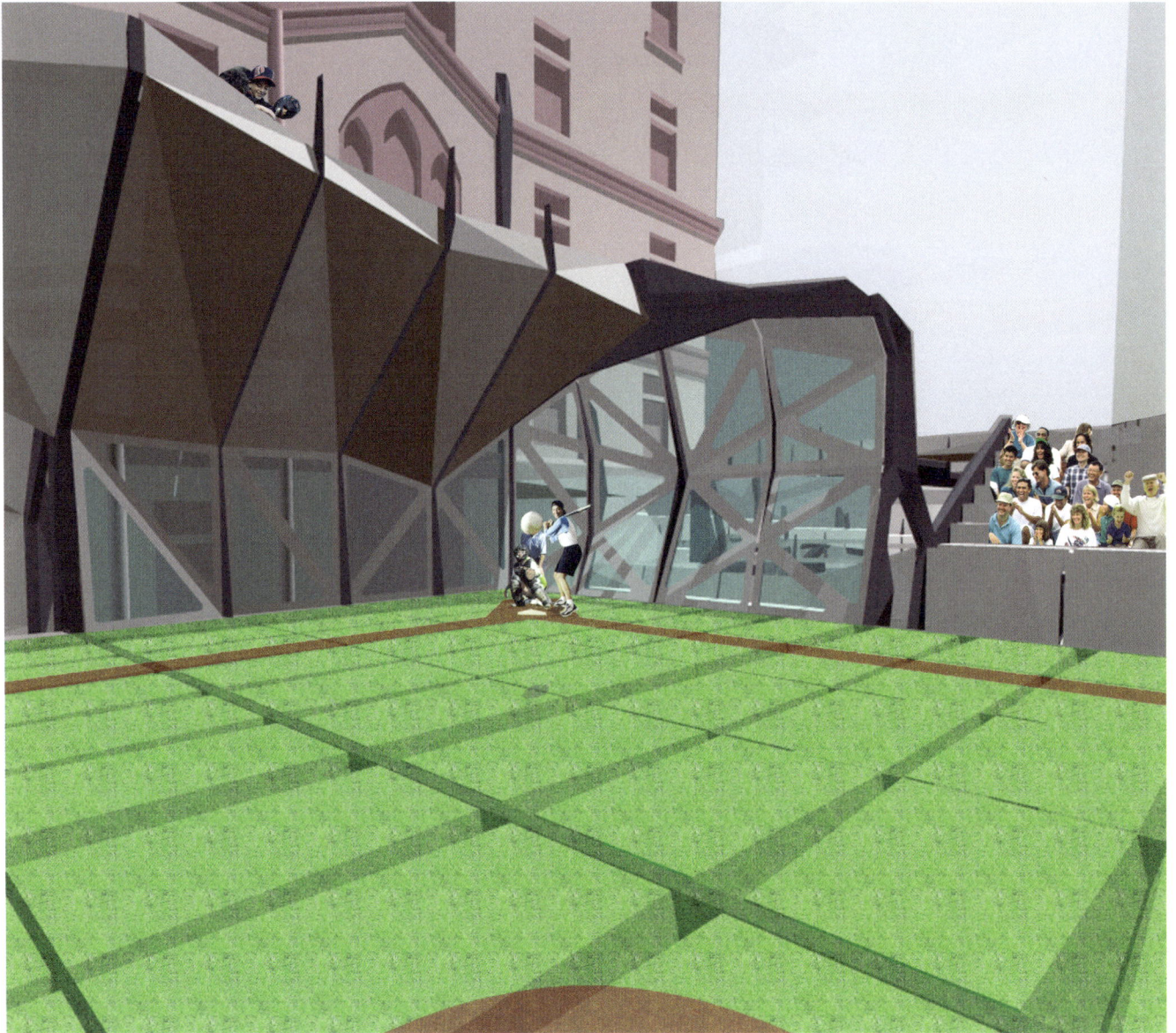

1.27

1.28

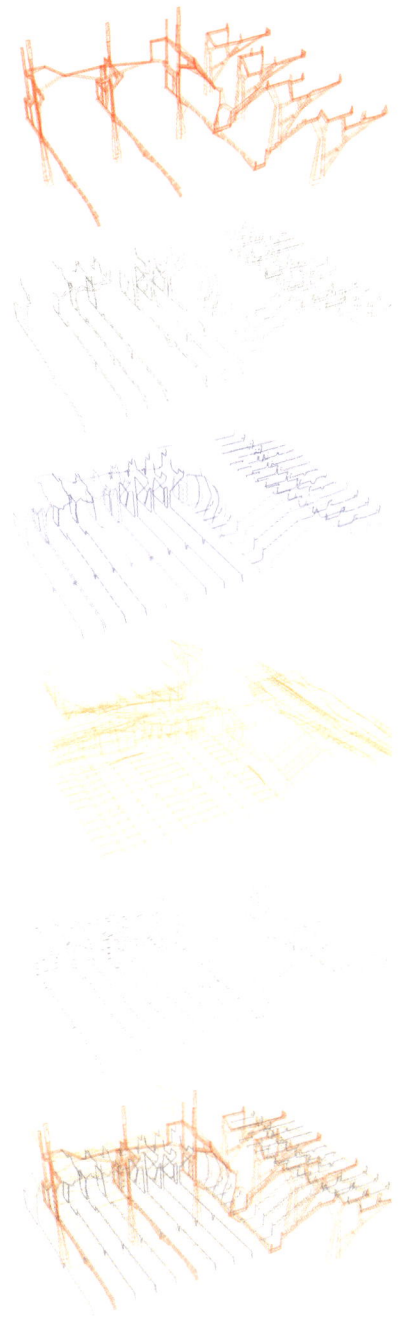

1.29

Damian Zunino and Ezra Groskin:
1.27–28 To study an assemblage of PoPS within existing conditions, we chose a site on Broadway and applied the principles of the "Hyper PoPS." The resultant district, a continuous, above-grade pedestrian level running above Broadway from City Hall Park to Battery Park, is created by a connection 23 feet above the street that serves as a recreational, commercial, and cultural space, reinvigorates a dark and underutilized stretch of a famous New York street, and provides exponentially more space within Lower Manhattan for public activity.

1.29 Not only were students required to develop architectural proposals in accordance with the studio brief, they were also to design modeling and structural techniques. In this project, the simple modeling technique of folding a surface in two directions to create rigidity was used in sophisticated ways while also incorporating program and service utilities. The secondary folds allow the plates to connect to each other as well the larger superstructure, which consists of outriggers that project the public plane up off the street level.

1.30 Diagrams of architectural solutions that address both tectonic and programmatic concerns.

1.31 To test this structural system, we created a scenario in which a baseball field was placed over Trinity Cemetery and a swimming pool was carved through the Trinity Building and the U.S. Realty Building. The program took advantage of one of the rare open spaces in Lower Manhattan, adding a usable field above an otherwise inaccessible area. The pool capitalized on the long, narrow formation of the buildings, linking them to maximize FAR bonuses and usable space.

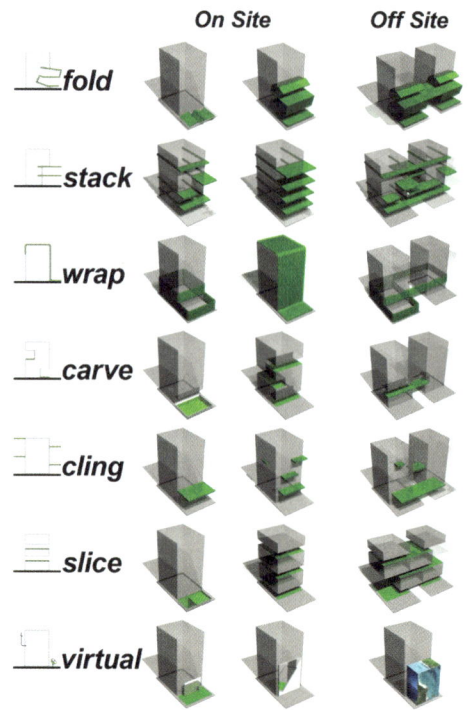

On Site   Off Site

fold
stack
wrap
carve
cling
slice
virtual

1.30

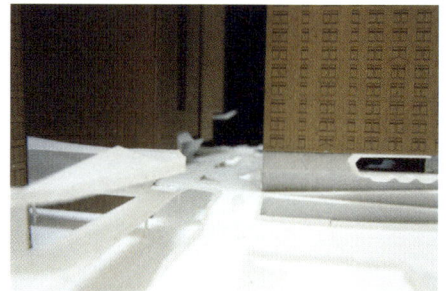

1.31

Gregg Pasquarelli: To activate some of these insertions, you need to see what's happening adjacent to them. I want to see the force of what's going on inside the building as it moves from the office space to another sort of transformation, which engages the whole pinball mechanism of the façade. It would also help with the issue of light and air. How much do you allow the Donald Judd model of sky-exposure plane and light and air to operate here? You don't revert back to 1910, where everybody is locked up. This type of modeling starts to deal with that issue. It's sort of like the Galleria Vittorio Emmanuel, in Milan. There, a five-story arcade was created at the intersection of two streets connecting the Duomo and La Scala. It is a pedestrian space lined with shops and cafés and galleries and is also an incredible space in itself. Does your project similarly generate a new type of arcade? But like your project, the Milan Galleria wasn't something that was built from scratch; it actually grew out of the surrounding forces.

Brady Stone and Brendan Lee:
1.32 We tackled the boundaries between public and private through the idea that you can use programmatic pixilation as a threshold, what we call the PoPS "In" and the PoPS "Out." Pixilation as an architectural technique allows for varying intensities to shift across that zone.

Yang Yang and Yong Mei:
1.33–34 Time is the biggest element affecting the physical space in the city. Certain programmatic adjacencies were based on the time it takes to get from one point to the next, rather than the physical distance between them. This concept, which we call "time cores," organized the urban-planning model, along with certain programmatic requirements at central nodes and other programs at the adjacencies.

Chris Sharples: What effects do you get as a result of the analysis of the model? Is

PoPs Retail Space

Retail Space

Retail Space

Passage to Large-Scale

1.32

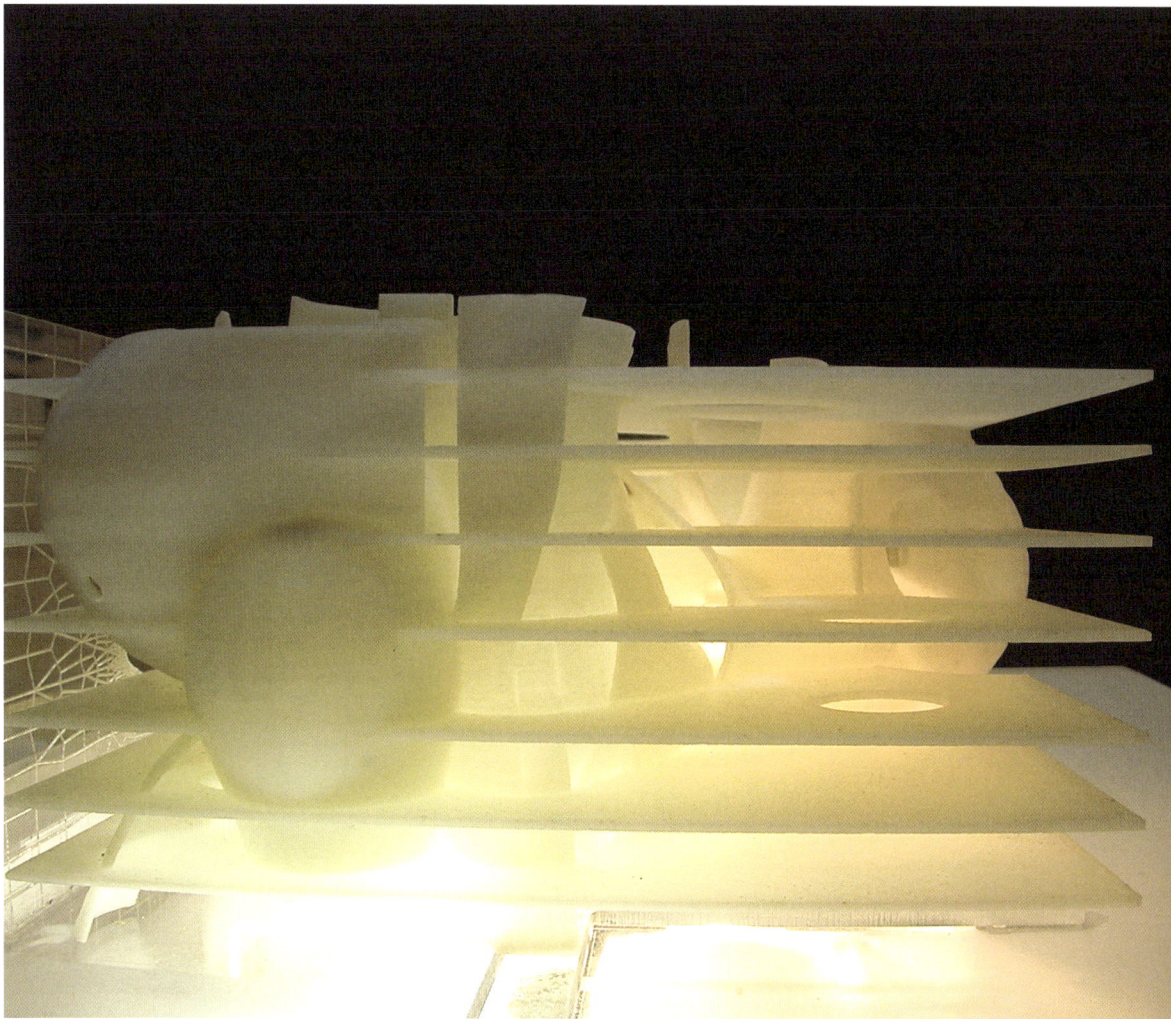

1.33

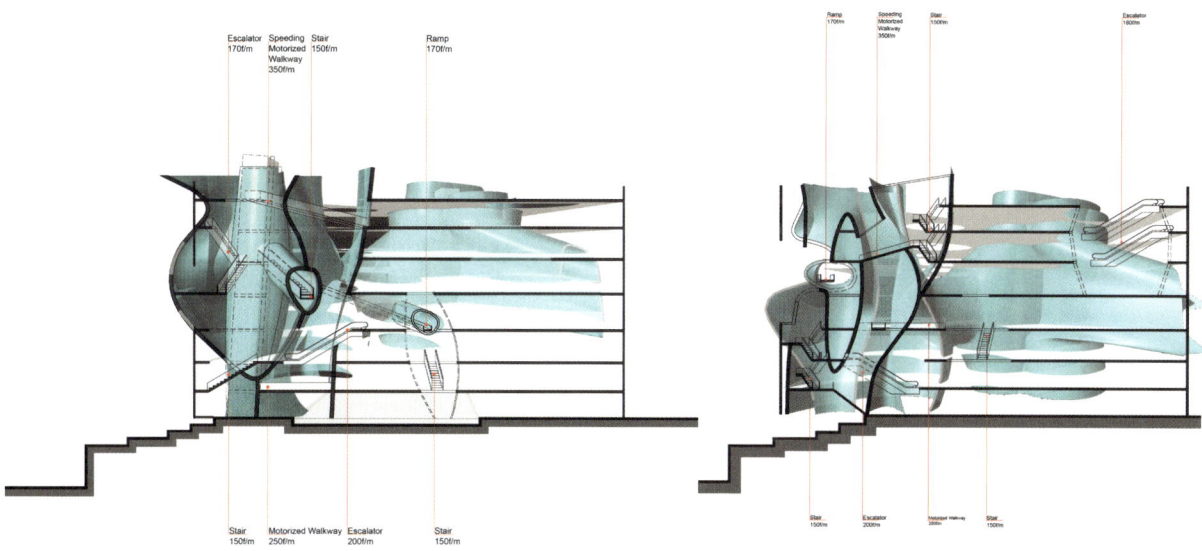

Escalator 170f/m   Speeding Motorized Walkway 350f/m   Stair 150f/m   Ramp 170f/m

Stair 150f/m   Motorized Walkway 250f/m   Escalator 200f/m   Stair 150f/m

Ramp 170f/m   Speeding Motorized Walkway 350f/m   Stair 150f/m   Escalator 160f/m

Stair 150f/m   Escalator 200f/m   Motorized Walkway 100f/m   Stair 150f/m

1.34

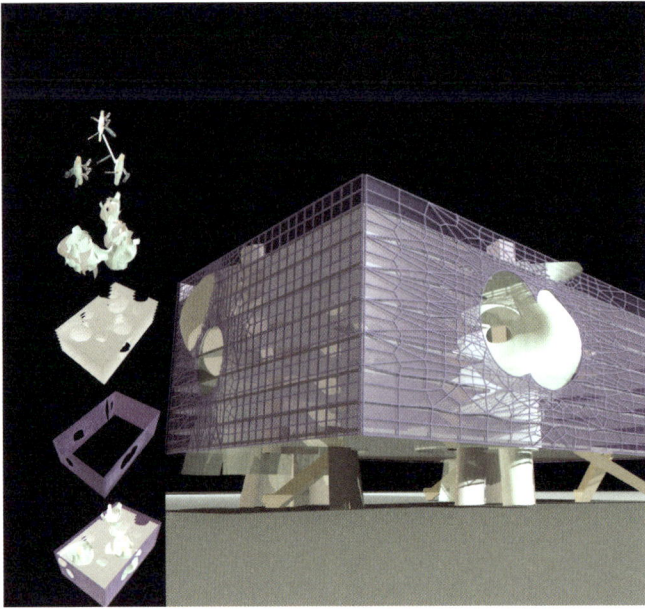

1.35

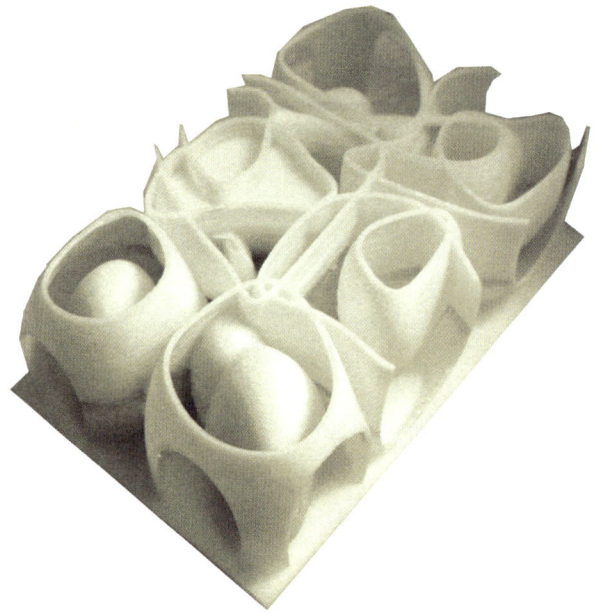

1.36

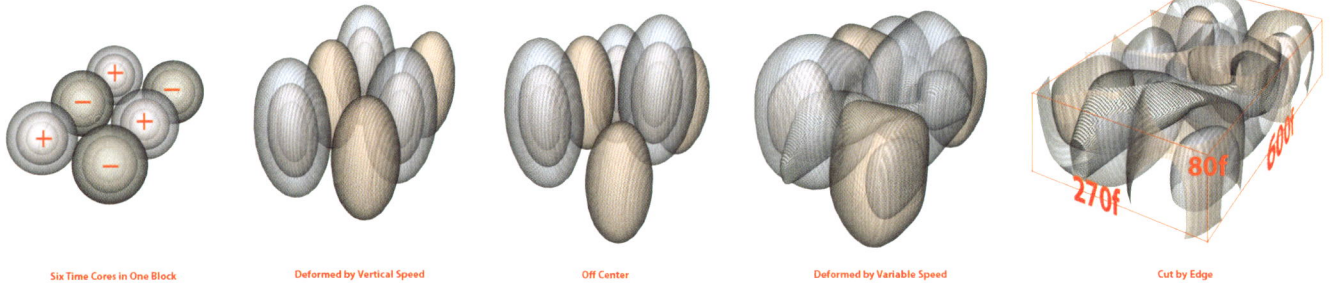

| Six Time Cores in One Block | Deformed by Vertical Speed | Off Center | Deformed by Variable Speed | Cut by Edge |

1.37

it working better this way or that way? What kind of behaviors are you trying to achieve?

Edward Mitchell: When you put the time cores in key spots, everything else will fill in—it becomes time-based planning. There is a local condition about the core of downtown and how far you start to get from the core that creates distortions within your transportation network.

Yang Yang and Yong Mei:
1.35 In exploring time cores, we found a way to balance the dynamic cycles of the 24-hour day. There is a maximum opportunity for mixed use at the moment where the layers of program overlap. Architecturally, we looked at circulation and categories of pedestrian movement: escalators, stairs, and ramps, each of which has a different speed. The distance is constant, and the time is variable; or the time is constant, and the distance is variable. The idea is the opposite of the traditional concept of the map.

1.36 3D print of diagram showing interconnected time cores.

1.37 How can the developer come in and transform the entire area? How is the FAR bonus defined so that developers must build certain key moments first

and then the areas between those moments? How do you achieve the maximum usage of the space so that it can operate 24 hours a day?

We began by revising zoning-use groups based on time, meaning how long the program can be used by individuals during the day. There would be an eight-hour program, a twelve-hour program, a 22-hour program, and so on. The next step in planning was to choose the programs from each category and make them work together in various combinations so that at any given time a space was active.

Spencer Luckey and Edward Richardson:
1.38 The central paradox of "Hyper PoPS" is that in creating incentivized public space and the resultant bonus development, the city becomes denser. This project's main intention was to exploit this relationship by treating the city in the same way that it treats itself, that is, by filling the voids at the fringe of the previous ring with more PoPS, which in turn beget more density.

1.39 We made this system using the pentominoes because they have a large surface area and a lot of malleable properties. We came up with different ways of aggregating them that were similar to how coral reefs develop. The basic diagram is office space on the street and housing on the water, with big box underneath; but the section becomes more and more complex as additional space and program aggregate. To continue to conform to the code, developers must constantly keep creating pockets of public space within the growing private mass or else, like coral, the entire system will suffocate and die.

42

1.38

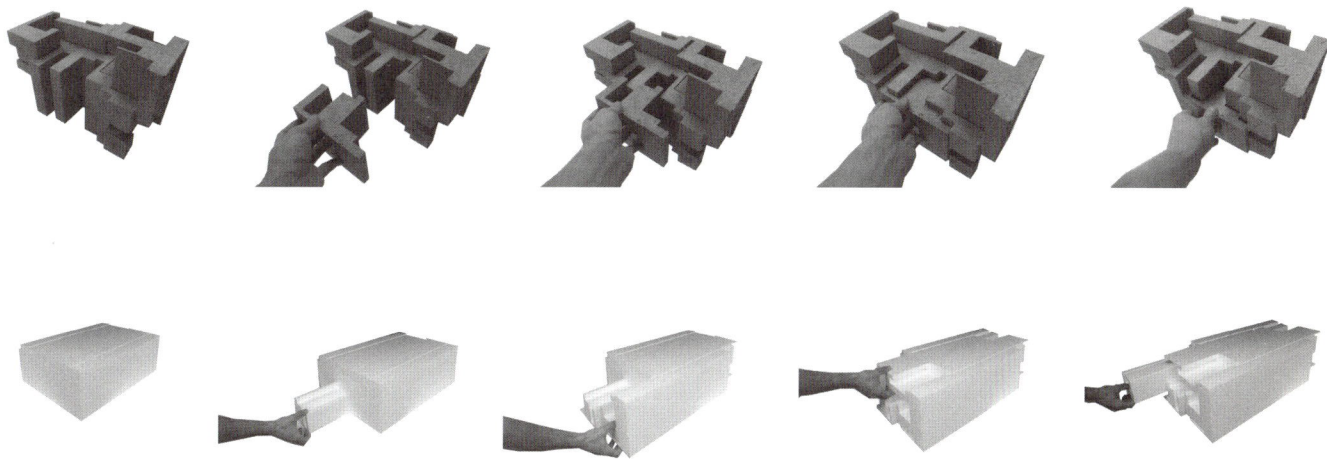

1.39

1.40

1.41

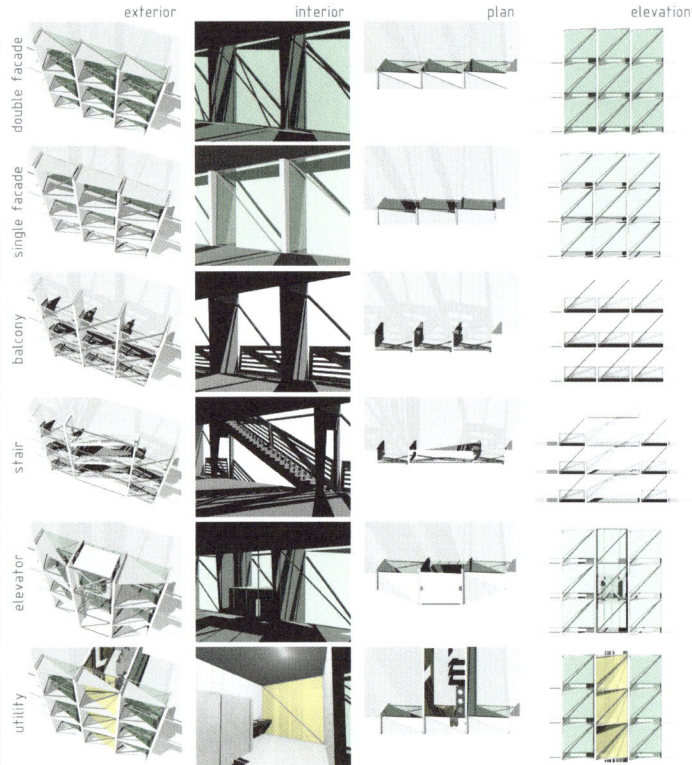

exterior   interior   plan   elevation

double facade
single facade
balcony
stair
elevator
utility

1.42

Ken Gowland and Esin Yurekli:
1.40 In this system, one grain of directional structure can support the other, meaning you can eliminate not just the static ground plane created by conventional building techniques that require columns and beams but also the distinction between public and private in the cross grain that results. By using the technique of "lofting" between systems, space in the threshold can be created by the very nature of making connections. Those spaces that are clearly public now have an indefinite relationship to those that are clearly private. It is not just, "Here's the building, here's the plaza"—it becomes a slippery space that is born from the juncture of the two.

Erin Carraher and Stephen Van Dyck:
1.41–42 Typologies employed to increase area of "Hyper PoPS" on- or offsite.

New techniques of modeling, organization, and construction were developed to explore the architectural and tectonic implications of the project at different phases which was a response to the idea of versioning as well as the call for rapid prototyping and mass customization.

This project is about the creation of a performance-based zoning code that introduces sustainable volumes into new, tall buildings through the use of large public spaces and programs. We proposed a new PoPs system that internalizes public spaces, removes the 20 percent bonus limit, awards bonuses through an open-source performance-based code, and programs adjacent spaces with a variety of public facilities. By removing the 20 percent bonus limit, the size of the bonus of the building would be limited by structure, circulation technology, and economics alone, not by prescriptive elements such as FAR and setback regulations.

Gregg Pasquarelli: You flip the code on its head, saying sustainability is the future and public space is what it is. The other marvelous invention is the vertical tessellations. You're saying it doesn't have to work the way it has since the nineteenth century. The hybrid inventions also combine the circulation with fresh air, which in itself is enough, and it could determine a lot about the volumes in your building and how you move vertically. If you can do that much, that's mind-blowing.

REINTERPRETING DENSITY

The paradox of "Hyper PoPS" is that it simultaneously increases the density of the urban fabric by allowing developers to build bigger and higher while it mandates additional increases in public space, sometimes enclosed, sometimes open. Three main logics emerged as methods that the students used to maximize public and private space, enclose rentable floor area, and open public recreation space: aeration, vertical redistribution, and interweaving urban fabrics.

Carving holes in the density of the existing urban fabric, whether by digging underground or extracting sections from existing buildings, allows light, air, and public circulation into densely built-up areas of the city. In exchange, new zoning rules are required in order to extend the boundary of the built fabric and give back the density lost in the process. Sectional shifts, either vertical or horizontal, allow for additional public space in already densely populated areas. Proposals included extending the public plane underground, creating a public *piano nobile* above the street, bringing the public into the upper levels of a building by making operations on the z-axis, and reconsidering PoPS as qualitative volumes. "Interweaving" is a subset of the above categories: it carves out fingers that stretch back into the city fabric, while vertical solutions knit the public up and down into areas that were previously exclusively private.

1.43

Damian Zunino and Ezra Groskin:
1.43–44 The method of creating the continuous open space of the PoPS assemblage was through a zoning amendment mandating that all building owners construct a minimum thirty-foot-wide connection to the adjacent sites over street intersections. In exchange, owners are rewarded with air-right bonuses at a rate of three square feet for every square foot of PoPS built, without limit. For existing buildings, the air rights can be sold and applied anywhere in Lower Manhattan. New buildings can apply 20 percent of their bonus to their building and sell any additional rights. The continuous, secondary pedestrian plane also allows owners to better use the second through fifth floors of their buildings, charging higher rents for previously unpopular space.

The PoPS bonus has historically been awarded as a one-shot bonus to the landowners. Economically speaking, this isn't a sustainable model; once the landowners get the bonus they have no financial incentive to develop a nice space. In our proposal, an ongoing exchange would occur between the public and private, creating additional incentives for developers to innovate and improve the public spaces.

Chris Sharples: In the ramped sections you can imagine coming out of the building and going back in a leisurely way, but I wonder if you can also imagine doing so immediately. What is the force generating what is going on in that building? Has it moved from the office building to another sort of transformation that engages the whole mechanism of the façade? Does it generate a new arcade within the façade? How does this then extend into the thickness of the building?

Gregg Pasquarelli: It retreats from just being a surface, which was your first gesture, and the building starts to deploy something that actually becomes construction, program, surface, and PoPS, all at the same time.

Keller Easterling: Not only does it engage a construction technology, a complete redefinition of what a façade would be, but suddenly the company that is building this has permitted it to happen. They've revalued x number of floors to make more and more and more money. It's really, really clever. And one wants to see you make even more of it.

Erin Carraher and Stephen Van Dyck:
1.45–46 Unlike the existing code, the code proposed here is performance-based, provides unlimited bonus opportunity, integrates the public into the building at higher levels, integrates light and air into the mass of the building, is measured in volume rather than

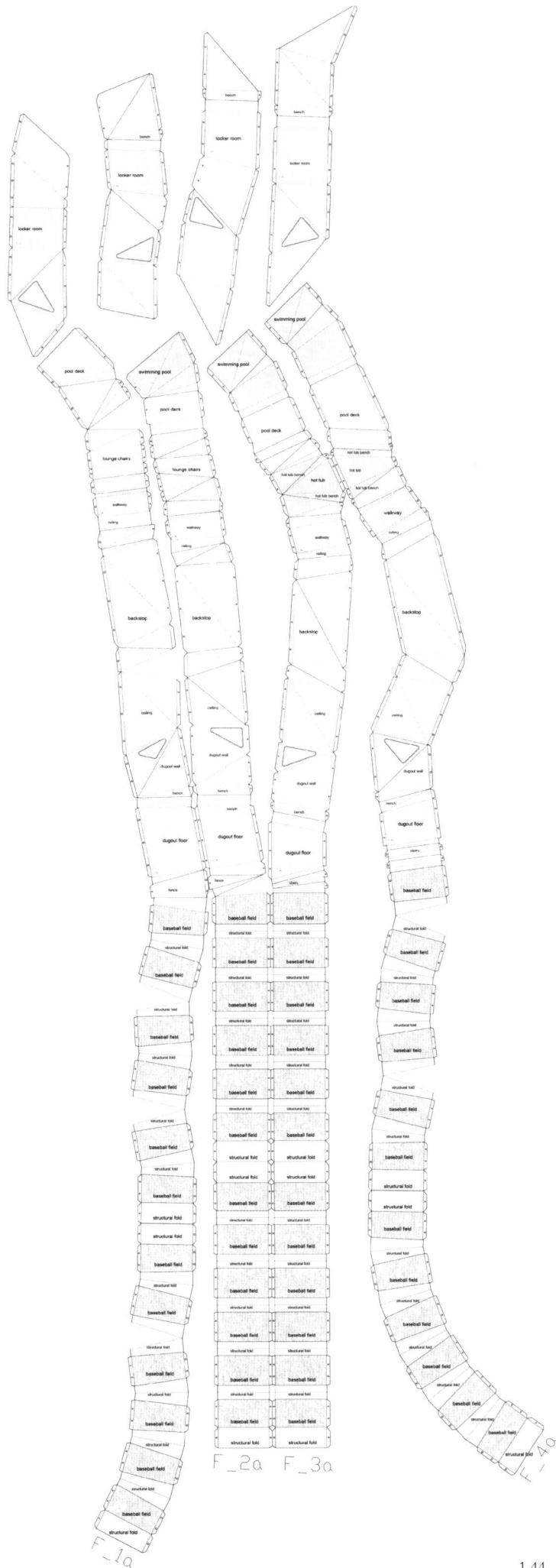

F_1a   F_2a   F_3a   F_4a

1.44

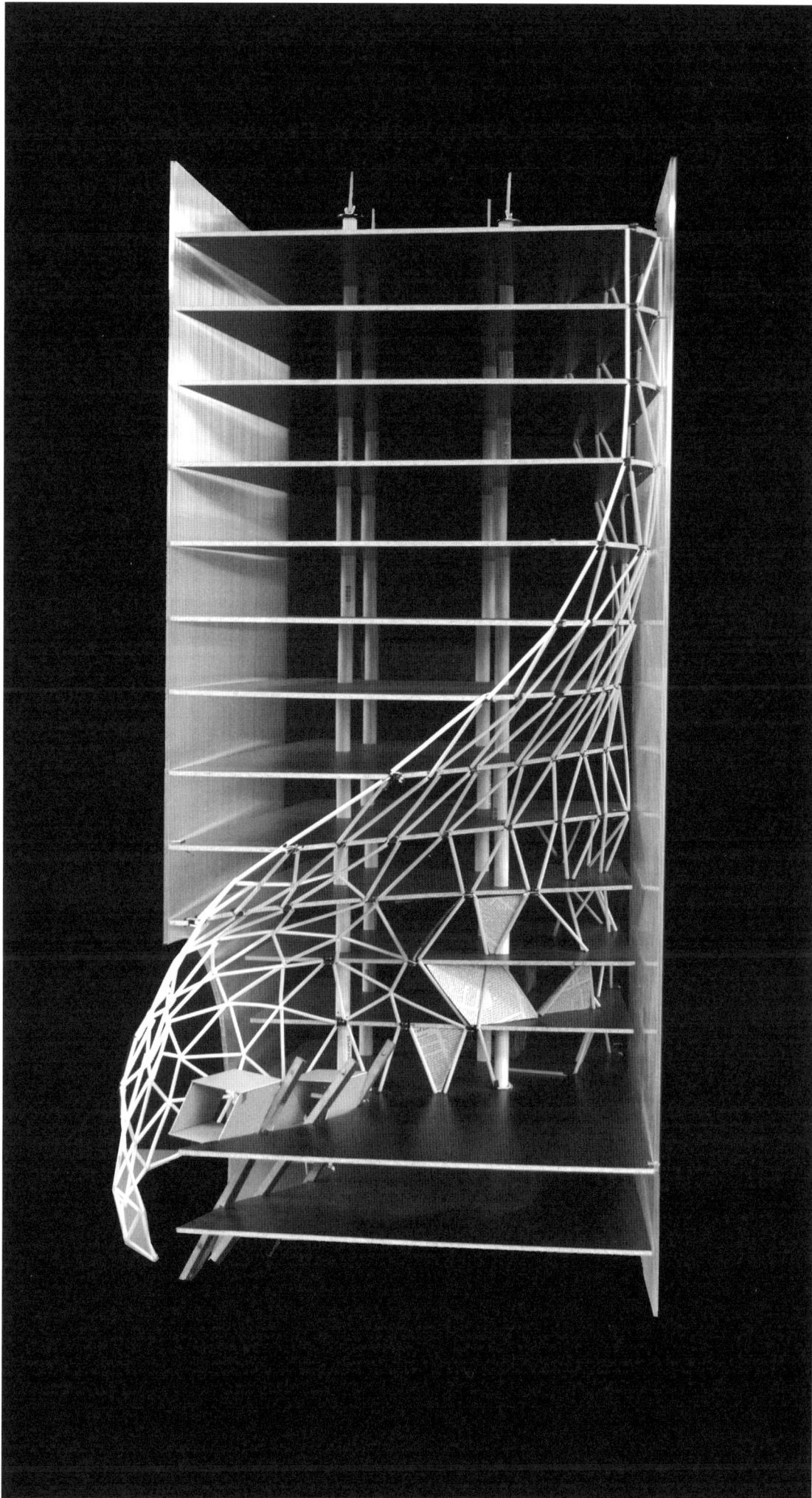

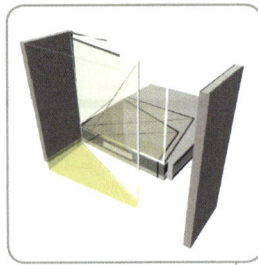

curtain wall double facade allows for air circulation between glass layers

floor slab system with upturned ribs to allow for air intake and utility passage

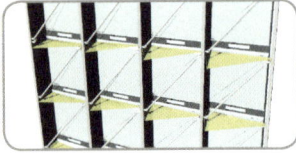

horizontal shaders vary angle to allow for different degrees of sun shading

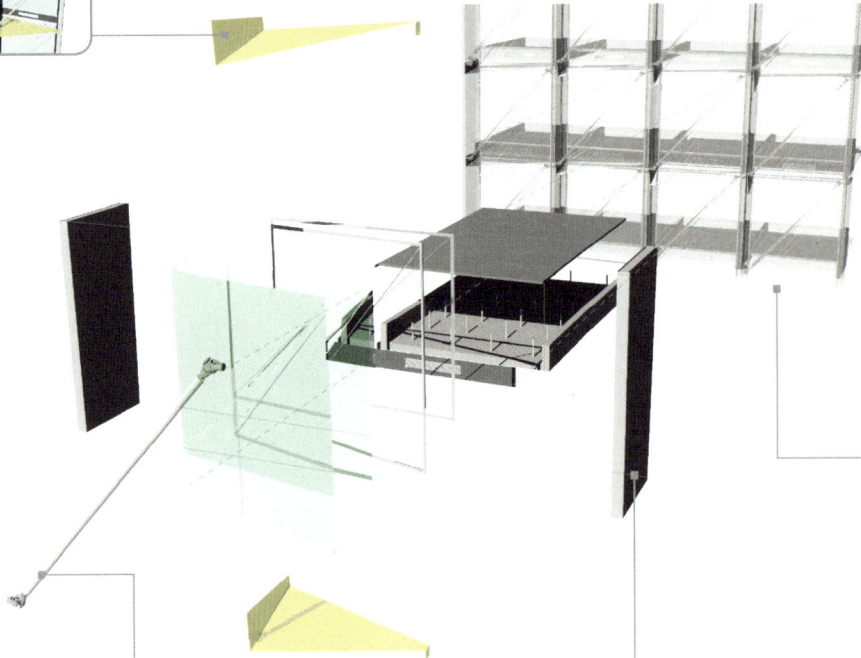

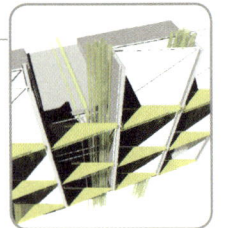

utility chase the thickness of the entire facade system increases, providing an allowable use with a unidirectional utility entry

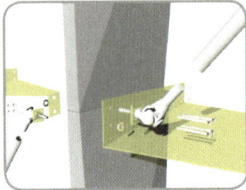

universal joint provides the point of connection for the column, shader, and diagonal bracing systems

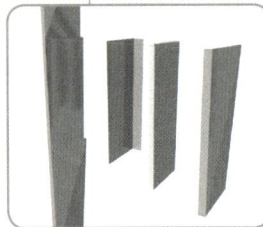

columns two bent steel sheets are joined to provide the formwork for a concrete column system and remain the material finish

1.46

1.47

1.48

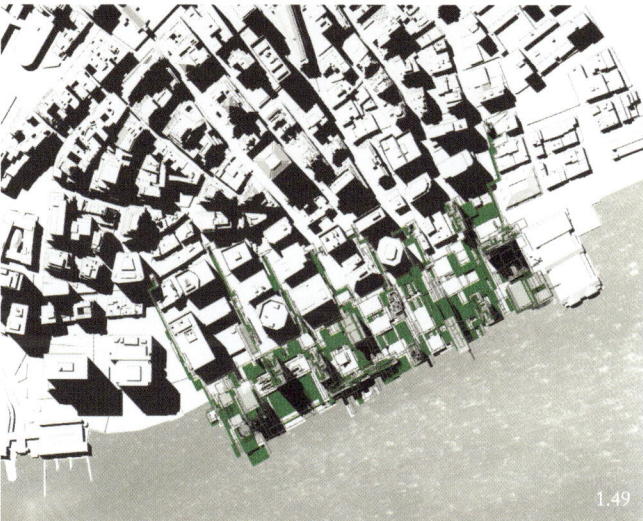

1.49

[Before]   [After]

1.50

area, and attempts to provide quality to the public in a quantitative way.

Gregg Pasquarelli: You need to say, "Nineteen sixty-one is over, it's not about the process, and we are about public good." It's not about light—certainly not about sunlight coming down to the street. "Public good" is making sustainable buildings.

Chris Sharples: It is very much operating on the models coming from Hong Kong and Japan. This is another model that has been injected into the grid system, and suddenly we're seeing a mutation.

Spencer Luckey and Edward Richardson: 1.47–49 As opposed to previous large-scale development projects like Battery Park City that achieved their ends through broad strokes by up-zoning the general FAR for the site, which resulted in huge buildings out of scale with the surrounding public space, we mutated the code to achieve our design density by controlling the scale of public space at a finer resolution.

PoPS have long been used as a tool by developers to make their buildings bigger, but there have always been limits to the system dependent on program or type of space created. As a strip of bare concrete is just as profitable to the developer as a well-designed space, the PoPS restrictions have contributed to the lackluster spaces that have resulted. By removing the PoPS cap and maintaining the existing FAR at the East River site, we proposed the developed area could achieve the desired density by providing massive amounts of PoPS space. The result is a highly aerated plinth of mixed-use commercial and retail space intertwined with PoPS that is attractive to the developer, who can now build without limitation on a particular site but only by providing more and better public space.

Brady Stone and Brendan Lee: 1.50 Diagram of the PoPS "In" PoPS "Out" spatial exchange system where in space dedicated to the public on the interior of a building is traded for additional space for commercial use at the street level.

William Sharples: This project creates the possibility of injecting the infrastructure needed for a 24-hour city because it aerates the situation and pulls you into the fabric. It's like in Midtown: if you know which lobbies to go through, you can cut through all of Midtown without having to walk the sidewalks. You need to really get into these cities and figure out what is going on. In the middle of London there's a Victorian market; you wouldn't know it unless you were driving down a side street and stumbled upon it. This can take on that energy, but you have to talk more about what

1.51

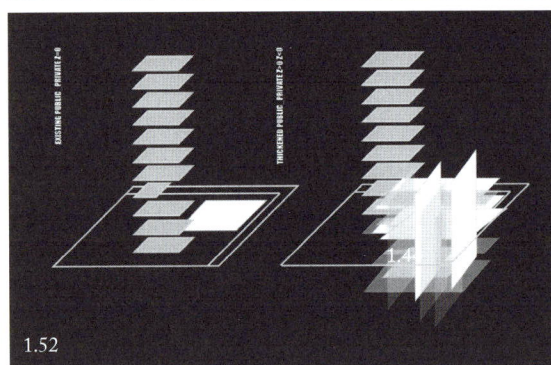
1.52

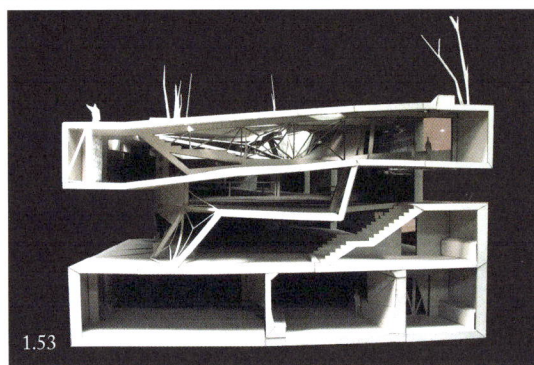
1.53

is the enterprise that's going to happen as a result of these new, carved-out spaces, not just sort of build out on the periphery.

Gregg Pasquarelli: If you take the amount of FAR that exists in Lower Manhattan and divide it by the linear feet of retail frontage, it's probably the worst ratio in all of New York. It's tiny. The students are saying the aggregate spaces can carve through the existing buildings, but at the same time there's a lot more density that needs to take place if they want to put residential, retail, cultural institutions, and joy downtown and continue to maintain the balance between it and the stuff. So the key question of the strategy is, how, with a single move, do you aerate the core but also build density?

Chris Sharples: Maybe it could become the new *piano nobile* of the city. It

reminds me of the Lever House: it has the public element to it, but there's a certain amount of blurring because there is the glass box on the second floor that now has a gallery but could also work as a commercial space. There's a strong relationship between the garden and the urban cloister. How do you draw them up to that *piano nobile,* to that open area? The process of getting you up there informs you about the PoPS "Out." It comes back to what you are trying to achieve in terms of the experience of the place. That's the problem right now with existing PoPS: people don't know what to do with them. People feel awkward and exposed, whereas this project starts to talk about nesting within this environment and giving them a purpose.

Ken Gowland and Esin Yurekli:
1.51–52 Rendering and diagrams showing transitional spaces that resulted when time cores begin to congeal.

1.53 This model is designed as one big truss, attached at points in an interlocking egg-crate pattern. Imagine an x-y grid that is extruded to give each line a thickness in the z direction: the lines are now planes, and the intersection points are now lines. If the lines and planes of the gird are shifted in elevation, there can no longer be just a static plane; pockets of space are created within the thickness of the system, as well as in thresholds where space slips from one side to the other and back again.

Chris Sharples: How do you move down into the next space, and how does this slippage work? The Whitney Museum of American Art has this problem with its moat, but it's sort of exciting to be on the street and look down into that area. If the tessellated pieces in your project were made of glass, those below-grade PoPS would be incredible. At night, you would see the glowing of all these PoPS throughout Lower Manhattan. It reminds me of Bruno Taut's crystal architecture but in reverse, extending like a geode into the city.

STRUCTURE AND TECTONICS

Versioning considers new construction techniques informed by digital technology. Methods of construction were integrated into the design process from the beginning in the form of innovative modeling techniques and research into interdisciplinary fabrication technologies, allowing a number of alternative building methods to emerge during the course of the studio. Certain projects developed building systems that operated as both surface and structure. These systems served such disparate functions as circulation and utility cores, programmed spaces, active or passive sustainable devices, and membranes regulating passage between public and private zones. Alternately, folded-surface systems maximized the usable square footage within a designated footprint while also dealing with the three main conditions encountered in doing so: spanning, ramping, and enclosing. By folding a surface in two directions, it creates rigidity while simultaneously incorporating program and service utilities. Projects using the methods of carving and casting extracted pockets of public space from existing or proposed densities and moved the displaced volume to areas in the city where densification was needed. This method moved beyond the consideration of the block or neighborhood and looked at the city at a larger scale of density and void and attempted to mediate between the two. Thickened skins bridged public amenities and private spaces and were manifest primarily as the subtle deformation of what was once designated the ground or wall plane. The effect erased the line between public and private.

1.54

Yang Yang and Yong Mei:
1.54–55 The idea is to reverse the traditional concept of the map. These diagrams show how the time cores are informed by the different types of circulation within the system. If you put in more vertical circulation, the time cores will deform vertically. If you choose other kinds of circulation, the whole architecture changes.

1.56 Sections showing transportation linkages among public and private sectors.

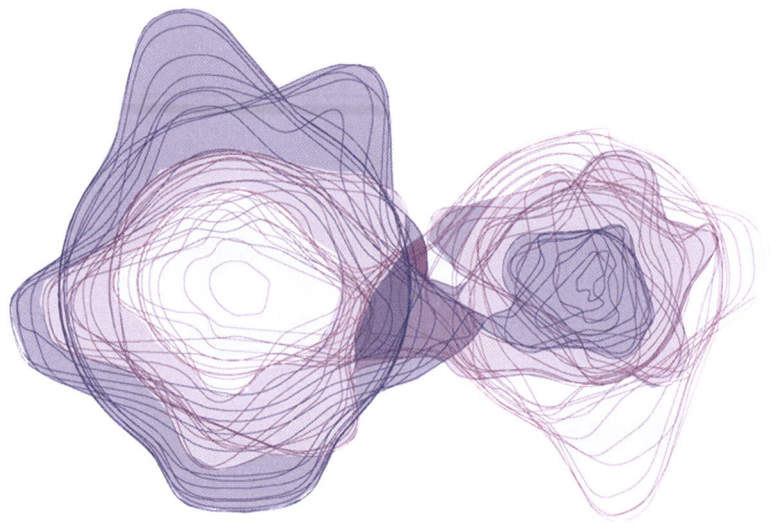

Gregg Pasquarelli: At what point is it just a diagram? At what point do you make it morphology? When is it just something that's helping you think? Its visibility is sometimes irrelevant because you're being inventive.

Ken Gowland and Esin Yurekli:
1.57–61 By operating within both the public and private realms, it is possible for the Hyper PoPS to perform as dense nodes of activity within the urban network, thus transforming sites of contention between public and private desires from a valueless terrain into the loci of a mutually advantageous relationship.

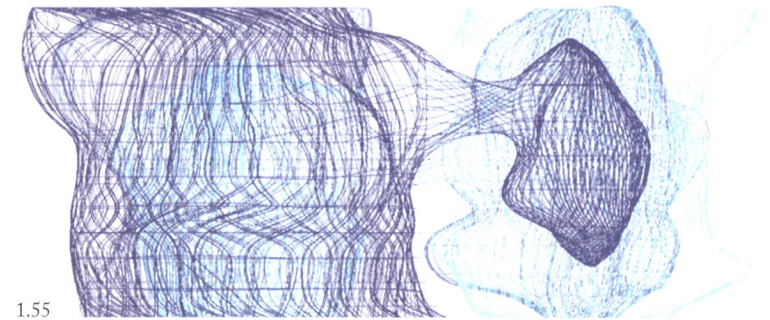

1.55

Gregg Pasquarelli: We're thinking of these sections of the structure as a bulkhead. When you think of a computational fluid dynamic model and start to see points at which there's intensity, how amazing would it be to see these three or four surfaces of plaza and—just by looking at the thicknesses and the way that it's continually differentiating—create a joint that is continually changing yet becomes the language for the architectural detail and the tectonic for the building.

Chris Sharples: Each piece is a unique puzzle piece—maybe that's the technology you might look at next. Take a section of that and realize how those pieces are very, very precise at a certain point in time.

Gregg Pasquarelli: It's great because slicing is always the first move, especially with this type of model, and then layering is the next easiest one. It's really good that you've recognized the limits of those models and moved beyond them; your ideas require you to use new technologies. You're milling and carving out three-dimensional space, which raises a whole series of technological issues you have to deal with. And then how do you start to deploy other materials into the

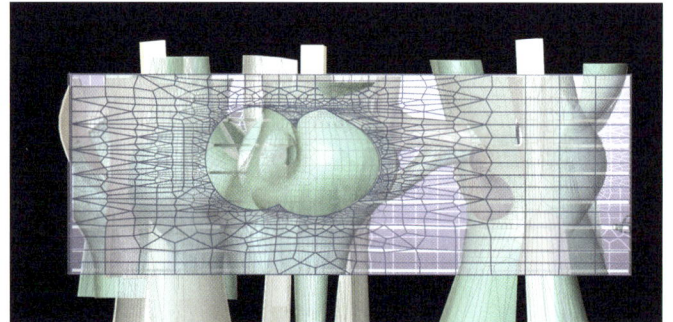

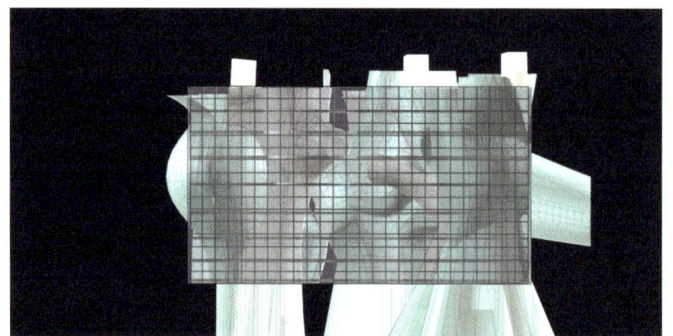

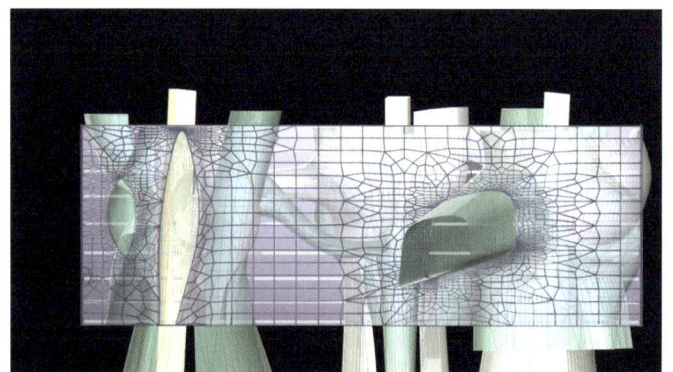

1.56

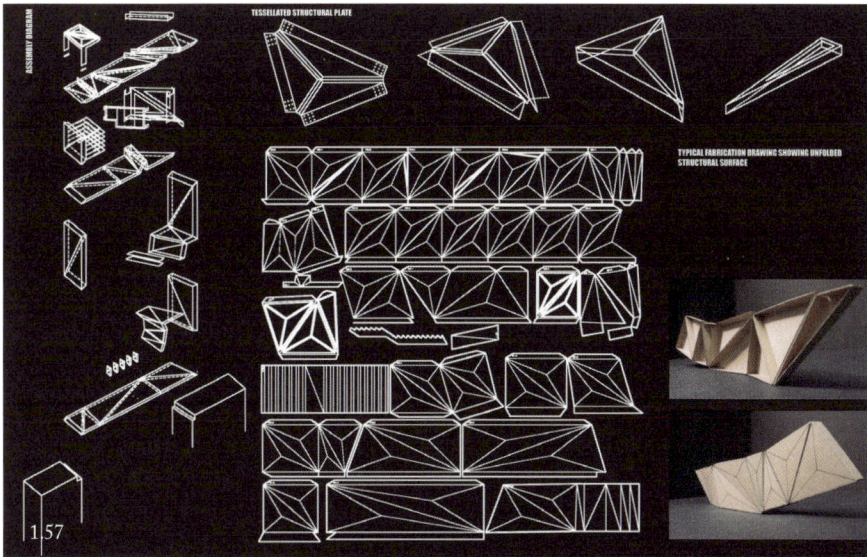

ASSEMBLY DIAGRAM

TESSELLATED STRUCTURAL PLATE

TYPICAL FABRICATION DRAWING SHOWING UNFOLDED
STRUCTURAL SURFACE

1.57

1.58

1.59

1.60

1.61

1.62

1.63

1.64

1.65

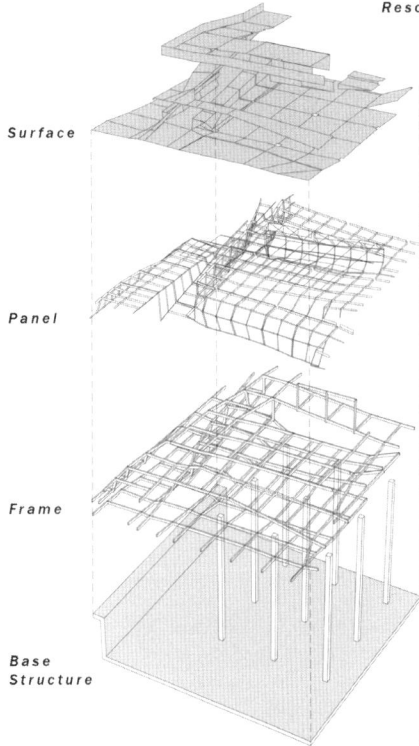

Surface

Panel

Frame

Base
Structure

1.66

folded system? It can't just be a unimaterial like it is in the chipboard model. As more and more specificity starts to come into play in the surface, program, and structure, then more and more materials come in, and the question becomes how to bring heterogeneity back into the model once you have five or ten different systems working together. That's where the research has to now move.

Keller Easterling: This engages with construction technology and completes the definition of what the façade can be. In addition, the company that's committed to this model would have trade-offs, but what they have done is revalue x numbers of floors of the building so they are making more and more money.

Erin Carraher and Stephen Van Dyck:
1.62–63 In response to the changes proposed in the zoning code to promote buildings that not only are sustainable in terms of low-energy consumption but also become sustainable by being used and loved by the public, we set out to create a multifunctional building system that operates within this code. We have developed a skeletal system that is structural, provides circulation and utilities, houses passive sustainable devices, and creates a membrane that regulates passage between public and private areas.

All the public spaces and the circulation systems combined account for 30 percent of the building volume, a number usually reserved for circulation alone. The new Hyper PoPS would enhance street life by bringing the public up to the light and air and aerating a new generation of public and semipublic spaces in the process.

1.64 Versioning was used to create multigenerational study models by altering one variable at a time and then playing out all scenarios of an idea before moving to the next phase of design. Complex taxonomies were created from which stronger iterations were culled to create more fully developed models that were fabricated and studied.

Gregg Pasquarelli: This is a strategy that describes quality through a code based on performance, rather than prescription. It's amazing because that is an almost impossible thing to do.

Spencer Luckey and Edward Richardson:
1.65 In our proposal, the developed area would only achieve the desired density by providing massive amounts of PoPS to aerate private spaces. According to the proposed code, the resultant architecture would be a highly aerated plinth of mixed-use commercial and retail spaces intertwined with PoPS and punctuated by a series of towers growing out of the plinth to accommodate FAR displaced during the aeration process. The more private space developers want to build, the more ingenious they need to be to

achieve the required aeration of the plinth. Like the architects of the Gothic cathedrals, they will need to test the limits of the structure-to-volume ratio, creating similarly innovative and impressive architecture.

Brady Stone and Brendan Lee:
1.66 PoPS "In" and PoPS "Out" proposes a weighted exchange of square footage between the building and the PoPS. A symbiotic economic relationship between building and open space catalyzes a new spatial relationship between the two entities. Local implementations of urban scripting are administered by a PoPS network, an economic and political organization akin to a BID. The PoPS network enlists a sponsoring organization to take a financial interest in the improvement of the area's public spaces.

Damian Zunino and Ezra Groskin:
1.67–68 The structural system maximizes the usable square footage within a designated footprint while also providing a connective system that can deal with the three main conditions encountered: spanning, ramping, and enclosing.

Keller Easterling: You need to hire a handler to help you campaign for your project, because I think it's really quite great and a really different species of proposal. Maybe it should stay different. For instance, the swimming pool seems like the perfect vivid thing that you use to say, "Here's this real estate possibility," which will then yield all these different things: it will pay for the bike racks, the bleachers, and the little-league field and inspire the next innovation within the system.

Gregg Pasquarelli: How do we make the skin become the grid or the grid become the skin? How do we begin to cut material and fold it in a way so that thickness, program, and structure become the same thing? To me, that's really the power of what computer-aided design can do. It's not just to make formless moves; it's the larger point in the studio. This is a time when there's a true paradigm shift happening in architecture and construction. You start to be able to be as poetic and beautiful as Calatrava without the dinosaur and bird drawings because it's actually happening; it becomes like bones, it becomes all of these things simultaneously, and yet we can do it without spending $1,000 a square foot. To me, that's where it becomes incredibly interesting.

55

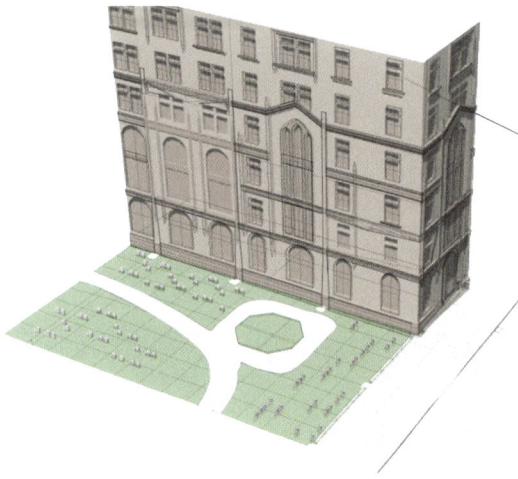

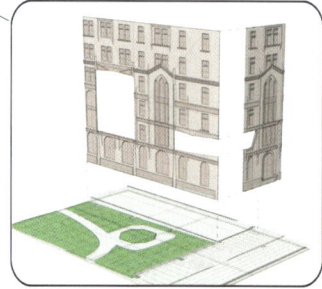

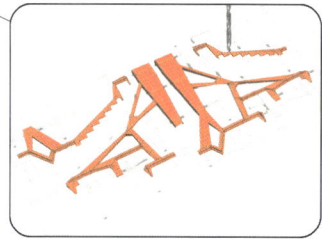

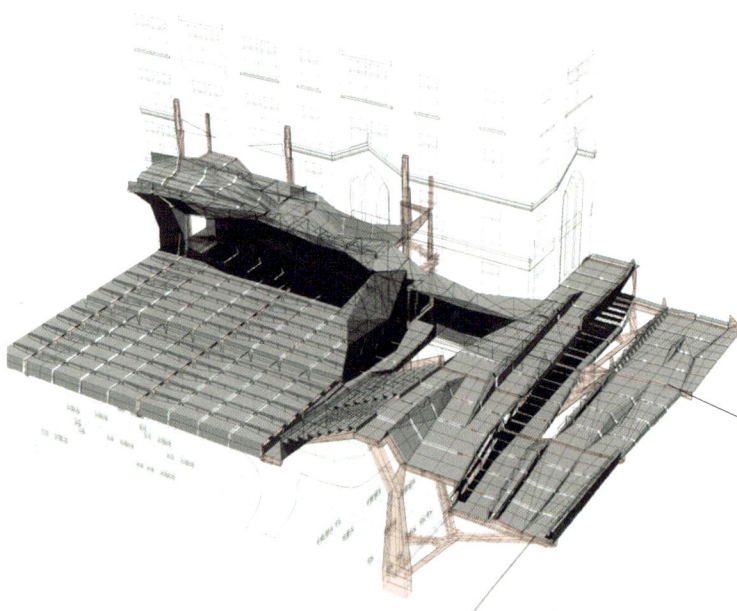

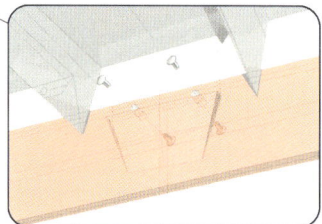

1.67

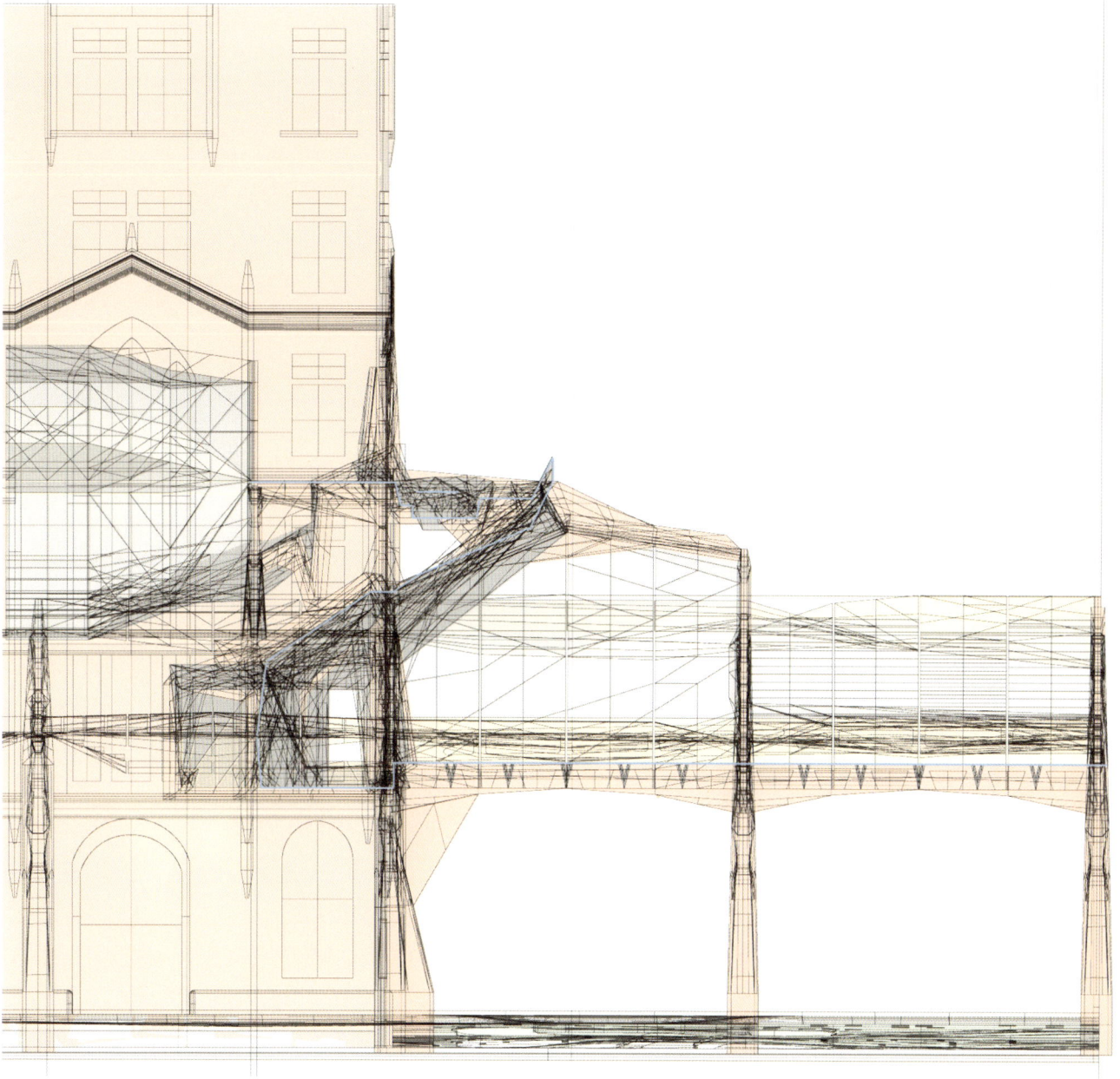

1.68

GALIA
SOLOMO

Galia Solomonoff was the Kahn Visiting Assistant Professor at Yale School of Architecture in fall 2004. Her practice began with Alan Koch, Lyn Rice, and Linda Taalman in 1999 as a founder of the firm OpenOffice, in New York, from 1999 to 2004. Since 2005 she has been principal of her own firm, Solomonoff Architecture Studio (SAS), in New York, and is working on projects in Harlem, Chelsea, the Lower East Side and Miami. As associate professor at Columbia University's Graduate School of Architecture, Planning, and Preservation, she teaches advanced studios and coordinates the first-year studios. Below she discusses her approach to architecture and urbanism with Nina Rappaport.

Nina Rappaport: Many designers today are crossing over to different disciplines: urban design, industrial design, art, teaching. How does SAS collaborate on multidisciplinary projects, and how might that relate back to the historical role of the architect?

Galia Solomonoff: The structures of production have changed, the complexity and role of architecture have expanded, and design is now understood as more central to everyday life and accessible to more people. Therefore it is more advantageous to think of ourselves as leaders and teams rather than single practitioners or heroic architects. The team takes the central role, credit, and responsibility for the work produced. I see myself as the creative producer within my team more than designer. SAS's recent growth necessitated that I learn very specific tools from the world of finance, law, construction, education, planning, management, art, etc. My central task is to envision the big picture, think of the narratives within which the projects are

inscribed, and consult with my team and consultants to move a common vision forward. Rather than going heroically against the flow, take the flow further; exploit the possibilities of the real, the opportunists, the political, the accidental, the unique, the defective.

NR: How has the organization of your office changed over time as you have shifted from working with OpenOffice to working on your own for three years as SAS? How do you control and direct a project as your expertise increases?

GS: I am interested in developing my own language as an architect, designing a practice not just buildings, writing the curriculum not just teaching, and taking the least amount of restrictions as a given. If a rule does not make sense, if it detracts from the architecture, if it is archaic, then it is imperative for us to challenge it. As licensed architects we have resources to exert more control over the building process. I retain as many consultants as recommended, but I do not delegate the responsibility of running or narrating the project to them. During the first ten years of my practice I learned the rules, now I am more assertive and can discern a direction for my practice, life, and work.

NR: Dia:Beacon was designed from 1999 to 2003 by OpenOffice, with the artist Robert Irwin and the art institution, to adapt an existing building. How did that project help inform your practice as you were jumping to a larger scale?

GS: Dia was a very good learning experience. Artists are stubborn, and we learned from them. The project required patience, clarity, and precision. It was a slow and cerebral maneuver—the opposite of

the type of first projects that most times young architects get to do. It made us mature and restrained, sometimes too serious. I am having more fun now, trying more things. Paradoxically, as time goes by I am given more opportunities to be more experimental and playful with my projects, even though the projects and budgets keep getting larger. Maybe it is because I proved with Dia that, although young, I delivered.

NR: You were working on Dia during the same time you worked with artists on their own studios and living spaces. What has been the most satisfying thing about working with artists? Is it the ability to have more aesthetic freedom and the kinds of opportunities that you have been able to carry through?

GS: The most satisfying thing is the clarity of the decision-making process of an artist, the drive, and assertiveness. It doesn't matter how many developers come to me, I will always work with artists. Artists and teaching keep me honest and sober. The effort and discipline of both is like a fitness routine for the design drive. With our office in Chelsea, I am surrounded by the art world. I go to galleries at my lunch beak and see art and artists, and it is as much my community as architecture.

NR: Do you feel there is a lack of an awareness of what is going on in the art world for most architects? What does this awareness do for you?

GS: What it does is raise awareness of materials, from duct tape to cardboard, to Tyvek to clay. SAS's choices of colors, materials, and finishes are influenced by our proximity to the art context and the fact that most of our income comes from artists (clients). It expands how you see things in the material world, the relationship between matter and ideas, matter and subject. It is essential to our practice.

NR: Does crossing over into the realm of art make for a more wholistic approach in architecture?

GS: Our approach requires an integral way of thinking. I see no boundaries between people; I like to see continuity in the way ideas, matter, and subject flow. Le Corbusier asserted that architecture had the mission to make people happier; I would say "more aware" rather than "happier." In the United States politics is a negative word, but democracy cannot exist without politics and every project has a political context. Architecture cannot survive without art or political agency.

NR: The intersection between the creative mind and the bureaucratic framework becomes interesting as a point of tension to influence creativity. Architects acknowledge restrictions and then figure out ways projects can be worked in and around those restrictions. Do you think organizational structures and programmatic restrictions help you form your projects? How does pragmatism help creativity?

GS: In a way, good projects manifest latent organizational structures. At different scales, the competition entry with OpenOffice for the Highline, Dia:Beacon, or small residential projects are a confluence of the constraints of the law, our desire—as well as some happy coincidence of our clients' and our own desires—and the availability of resources. Since it is always someone else's money, we need to foster a common desire/vision of the thing.

NR: Turning to urbanism and urban issues, how do you see architecture as an individual object in relationship to urban design both in your own work and in studios that you have taught? As an architect, what do you think your role is in designing cities or parts of cities?

GS: The city is an arrangement of different things, and when you have a chance to design a building that will affect the life of one, two, or eight hundred people, you have a chance of reinscribing the narratives of those people. If I am doing a residential building in a neighborhood, I am not only responsible for a piece of architecture, I consider how I script the lives of people. Do I want them to enter their private domain directly from the street? Do I want them to go through a garden? Would they get their morning coffees in their home or before they enter the train? I am not manipulating their lives, but I am trying to think about as many scenarios as I can for their private daily routines. The difference between the architect and the urbanist is that I am thinking about the intimacy of their daily lives and also their influence on their block and vice versa. It is a little bit like a butterfly effect: once you put new people on the block, you've altered the eco-system. From the architectural point of view, it extends from the very small layer of the closet, bathroom, and kitchen to the sidewalks, the subway platforms, cityscape, and the skyline—from the intimate to the urban to the regional.

But I also think about the building as an artifact in the urban fabric. In an area of town that is not recognizable for having tall buildings, it often makes sense to have a tall building so that, for example, in New York, when you see the skyline peak up at 96th Street and almost nothing to the north, less lights, less tall structures, it makes sense to have something above the normal height of the area in Harlem, where we are now working. Or in the East Village, the blue building by Bernard Tschumi is a new landmark for that area that also triggers all kinds of ways of reorganizing the urban fabric. It is a double bind for an architect: as you are thinking about the small things and the larger picture, you are making decisions and negotiating a position that straddles both.

NR: In terms of the layered and multiple ways to occupy and view a city, how do you work within these layers? How do the various perspectives and architectural approaches—tabula rasa, new urbanism, on innovative design—offer solutions for the city? How do you as a contemporary architect integrate your work with what is existing and then jump into the potential for the future of the city?

GS: In terms of future and past, when I reread Le Corbusier I feel as if his attention and focus on the future didn't allow him to see the possibilities of the past. He was so focused on his own imprint and changing the world that he didn't appreciate what was there. I don't think he was totally sincere in terms of his negativity toward the past and his relationship to the present. I think my generation's position is more like storytelling within a larger story. It is not as if we are writing a big new book. No one person can claim full responsibility for the transformation of the Meatpacking District, or Harlem, or the Lower East Side. SANAA's building for the New Museum of Contemporary Art, on the Bowery, is part of the story of change that will be a catalyst for that area of town. Certainly the UN development or the WTC, which are big chunks of land and new ground or Battery Park City, with a very scripted master plan and

Solomonoff Architecture Studio, rendering of interior of Baptist Church, New York, 2007.

Solomonoff Architecture Studio in collaboration with designer Etsumi Imamura, Stimulus, clothing store prototype, Tokyo, Japan, 2006.

aesthetic guidelines, require different approaches compared with the Meatpacking District or the Lower East Side, which are intricate, careful pieces. A skillful architect is assertive and introspective in making his or her own piece but also carefully tying it to the context.

NR: New York City architects were for so long stuck in the grid, hemmed in by the zoning laws, and unable to shift even for light and air. Projects such as Portzamparc's on 57th Street broke the grid and Herzog & De Meuron tried with an exaggerated zoning envelop for the MoMA competition. How do you take advantage of the opportunity to re-orient new buildings off the grid in the nongridded areas of the city, like the Atlantic Terminal, and make them respond in different ways to the rigidity of the city framework? Is this occurring in your new projects?

GS: For a long time the grid of the city and the zoning were used as crutches to retain a New Yorkness, and now because of younger and/or European outsider architects who have intervened in the city and others who might be less respectful of these rules, it is not taken for granted anymore. The responsibility to a site, such as the Atlantic Terminal site or the Hudson Yards, is much larger. One needs to think and imagine the transforming effect that Grand Central, Park Avenue, and Central Park had in the city and imagine New York without them to appreciate the real responsibility of tackling Atlantic Terminal or Hudson Yards. In Brooklyn, they are talking about which of the avenues should be the main artery and which streets should cross it. Those are decisions traditionally thought about by urban planners, but since Koolhaas, fortunately they are also the territory of architects, too. *Delirious New York* is a fundamental book to teach because it connects the responsibility of the architect with the script of the city. Every time I read that book with students I am convinced that my profession is instrumental in making a better world, and I demand of myself—and my students—more.

NR: When OpenOffice was one of the teams selected in summer 2004 to compete for the Highline redevelopment, how did you apply the approach of working within constraints and your interests in urbanism to your proposal?

GS: Ours was the most urban section I have seen in a project. There is a park as well as the integration of public space and private domain. The city offered private owners air rights around a void in exchange for the park to make them happy. As for a master plan, we wanted a design approach for the city, the property owners, and the park, very much like Dia. It is an intricate group of negotiators. We don't have that many opportunities to mix the different stories of the city, and the Highline provides a place where there is an artifact that was used one way in the past, and now you can rescript it with totally different uses: an elevated park, a place you can walk around walk without cars, a sky lobby for an adjacent building. It is such a great concept for the city. The people that own land near it always said that money doesn't grow on trees, but here it was proven that it does grow on shrubs—the big voids generate value around it. In a strategic plan, you have to be able to say which voids in the city should be kept while providing access to as much diversity as possible. As the city grows, we need to add not only housing but the infrastructure necessary to support it, everything from sewers, to subways, to parks and schools.

NR: Do you see similar opportunities in the residential project in Harlem?

GS: What I love about Harlem is that when everyone else in New York is shopping and eating brunch, there are hundreds of people going to churches and singing their hearts out. It is a very soulful place. I went to City College and Columbia, so I have been around those blocks and always felt the soul, the anguish sometimes, and the creativity. Whatever changes in Harlem, it should retain that kind of Sunday-morning community. And if we can design a condominium to retain a church, it will keep the storytelling within the city. In that sense I love that the project we are doing is keeping these uses together.

NR: How does teaching enhance your practice?

GS: It provides me with a community and an audience that I am attuned to and that I need to respond to. I teach because I hope to spread the base and interests of architecture and create a sense of renewal for others and myself. I get stricter as I gain experience, and my students get more sophisticated, so we all gain from it. I have less time and push them harder, and they respond better. It is like when you train for a sport everyday: you get more proficient at it. I am on a regime of exercising with the students, and when I get to the office I am more efficient. I am more focused and sharpened by teaching. It enriches SAS. Over time, we are building a layered community and playing deeper roles.

OpenOffice with Robert Irwin, Dia:Beacon, Beacon, New York, interiors showing Richard Serra sculpture installation, 2003.

OpenOffice with Robert Irwin, Dia:Beacon, Beacon, New York, interior gallery space, 2003.

Solomonoff Architecture Studio, rendering of East 7th Street townhouse extension and garden, New York, 2005.

Solomonoff Architecture Studio, interior of East 7th Street townhouse project, New York, 2005.

BROOKL
CIVIC S

The studio investigated the Brooklyn Atlantic Yards, where Forest City Ratner has proposed a stadium designed by Frank Gehry and the local community is demanding more input. Working first in teams and then completing individual projects, the students were asked to find what an alternative and relevant urban insertion might be. They were asked to interpret programmatic needs, make design decisions, and create a project that takes maximum advantage of the site and its layered history. The studio took the stance that the emergence of relevant urban form is the consequence of multilayered, coincidental and/or contradictory logics: old/new, popular/elitist, generic/specific, high/low, political/ fashionable, intellectual/mundane, ideal/defective, practical/theoretical, pragmatic/philosophical, and dense/sparse. They recognized that relevant urban form embodies and retains at least one major contradiction within it.

Organized in a three-step process—fieldwork, program work, and formwork—the studio considered urban issues in a seminar format while designing a selected track of land. As seen in the following studio section, they began with a discussion of three urban paradigms, the first being The Conflict, where amid globalization and Internet accessibility the question was, how do you tease out the significant data of the given site? What is local, federal, or global? How do we respond to geography, geology, land use, sociological data, history, or economics? To investigate questions and inject variables into the design equation, the students researched these questions and presented responses in a discussion with various stakeholders.

The second urban paradigm was The Means to What End, wherein every piece of land responds to delineations of territory. The site expected conflicting markings and programmatic allocations began to appear: the railroad yards, the previous site plans, the neighbors' desires, the connection to infrastructure, and the proposed development plans. The students asked, how does a given piece of land connect and function with everything else? What kind of space has the modernist obsession with the programmatic segregation of speeds and the modes produced? What is today's take on the earlier fantasies of grade separation and programmatic segregation? What is the relationship of public space to public infrastructure? How do we go about imprinting a program on a given site and community? Are these ideologically driven choices or purely practical ones? The studio observed programmatic contradictions/coincidences as each student developed his or her own program.

The third paradigm was that of The Overall Form, so that after the program was decided upon, two parcels were selected for non-housing development. Students made proposals for one of the parcels and were required to design a new multimodal transport hub with cultural, retail, and housing components as well as their own programmatic concepts, which they then developed further. Some students focused on expanding public space at many scales: the house, the neighborhood, and the city; others made linear designs inserted into the site with a network of parks as infrastructure, where housing and programs would flow around an arena. Some considered ways to incorporate housing throughout

the site, so that it would grow according to market needs; still others saw potential in activating underground space in the rail yards. Surprisingly, most students maintained the stadium, finding ways to reduce it or incorporate it into a new scheme.

Discussions in the studio evolved around the issues of the role of the architect as an urban designer and the potential for a new role as civic leader. Most of us agreed architects should be responsible politically, socially, and economically for their decisions in urban design issues.

—Galia Solomonoff

scale				
—	**small street**	anywhere, Tokyo	-narrow intimate street where pedestrians must interact in close quarters -no vehicular traffic allows for total wandering	2-3 stories max 8-12 ft
	corner bodega	brooklyn, NY	-ground floor retail space approx 300-400 sf -proximity to subway or bus stop affects success	typical bodega signage - blends in corner or high pedestrian traffic location ideal
	cleveland arcade	Cleveland, OH	-mixed-use arcade cuts through city block allowing sheltered pedestrian traffic through to interior street -space remains well lit with glass canopy	glass roof protects for "year-round" shopping -lets light in 5 levels interior commercial office commercial office commercial office retail retail pedestrian traffic can cut cross-block through arcade
	city blocks	Mitte, Berlin	-interior courtyard of blocks open to secondary pedestrian flow providing another layer of retail, public, and residential access at an intimate scale removed from the steet outside	courtyard inside block at more intimate scale than ouside less noise and no traffic access to shops, cafes, and private residences typical block - street relationship on outside pedestrian traffic may or may not meander in
	miyashita park	Tokyo	-a 1,100 ft long by 100 ft wide park sits parallel with rail lines -the park is above car parking and spans the streets below allowing traffic to pass beneath -the park is accessed via pedestrian bridges over the streets	adjacent railways main roads pass beneath park man-made park surface [1,100ft long] parking beneath pedestrian access points
	promenade	Brooklyn, NY	-a 1/3 mile long pedestrian park cantilevers out over the brooklyn-queens expressway -the park provides uninterrupted views to manhattan and acts as a barrier between the expressway and brooklyn heights -private gardens along the back of residences are visible, but not accessible by the public from the walkway	private residential buildings public access to promenade private gardens along promenade pedestrian path and benches east/west levels of brooklyn - queens expressway 1800 ft public park
+	**highline railway**	Manhattan, NY	-a 1.5 mile long rail system [no longer in use] winds through the west village in manhattan -the tracks are elevated well above street level and connect between buildings -a masterplan is currently in the works to make the "highline" into a public park	connection between multiple buildings streets pass by beneath 1.5 mi. park above streets

2.1

streets

adjacent blocks

corners

parking

street entry

parking egress

street crossing

passage entry

towers

open spaces

open space access

mixed use circulation

residential circulation

sunlight shafts

nodes of confluence

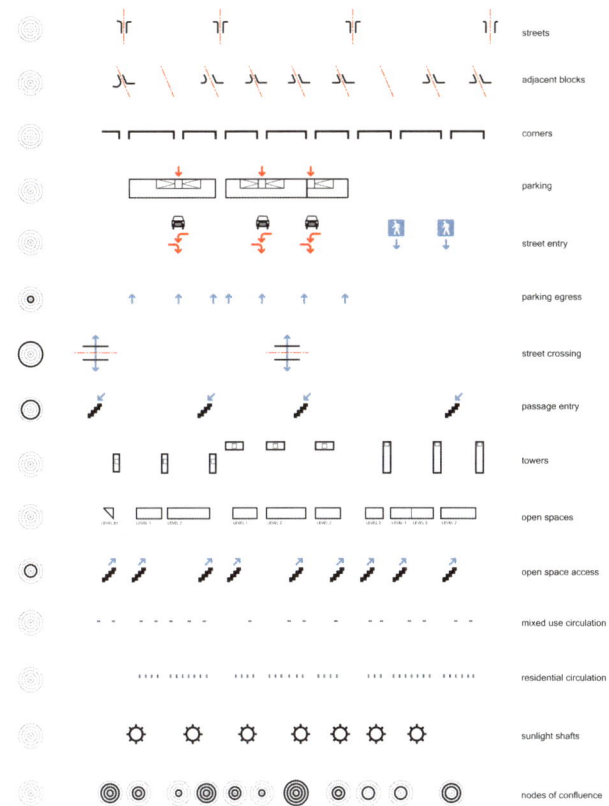

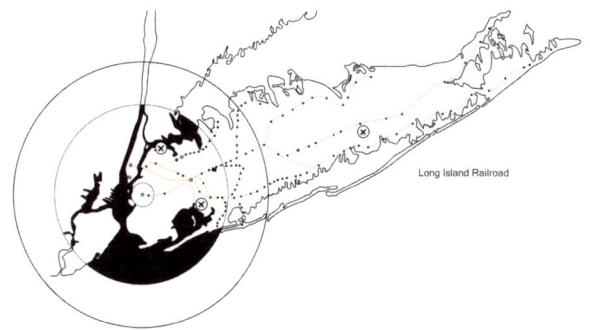

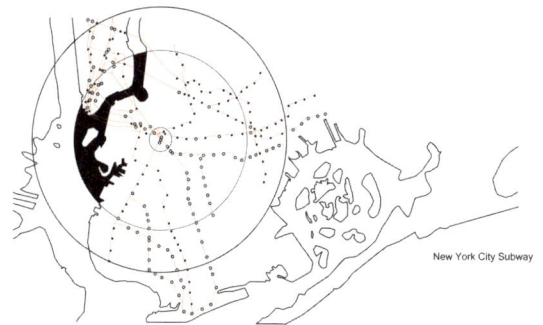

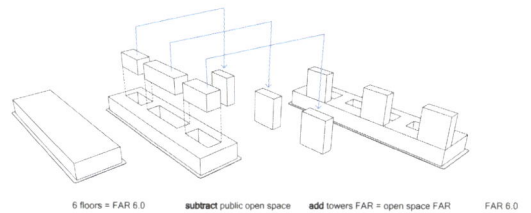

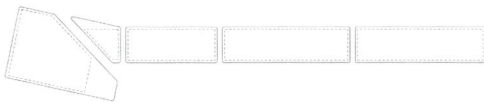

passage node diagram

2.2

Long Island Railroad

New York City Subway

6 floors = FAR 6.0   **subtract** public open space   **add** towers FAR = open space FAR   FAR 6.0

2.3

2.1 Diagrams showing urban projects, their situations, and the characteristics that make them successful. (Matt Hutchinson)

2.2 Mapping diagrams of the New York City metropolitan area showing the Atlantic Yards site positioned at the intersection of the Long Island Railroad and ten subway lines. Passengers transfer between the rail lines and subways, creates a large amount of subterranean activity. (Brett Spearman)

2.3 An overall map of Brooklyn locating the Atlantic Yards site and its relationship to Prospect Park, Fort Greene Park, and the smaller Brooklyn blocks that make up the surrounding neighborhoods. (Matt Hutchinson)

SITE HISTORY

Background: The Forest City Ratner Proposal for the Atlantic Yards, Brooklyn

Residential sales and construction have defined the post–World War I New York real estate market, pushing out low- and even middle-income residents.[1] Industry is also pushed out, as city zoning changes leave once-guarded industrial areas unprotected under new mixed-use regulations; indeed, as the city loses its high-paying blue-collar jobs, residential conversions of former industrial loft buildings gain in popularity because of their high ceilings and large footprints. Uses change and new popular neighborhoods are created through gentrification. Developers are instrumental in many zoning changes[2] through their political influence, money, and project proposals promising a safer and more beautiful city, as well as projections of an increased tax revenue for both the city and state.[3]

In Brooklyn, the developer Forest City Ratner (FCR) is working on the controversial Atlantic Yards site, at the intersection of Flatbush and Atlantic avenues and bordering a four-story residential neighborhood and two major commercial thoroughfares. Currently, the site has a main transit hub for Long Island Railroad and the MTA, as well as industrial and residential buildings. The FCR plan is to build over the railroad yards and raze the existing buildings in order to develop seventeen residential towers (some 57 stories tall) and a $435 million-dollar arena for the New Jersey Nets basketball team, which Bruce Ratner owns.[4]

Bruce Ratner obtained the site's property through questionable means. His company purchased the private portions of the site by offering the owners twice the market value for their homes or businesses and having them sign gag orders in order to prevent negative publicity.[5] When Ratner purchased the publicly owned portion of the site, which accounts for 40 percent of the FCR plan, he was allowed to buy it for $100 million. Interestingly, this purchase circumvented a law the state passed before that stipulated the MTA must accept the highest bid, which at the time was a $150 million offer from the Extell Corporation.[6] However, the law didn't come into effect until later in the year, and the Metropolitan Transit Authority was allowed to pick the political favorite—Forest City Ratner—and rejected the higher bid from Extell Corporation. Extell's bid was designed to appeal to the community, offered a less-dense scheme that did not use the state's eminent-domain law, and allowed the project to go through the city's land-use review process that the FCR scheme has managed to avoid.[7]

The use of eminent domain to purchase the remaining privately owned properties on the proposed development site is usually reserved for government projects and public infrastructure; here it was used for a private enterprise. The private properties are being seized by the government, citing "blight" in an area where functioning businesses and middle-income home-owners occupy newly renovated and healthy buildings.[8] Through political influence, FCR was able to circumvent many government regulations to its advantage. In the past, major projects were initiated by a development idea proposed by the government and tested by an Environmental Impact Study;

the project would then either be designed and built by the government itself or contracted out to the highest bidder. In the case of the Atlantic Yards project, FCR initiated the plan, received government support, and then went through an Environmental Impact Study that never included formal public project approval.[9]

The most controversial aspect reviewed by our project is that a large amount of the development cost is being funded by the taxpayers. Through direct contributions from the city and state, tax credits, and tax exemptions, Forest City Ratner's known public subsidy for the site is around $1.6 billion, but this does not take into account the discounted price Ratner paid for the site.[10] FCR defends the financial integrity of its plan, saying it will bring in $5 billion in net tax revenues over the next thirty years and thousands of jobs to the area.[11] However, FCR's financial gain will possibly outpace the public's.[12]

At the same time, FCR's proposal has become less valuable to the public good. In the beginning, the project promised 50 percent low-income housing and 50 percent market-rate housing. However, this 50/50 split only applied to the rentals, not market-rate condominiums, and since the project has become more expensive, the number of condominiums has increased, thereby decreasing the amount of low-income housing and public benefit.[13]

The Atlantic Yards project received fierce opposition from "Develop, Don't Destroy Brooklyn" and Brooklyn Speaks, two local groups that were supported by community leaders, politicians, and organizations such as the Municipal Arts Society and the National Trust for

Historic Preservation. In the end, their concerted effort didn't have the financial means to combat Forest City Ratner's million-dollar public-relations campaign, which lobbied, ran commercials, and sent direct mail. On December 20, 2006, the Atlantic Yards project received final government approval from the Public Authorities Control Board. [14]

While the project still has to respond to several lawsuits, Forest City Ratner is confident it will win.[15] If it does, brownstones and townhouses will be dwarfed by towers ten times their size, streets will be de-mapped to create superblocks, Nets basket-ball fans will inundate the neighbor-hood for events—and it will set a precedent. Our studio considered a wide range of alternatives.

—Julia Stanat

1. http://www.tenant.net/Community/history/hist02a.html.
2. http://atlanticyardsreport.blogspot.com/2006/03/rezoning-for-atlantic-yards-project.html.
3. Ratner's Atlantic Yards City Council proposal: http://www.theslatinreport.com/content/features/Ratner_Rail_Yards_presentation.pdf.
4. www.developdontdestroy.com.
5. Gallahue, Patrick. "Tout of Bounds," New York Post, June 16, 2004.
6. Bagli, Charles V. "Rival Bid Tops Ratner's Offer to Development Brooklyn Site," New York Times, July 23, 2005.
7. Ibid.
8. Hill, Isabel. "Brooklyn Matters," Building History Productions.
9. Angotti, Tom. "Atlantic Yards: Through the Looking Glass." Gotham Gazette, November 15, 2005.
10. "The Anatomy of a Sweetheart Deal: Public Subsidies and MOU for Dummies for Forest City Ratner's Atlantic Yard's Proposal." www.developdeontdestry.com, April 12, 2005.
11. Ratner's Atlantic Yards City Council proposal: http://www.theslatinreport.com/content/features/Ratner_Rail_Yards_presentation.pdf.
12. http://www.developdontdestroy.com/economicstudies/KimPeebles.pdf.
13. www.developdontdestroy.com.
14. Confessore, Nicholas. "State Board Approves Atlantic Yards Project," New York Times, December 20, 2006.
15. Confessore, Nicholas. "State Board Approves Atlantic Yards Project," New York Times, December 20, 2006.

Brooklyn Today.

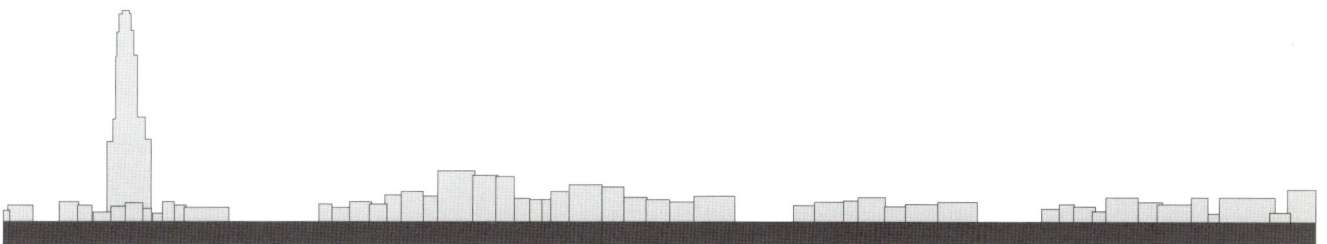

Brooklyn Tomorrow?

2.4

2.5

2.6

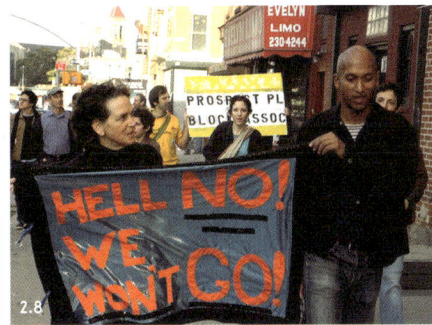

2.4 A before-and-after study from Develop Don't Destroy Brooklyn showing the impact of the development scheme on the neighborhood.

2.5 An aerial view of the Atlantic Yards, Brooklyn.

2.6 Frank Gehry's proposed scheme for the Forest City Ratner project.

2.7–8 November 13, 2005, walk-a-thon, "Walk, Don't Destroy Brooklyn."

PROJEC

MORPHOLOGICAL PLAY

The approach propositions the designer to create an iconic form for the complex and unconventional relationships between elements like the arena, street, housing, and commercial space. Concentrating on the singular viewpoint of the form of the design enables the project to produce the highest quality of interior space. Operative actions such as poking, shmushing, and stretching allow the designer to build space that would otherwise be inconceivable.

2.9

Noah Shepherd:
2.9 View of street extension. A half-mile street extends from Atlantic Avenue in and up the building to the seventh-floor level. The extension increases the street frontage of the building, allowing for additional retail and public spaces within the site. At the highest point of the street is a public beach at the level of the adjacent brownstone roofs. The project is an attempt to move away from a program-driven design process. Such a process must establish basic minimums and standards, which are then replicated to fill out the planned bulk and arranged in response to the specific site conditions. As an alternative, an investigation of a subtractive design process disclosed various floor plates and unplanned uses throughout the development. Compaction and carving standards were discarded in favor of local, specific negotiation between uses and contingencies. This process was opposed to accretion.

2.10 View from the east on Atlantic Avenue. The form is derived from a loose study of standard building practices for similar projects. The floor plates and vertical elements are held constant; only the edge condition and façade vary.

2.11 View of the model from the west. In the foreground is the street extension at its highest level. Beneath the street-extension level, the building mass is deep, providing internal spaces for parking and building services; above the street, the building is composed of thinner floor slabs, creating more space with access to light and air.

2.12 View from Flatbush Avenue. I placed a tower at the western end of the site. The height of the building is 512 feet, matching the Williamsburgh Savings Bank. The form of the building is intended to dance with the bank building.

Jeffrey Kipnis: There are buildings in the world much bigger than this. Yokohama Port Terminal is a half mile long; this is nothing. You're mild. On that urban site, the gesture of the tower, which is going to then integrate the alien world with its own autonomy into the context, is bizarre to me. You have built a medieval city. It is autonomous; it has a kind of distinct plane. No planner would call this planning. Walking from one side to the other does not have porosity for the project but it has building porosity, which are different in an architectural scheme.

Enrique Norten: I think that your project is a very good example because it takes one strategy all the way through and resolves everything formally.

Anthony Vidler: It becomes provocative aesthetically but not programmatically. And the provocative aesthetic of that interior street image is very consistent in its attempt to say what happens when you poke down and through it—that is an aesthetic strategy. But it also could have been a fundamental guide to a very radical programmatic strategy that took the program and poked the program in a very fundamental way. If you don't understand what "poking" means, then you're not going to get how to poke a program in the same way that you've poked the project.

Galia Solomonoff: Consistency is not necessarily indicative of a well-designed project; there could be multiple points of view, so the design doesn't need to be consistent for every approach. You could re-anchor your project by thinking about cycles of use and how these differ from that of traditional planning. One approach is more the way an architect operates, and the other is how a planner operates.

Jeffrey Kipnis: Don't you think New York kind of gives you that kind of inconsistency? Do you think the grid has anything to do with this?

Galia Solomonoff: The grid provides an armature for inconsistency.

Jeffrey Kipnis: The planning has a consistency that enables the architecture to be inconsistent. Or does the architecture have consistency to let the planning be inconsistent?

Marshall Brown: It is completely conservative to say that either it's consistent or it's differentiated. What is the differentiation between planning and architecture? How about transformation? How about the transformation or the

2.10

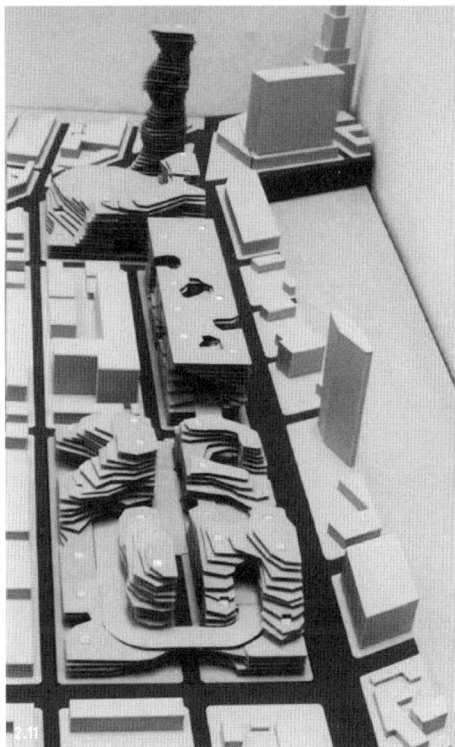

2.11

2.12

progression or the evolution from planning to architecture?

Galia Solomonoff: Well, what about the Bordeaux House? Is that consistent?

Jeffrey Kipnis: It's not an urban house. The elevated part of the building is consistent, and it works as the armature of consistency to allow all the differences around it to operate. It's a completely different size.

Keith Krumwiede: It's a question of resistance. There's nothing that's resisting you because there is no matter in this project.

Marshall Brown: The Bordeaux House is not consistent, but that is not the point. Consistency, I'm going to insist, is not the point. What it has, other than consistency, is a compelling and coherent narrative. There is a kind of role that it creates and lives in.

Anthony Vidler: I was simply using the notion of consistency as a strategy. He could think of that not just as a sculptural end product but as an analog to thinking programmatically. That program could then resolve itself in a very unique and radical way and make something that isn't simply a stylistic gesture that emptily has to be filled by program.

Jeffrey Kipnis: Consistency is not hegemony. Consistency is not totalitarianism, I agree. I think the problem is that the critique is important to understand the difference between the generative capabilities of consistency and the impossibility or the intolerability of hegemony. For example, Bertrand Russell—I know he's not in very good stead these days—said that you can't have any architecture at all without consistency, and he gave the following example: Something is better than nothing; nothing is better than God; therefore something is better than God. That means you can allow an inconsistent notion of nothing. So you do need an armature, which gives you consistency, but it's a very loose idea.

Aniket Shahane:
2.13 FAR diagram. Using the "uncoiled concourse" and its programs as a given, a strategy is generated that can be used to calibrate the residential envelope based on FAR demands and vice versa.

2.14–17 Project perspectives. These opportunities can help guide the development that takes place at various points along the site in space as well as in time. The scenarios are attempts to test different parts of the site in order to accept and take advantage of this potential.

Matt Hutchinson:
2.18 Digital model with a view down to the public arena from the cantilevered lobby in the basketball arena, with the continuous "park" surface visible throughout.

2.19 The green block interiors spill out into the street, suggesting a new relationship between the normally disparate functions of city life. The old stoop is replaced by a green incline, inviting people to interact socially and enter into the interior.

2.20 Aerial view of digital model.

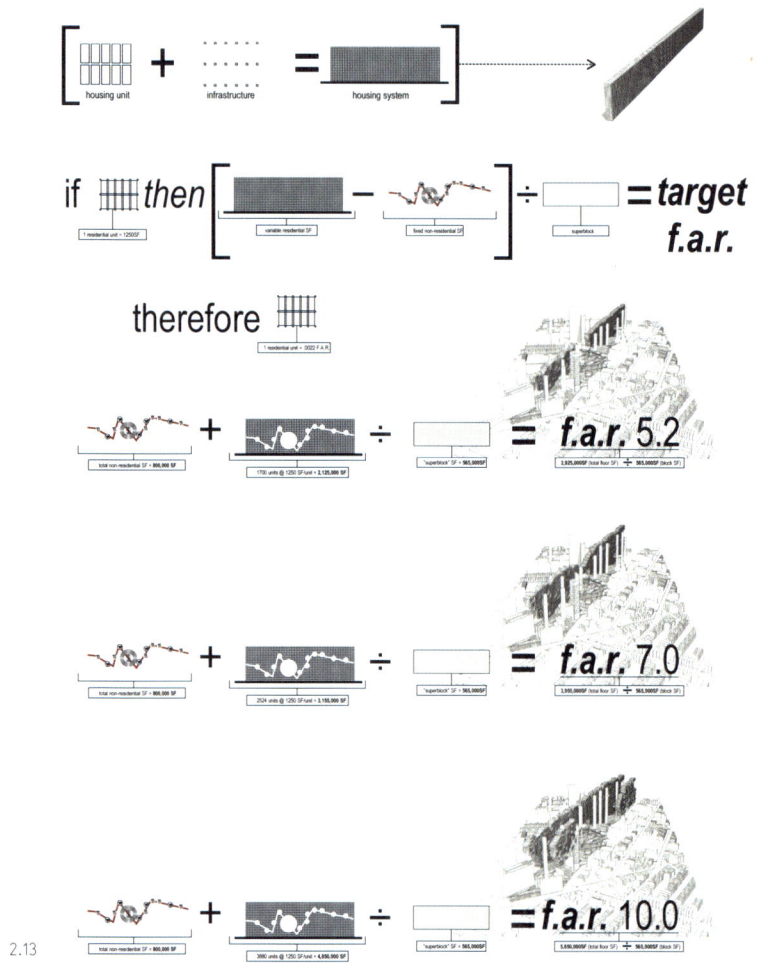

2.13

2.14

2.15

2.16

2.17

2.18

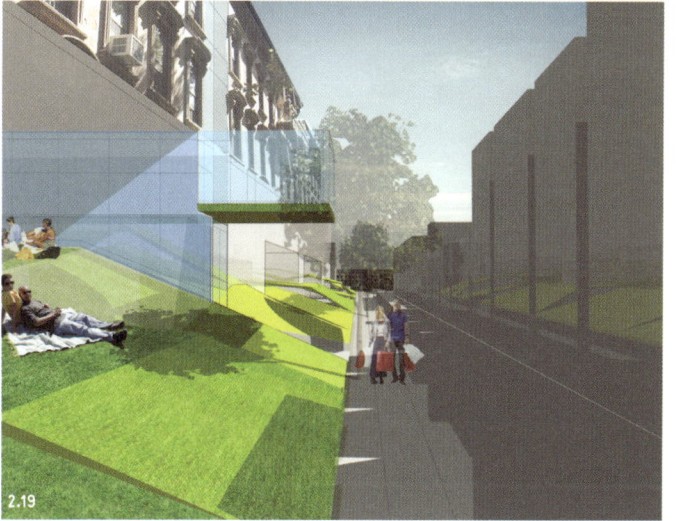
2.19

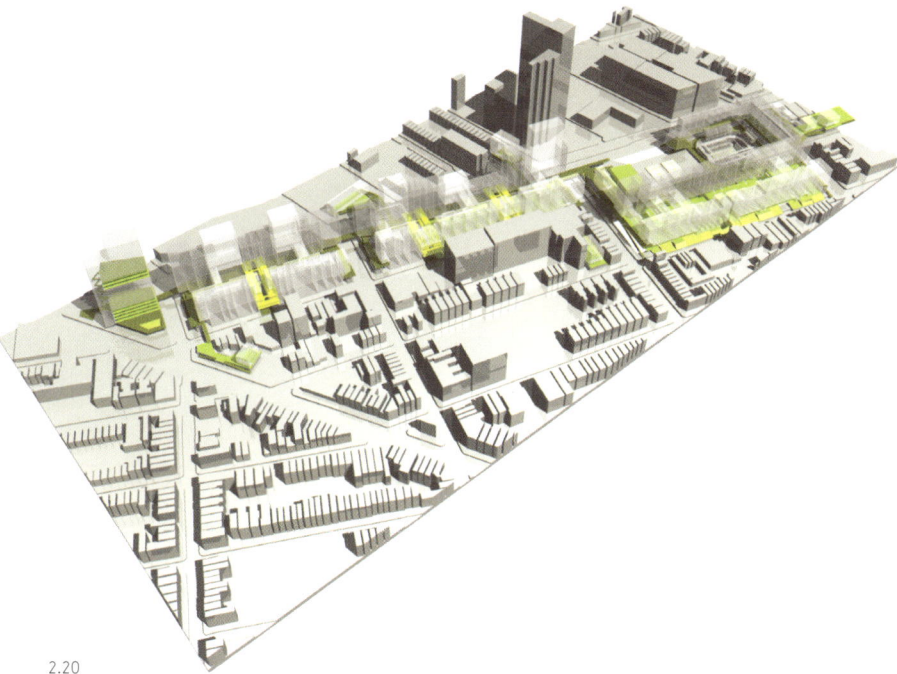
2.20

PUBLICNESS

The site sits on the city's third-largest public transportation hub (after Pennsylvania Station and Grand Central
Terminal) and includes connections between ten major subway lines, as well as the Long Island Railroad and the
city bus system, a condition that was impossible to ignore. Rather than listing it as one of the programmatic elements in the project, some students chose to use this public transport hub as their main generative device for the
design. This approach allowed the design to have a more sensitive connection between the proposed buildings
and the existing transportation infrastructure below. In most cases, this connection allowed light to enter into
an otherwise dark rail system and then reveal the streets and plazas designed aboveground. The infrastructure
extends into the building, distorting the boundary between large-scale transportation and pedestrian walkway,
thus imagining a dynamic formal environment that transforms the arena into a component of the pedestrian loop.

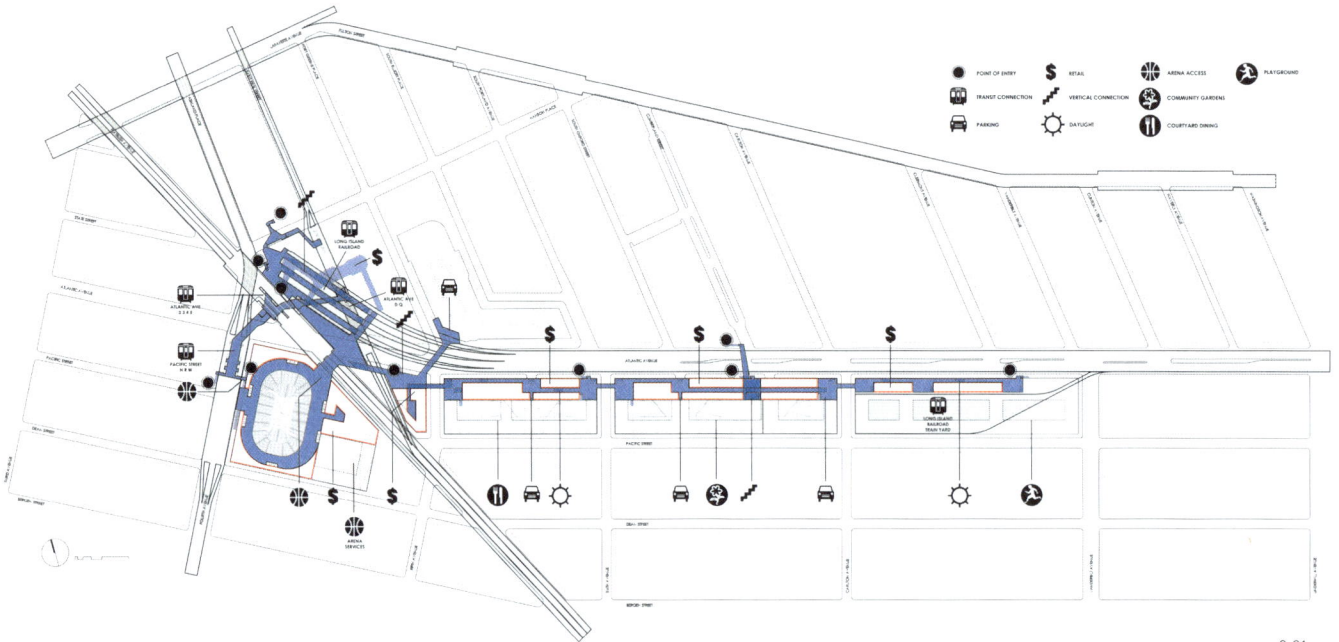

2.21

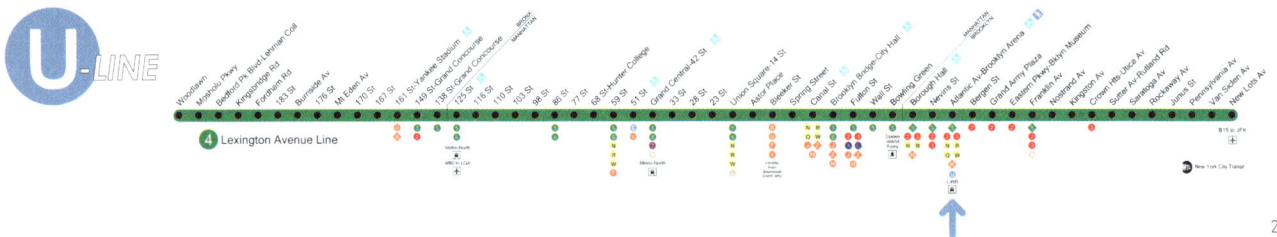

2.22

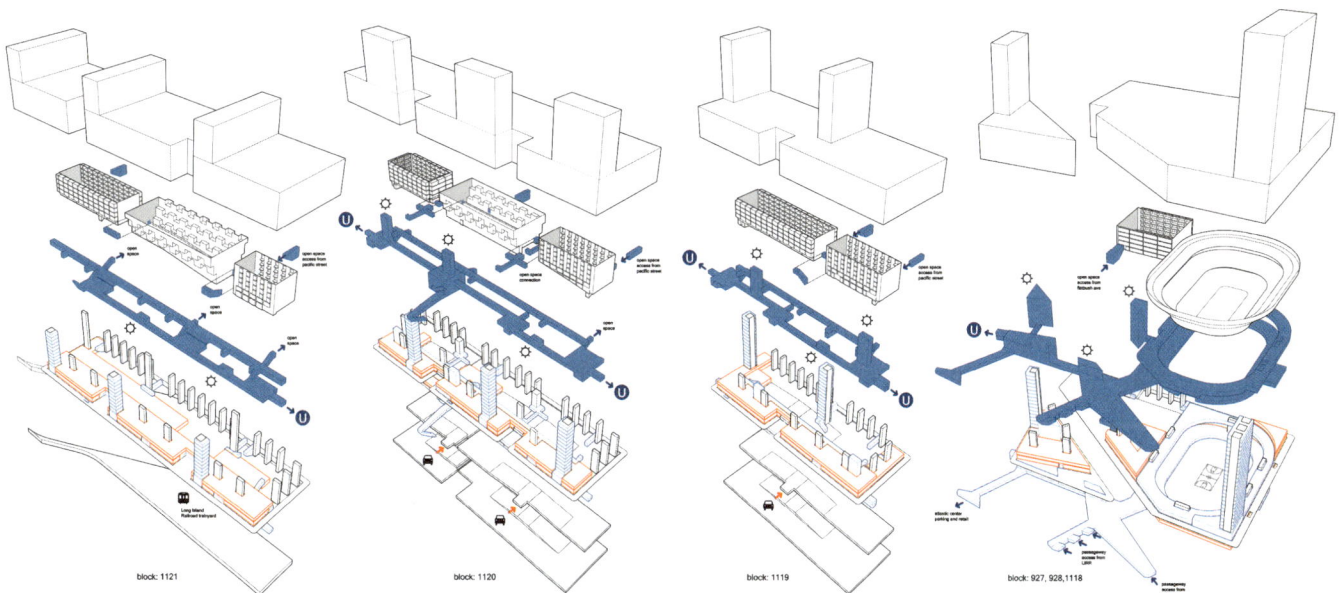

block: 1121   block: 1120   block: 1119   block: 927, 928,1118

Brett Spearman:

2.21 Project plan diagram. The Atlantic Terminal is a catalyst for the new development and the source of large numbers of commuter/consumers transferring from the Long Island Railroad to the city's subway and bus lines. In this project, the development surrounding the new Brooklyn arena is shifted to the intersection of Flatbush and Fourth avenues, centering the project on Atlantic Terminal and creating an underground hub that links the existing Forest City Ratner project with the new mixed-use community. The project outlines public spaces within the Brooklyn block, including public courtyards and a retail spine that connects the underground parking to streets and the arena. Voids, carved out from the surrounding spaces, allow for a view of the mix of uses, and a public corridor encompassing the arena provides the general public with a view into the arena from a shopping concourse.

2.22 Subway-stop diagram identifying the Atlantic Terminal and all possible transportation connections.

2.23 Exploded axonometric diagrams. The site is positioned at the terminal for the Long Island Railroad that serves Lower Manhattan as well as a convergence of subway lines in Brooklyn. Passengers transferring between the rail lines cause a large amount of subterranean activity.

Winka Dubbledam: Diagramming is abstraction, not reduction. You are reducing your idea to the point where it's flat, literally flat. Diagramming is used in order to test different scenarios. How is your idea reflected in an architectonic expression? This generator you created with your diagram should actually generate something in the architecture above it. What happens to the ceiling of the bottom of your building? The type is very, very traditional. If you refer to the World Trade Center, it was sitting on a big underground shopping mall. Before it collapsed they had just finished renovating it because it wasn't working. People got so disoriented because they couldn't see up to the sky. They tried to solve it by making a huge opening to the city and let the city slip back in—it was to become more fluid.

Keller Easterling: I'm excited about the way you are just looking at that blue space. How the crowds get in and out of the subway—the urban strategy is focused on that movement. You should reject the way we typically look at this, which is usually an underground concourse that we understand technically. You could look at it more geologically. People walk around in the city, and the project doesn't need to be completely continuous; now it can mutate more geologically, so that it's more like outcroppings. It becomes the reason for building, the reason for mapping.

Brett Spearman:
2.24 Interior courtyard perspective. The nodes where access occurs expressed in section with the accumulation of functions at the base of the development.

2.25 This early site model distinguishes between the passageways in blue and open spaces in white.

2.26 View of arena model. The site model subverts the buildings and the plane of the street in order to show the organization of the passage network within buildings and underground.

2.27 An overall model view.

2.28 Sectional perspective view to the courtyard.

Noah Shepherd:
2.29 Use diagram. In contrast with the master-plan use map, the building is capable of accommodating continuously varying uses. In an atomized use diagram, each circle represents a pocket of activity throughout the complex, with local accumulation of similar activities over time.

2.30 Section through arena. The arena is a public room, albeit one with limited access. On the three corners of the site are six-story openings into the arena, providing limited and partial views of the game from the street. Above the arena is a space that will be primarily occupied as office and hotel space.

2.31 Perspective looking from the intersection of Atlantic and Flatbush avenues. A homogenous volume of building at the macro scale combines the local heterogeneity, which creates local patterns of use while accommodating the largest possible variety. The tall tower in the foreground is the same height as the Williamsburgh Savings Bank tower to the north.

Enrique Norten: In the programmatic provisions of this project, the stadium is brought into an urban condition. In the United States, the arena is in the urban condition of an object sitting in a lot of concrete because it's all parking, and they add high-tech decoration to it. Because of your programmatic possibilities, you have the opportunity to deal with it more traditionally. For centuries, in Europe and Latin America, the arena really becomes more a part of the architecture because it's completely surrounded by a condition of housing, shops, etc.

Mathew Ford:
2.32 Model photo. This project ties into the existing transportation infrastructure and creates a plaza that provides the main approach to the new arena and also negotiates the abundance of vehicular traffic surrounding the site. Working from the idea that large volumes of traffic provide the illusion of

2.24

2.25

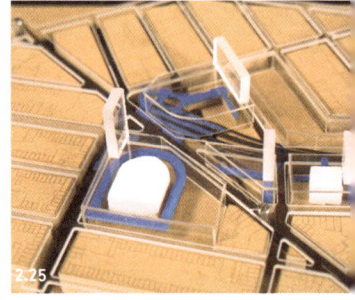
2.26

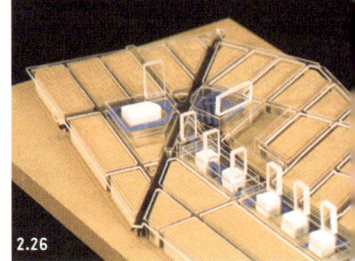
2.27

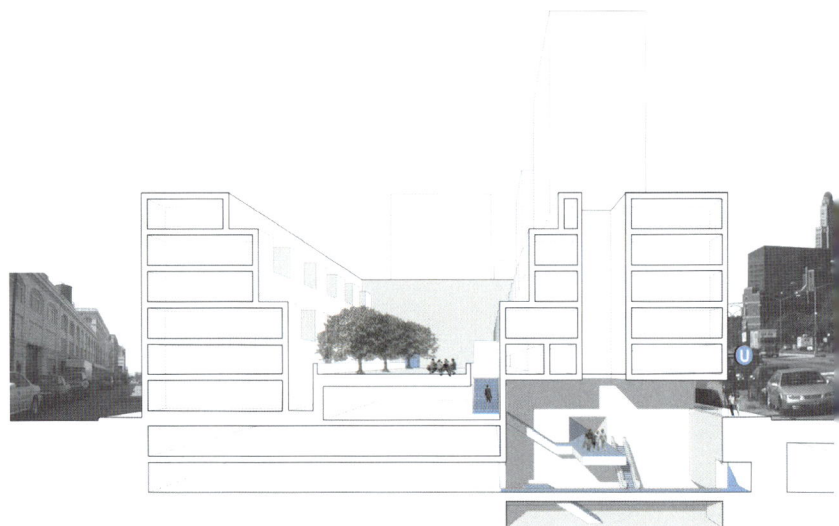
2.28

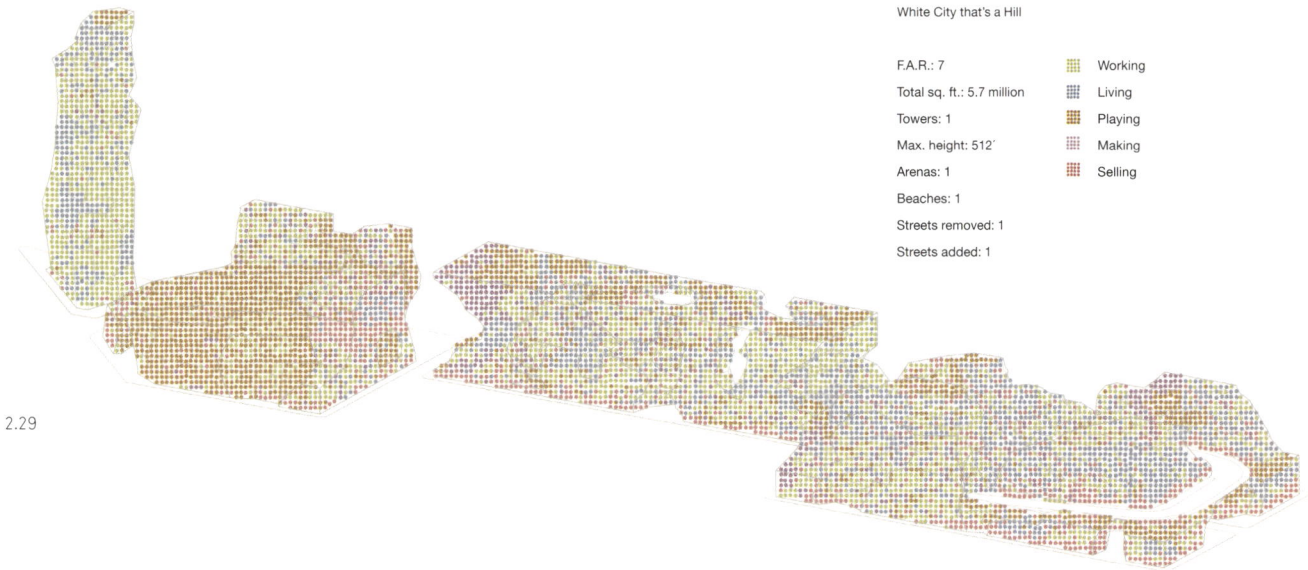

2.29

White City that's a Hill

F.A.R.: 7		Working
Total sq. ft.: 5.7 million		Living
Towers: 1		Playing
Max. height: 512´		Making
Arenas: 1		Selling
Beaches: 1		
Streets removed: 1		
Streets added: 1		

2.30

2.31

energy, this plaza exposed each of the interwoven transportation systems that approach the arena.

The plaza is drawn between the seating areas of the arena and the adjacent slab of office building. The office building provides a street front along Flatbush Avenue and is delaminated from the arena by the penetration of the plaza. Circulation physically and programmatically connects the two buildings, activating an atrium that terminates the received plaza. Spatially large programs typically desirable for office space, including spaces for physical activity, dining, and large conferences, are provided in the residual space of the arena. Likewise, the concourses of the arena penetrate the office slab, offering concession, retail space, and outdoor terraces with views of downtown Brooklyn.

Examining the programming of two building types, the arena and the office, over the course of the day, this project takes advantage of the respective off-hours and weaves the two types together into an efficient and desirable combination.

2.33 Image of building's relationship to the subway system. Atlantic Terminal is the third-largest transportation hub in New York City. With connections to four of the five boroughs and Long Island, the site requires the necessary transportation for a professional arena and large office building.

2.34 Project axonometric.

Julia Stanat:
2.36 A perspective from the intersection of Atlantic and Flatbush avenues. In order to cater to the loud Atlantic Avenue as well as the private residences, a screen for advertisements on one side that appears completely transparent on the other was used as a dividing device between the residential buildings and the busy street.

2.37 An interior perspective with the overlap of green spaces, streets, and housing.

2.38 An aerial view of the project. A system of layering visually connects and physically separates private and public green spaces, parking lots and residences, as well as retail and commercial establishments.

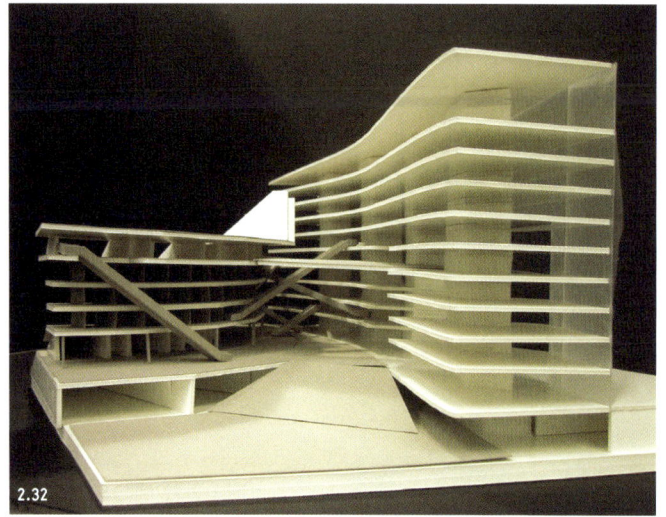

2.32

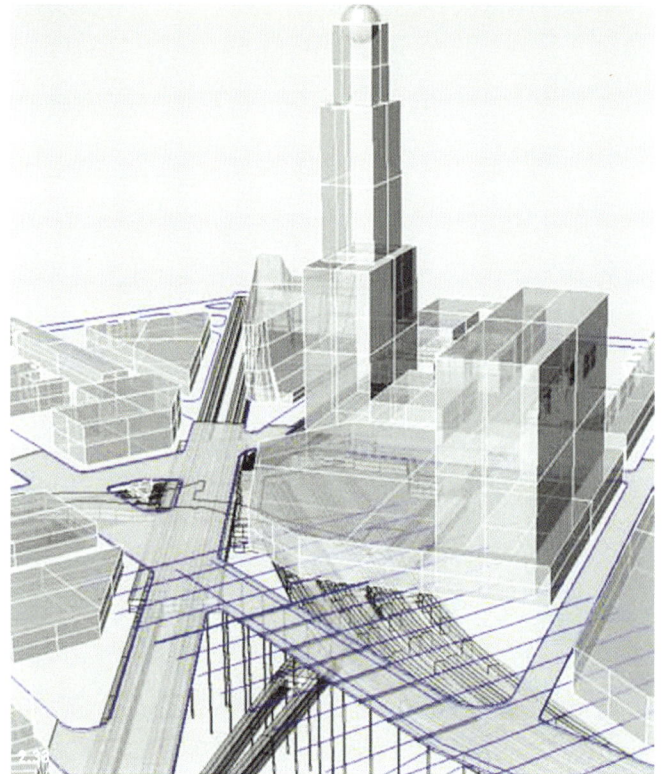

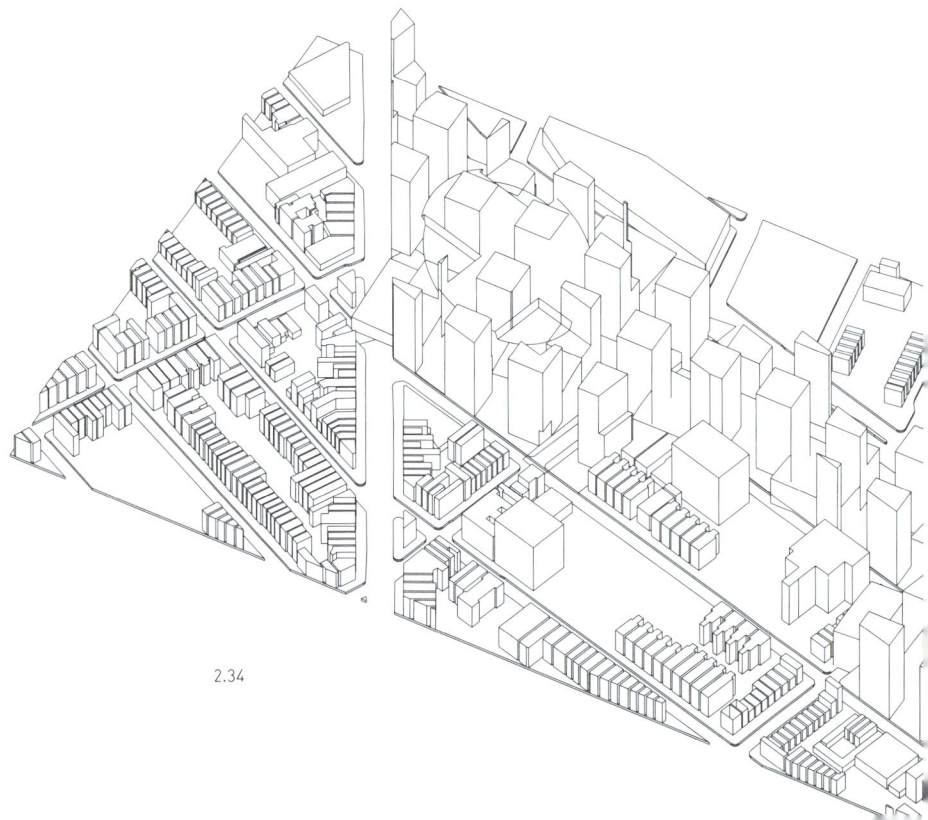

2.34

2.36

2.37

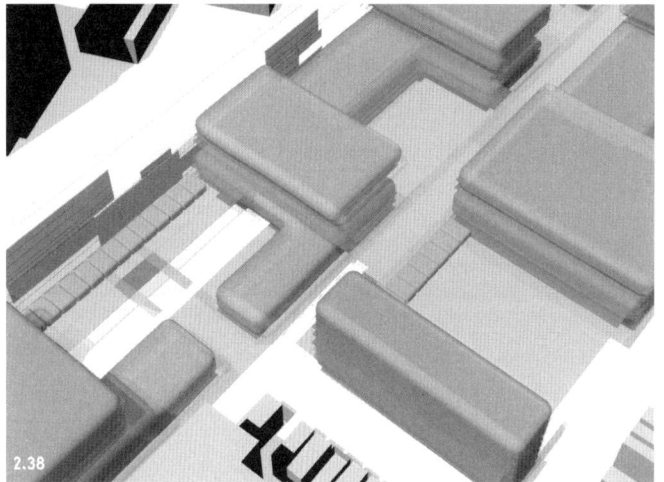

2.38

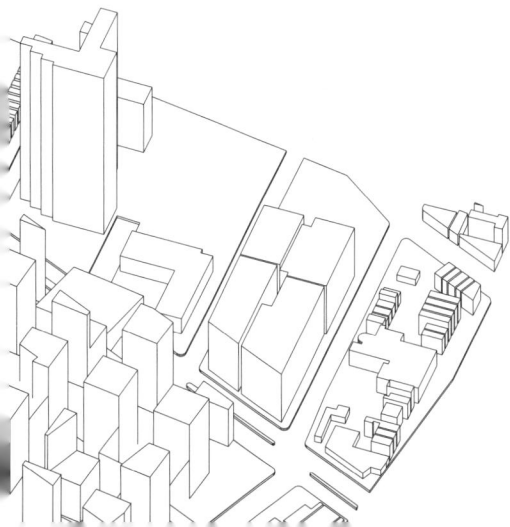

DOWNTOWN SUBURBIA

The arrangement and disparate scale shift between large urban and private suburban space is critical in a site that separates a major commercial thoroughfare and a three- to four-story residential neighborhood. This is also the condition that currently makes the project so controversial. The core strategy in some projects thus became to somehow dissolve this issue with the use of a programmatic blend that would allow the two scales to coexist. Some projects identified existing site conditions and placed their programmatic elements accordingly, such as housing and green space facing the residential neighborhood with commercial space siding on Atlantic Avenue. Some tried to reinterpret existing conditions, such as the residential stoop. Scale was a central issue for these projects, and the participants found ways of negotiating between the opposing sides by weaving small-scale sidewalks—suburban—through large-scale buildings—downtown, connecting the residential neighborhood to Atlantic Avenue. Some students created a barrier by placing tall buildings along Atlantic Avenue and then softened the site in a more congenial way toward the residential neighborhood to the south.

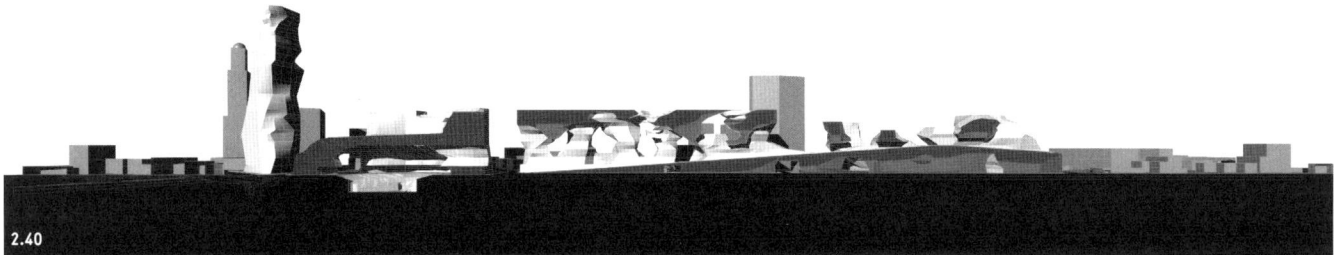

2.40

2.41

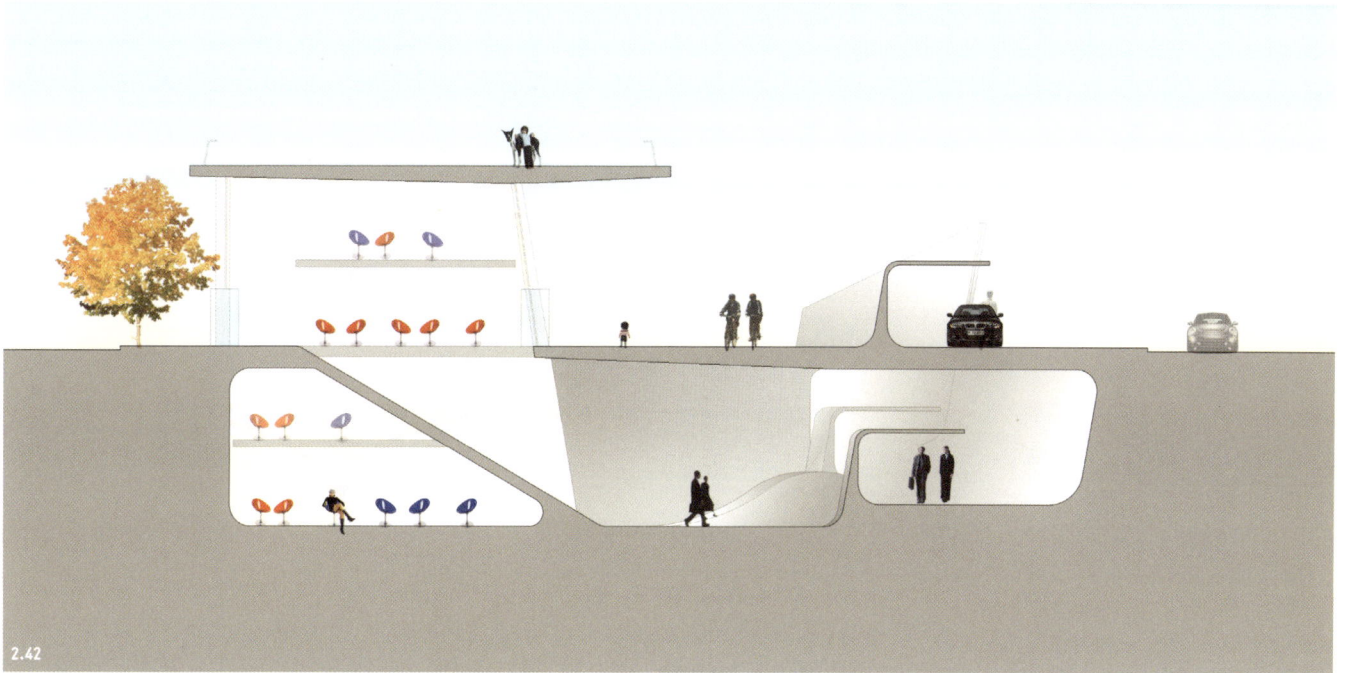

2.42

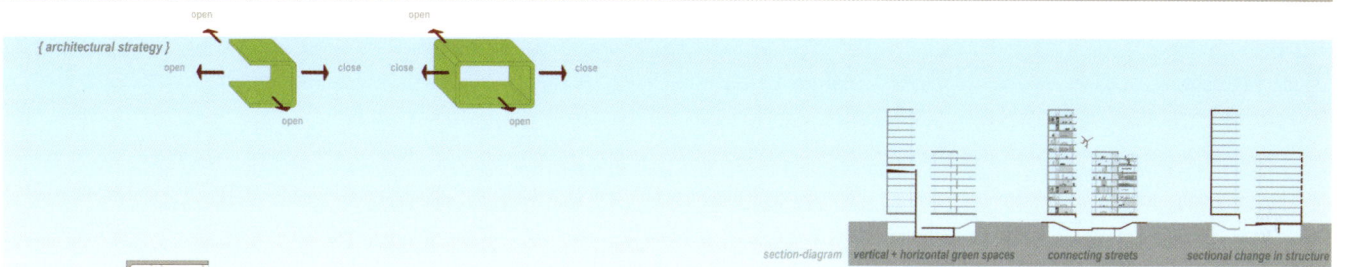

{ architectural strategy }

open   open   close   close

open → ← close   close → ← close

open   open

section-diagram   vertical + horizontal green spaces   connecting streets   sectional change in structure

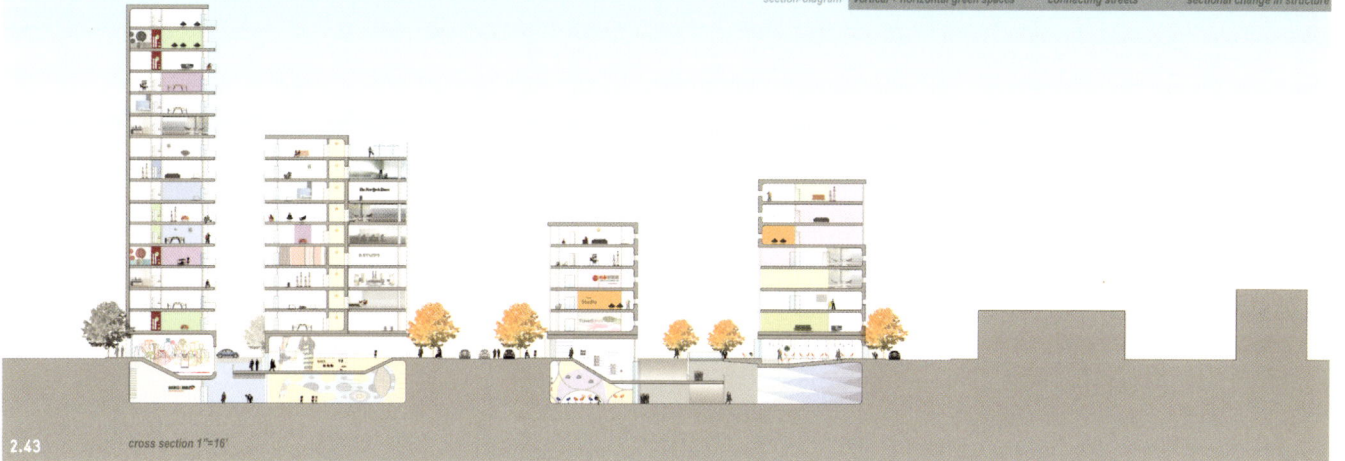

2.43   cross section 1"=16'

Noah Shepherd:

2.40 East/west section through the site with the tower at the west end, the Williamsburgh Savings Bank to the north, the basketball arena near the center, and the street extension going up and into the buildings at the eastern portion of the site.

2.41 A horizontal building section at the fourteenth floor. Through the creation of voids throughout the building, each location in the building is different in regard to floor-plate dimensions, proximity to the street, and provision of light and air. A primary concern was to investigate high-density buildings that permit continuously varied conditions of physical space, which could be used in a flexible manner. The variety of the physical characteristics of the floors, coupled with the regular provision of services and circulation, result in a building for multiple and changing uses.

Tracy Yu:

2.42–44 Project diagrams and images. Instead of the current Brooklyn block configuration where only the periphery is publicly accessible, this new master plan calls for pedestrian passages through the blocks. Pacific Street, Atlantic Avenue, and Dean Street are allowed to intersect at the middle of the blocks but in a quieter, more humanistic way.

The building designs take on a series of c-shapes to encourage a flow of activity and give directionality and character to public and private spaces. The site calls for a mixed-use program and has four programmatic nodes: residential, commercial, retail, and athletic facilities. They are sprinkled throughout the site vertically and horizontally, resulting in a three-dimensional, mixed-use urban matrix.

existing

proposed

{ urban strategy }

streets
building scale
arrival/departure points
noise of activities
site program

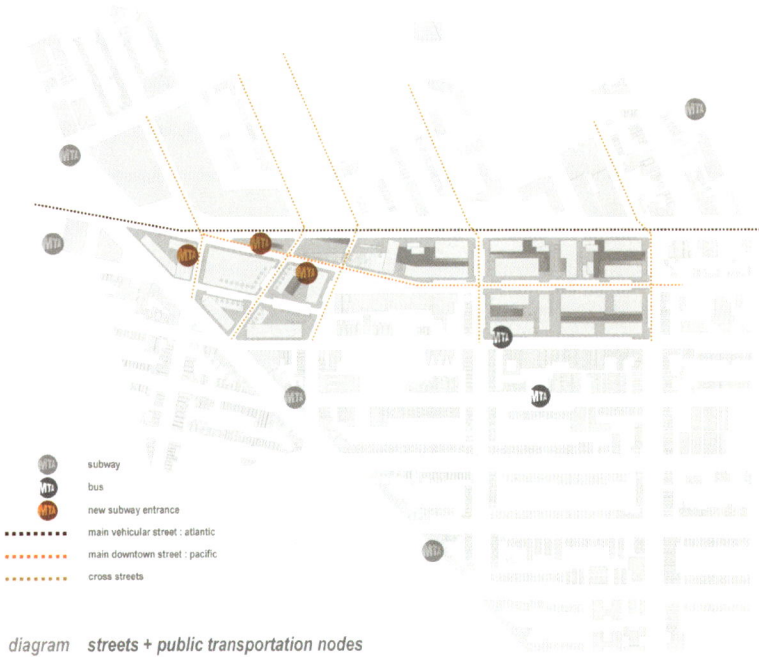

subway
bus
new subway entrance
main vehicular street : atlantic
main downtown street : pacific
cross streets

diagram **streets + public transportation nodes**

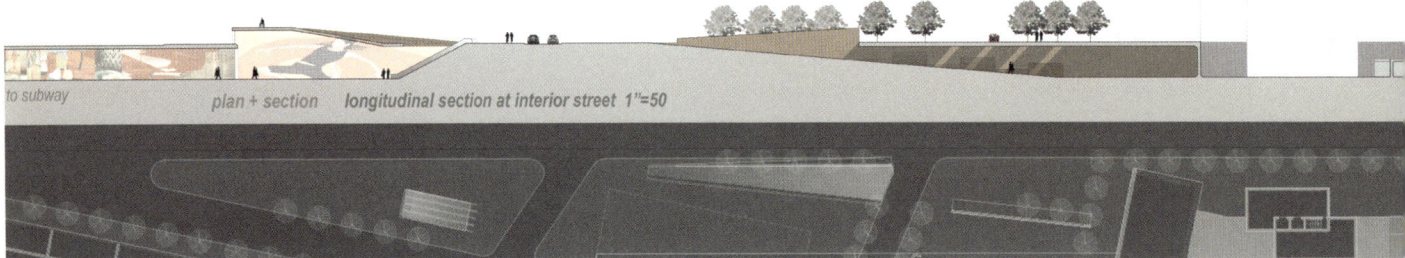

to subway

plan + section **longitudinal section at interior street 1"=50**

2.44

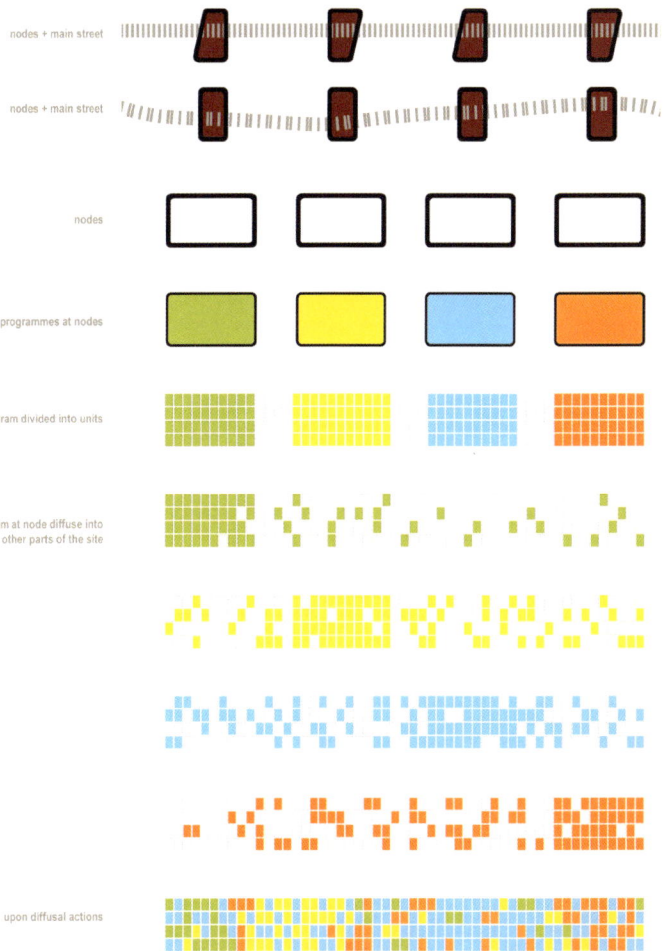

nodes + main street

nodes + main street

nodes

programmes at nodes

program divided into units

program at node diffuse into
other parts of the site

upon diffusal actions

adding main street into the fabric of program

retail + residential
day time use of site

retail + commercial
night time use of site

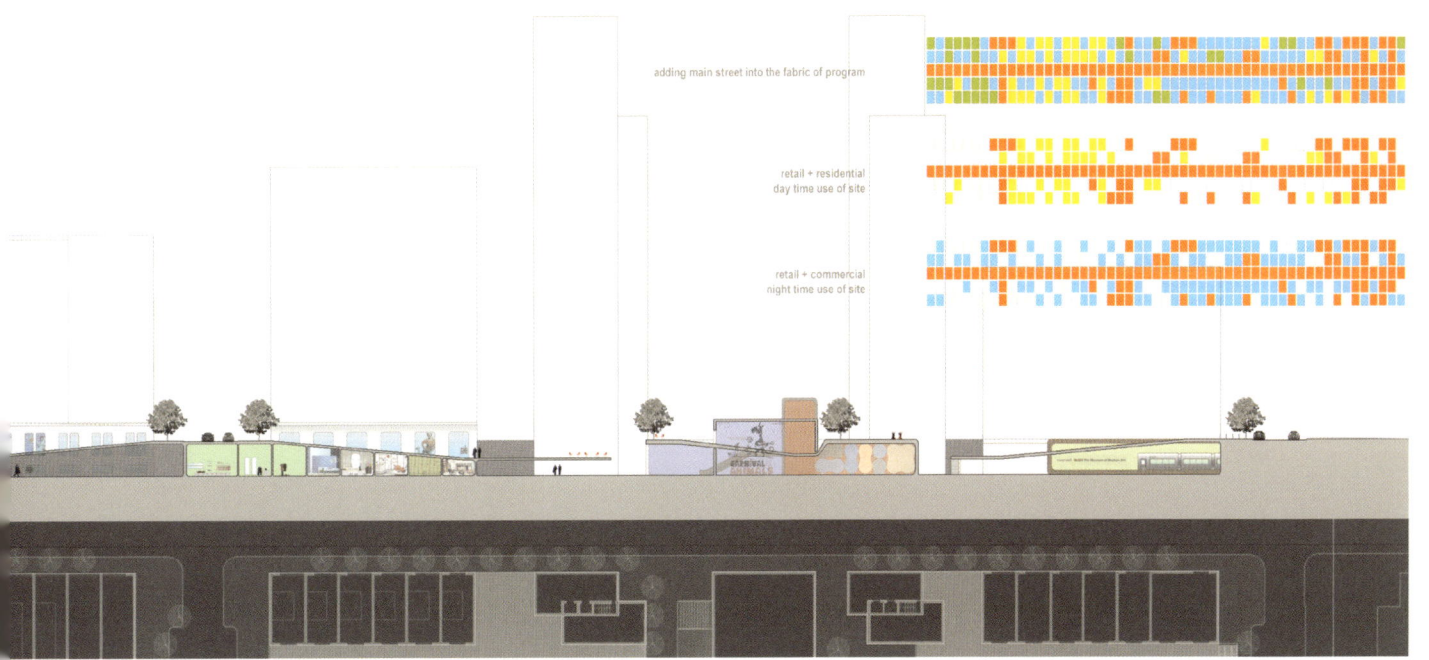

James Fullton:
2.45 Master-plan drawing illustrating the massing of the project along Atlantic Avenue. Diagrammatic sections on the left illustrate the program of each of the three major blocks of development along Atlantic Avenue.

2.46 Plans and sections of the arena and entertainment center. The section illustrates the way in which the arena is sunk into the landscape and an occupiable roof truss rises above to house the entertainment program. The plan shows the location of the public plaza in the southwest corner of the two-block project.

2.47 Diagram illustrating the potential location of an "Atlantic triangle" neighborhood between the established Brooklyn neighborhoods of Fort Greene, Park Slope, and Prospect Heights. Conceptually, the Atlantic Yards redevelopment forms the entire northern border of this triangle along Atlantic Avenue. The triangle is also bounded by Flatbush Avenue to the west and Vanderbilt Avenue to the east and is anchored at the corners by Atlantic Terminal, Prospect Park, and the arena established as a part of the redevelopment program.

Marshall Brown: What's the goal of having a FAR of 14? I understand that it's bigger, but what's the idea besides making more money?

Anthony Vidler: On that tack, on some occasions you are going to have droves of people coming to this thing. How are you going to organize the circulation for the parking, and how do you access the whole? Your have increased the density; you have added an entertainment center to the stadium. How do I get in and out without clogging traffic?

James Fullton: We did an analysis at one point of other people's projects around mid-term, and the idea for mine was the idea of a ground plinth and tower. Most of my parking is in two above-grade floors and two below-grade floors in the plinth level of these residential blocks. It allows me to house four levels in this entire block, as well as partial above-grade parking, because it is built above the rail yards.

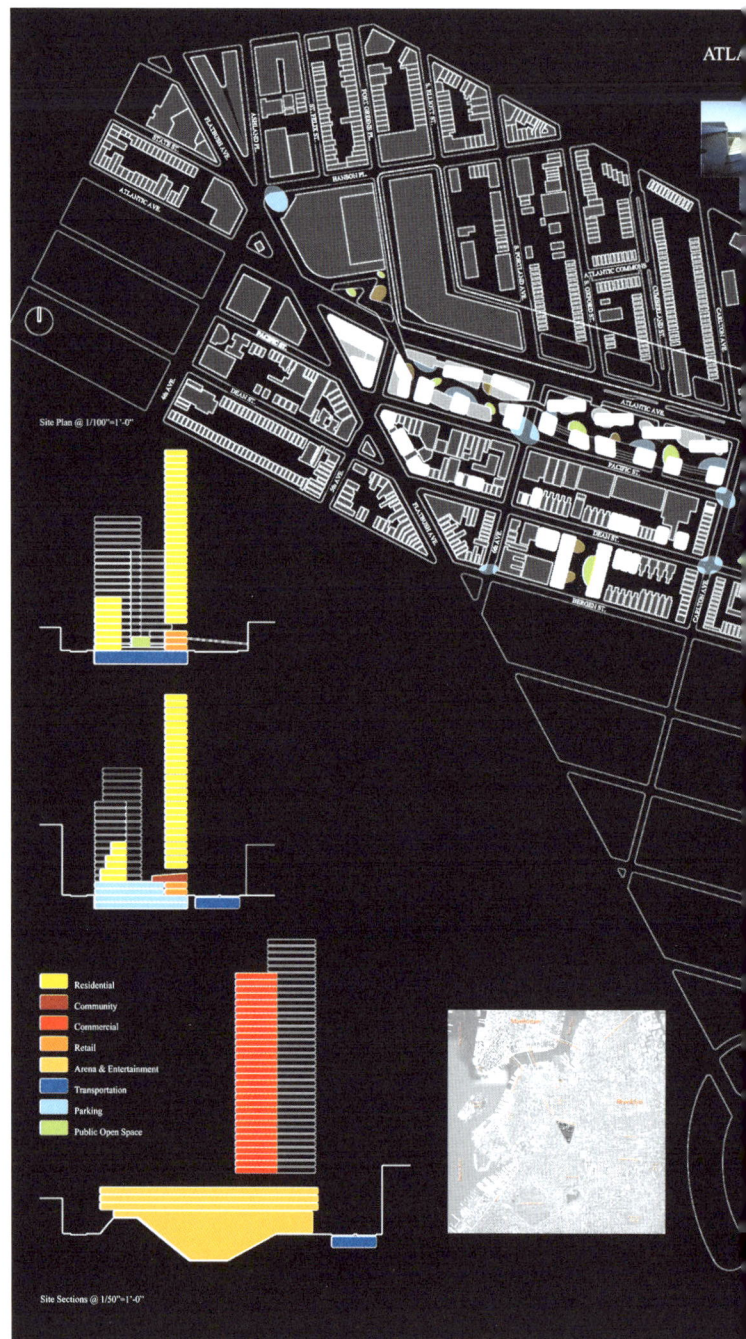

2.45

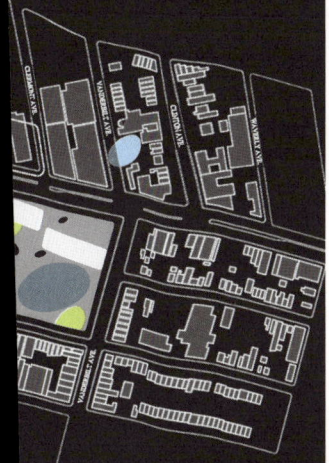

Typical Office Level Plan Showing Roof @ 1/50"=1'-0"

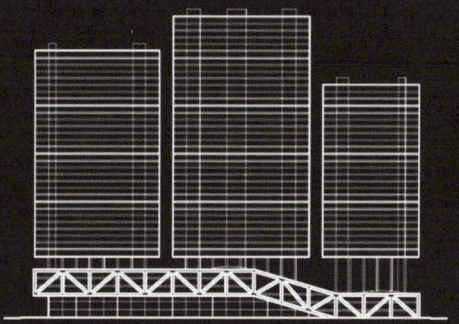

Total Program (sqft):	
Residential	2.3 million
Community	65,000
Commercial	2.0 million
Retail	0.25 million
Arena & Entertainment	1.0 million
Parking	0.3 million
Total	6.0 million

Floor Area Ratio Comparison:	
Atlantic Triangle Redevelopment	14.00 (average)
Atlantic Yards by Frank Gehry	10.00
Typical Brooklyn Residential Block	1.54
Radiant City by Le Corbusier	1.37-2.00

Truss Level Plan @ 1/50"=1'-0"

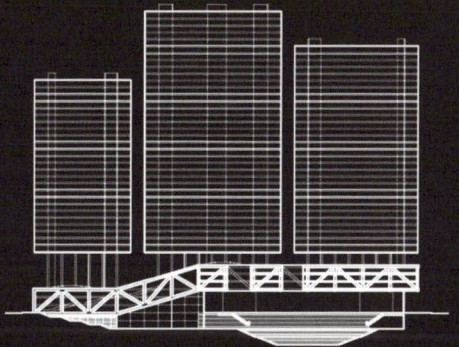

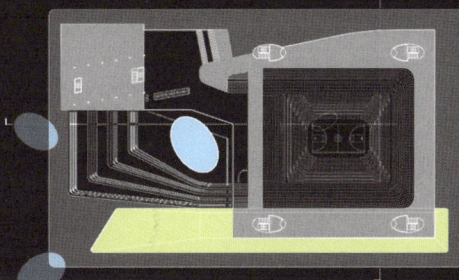

Ground Level Plan @ 1/50"=1'-0"

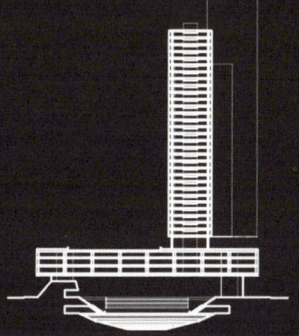

2.46

Fort Greene

Park Slope

Prospect Heights

2.47

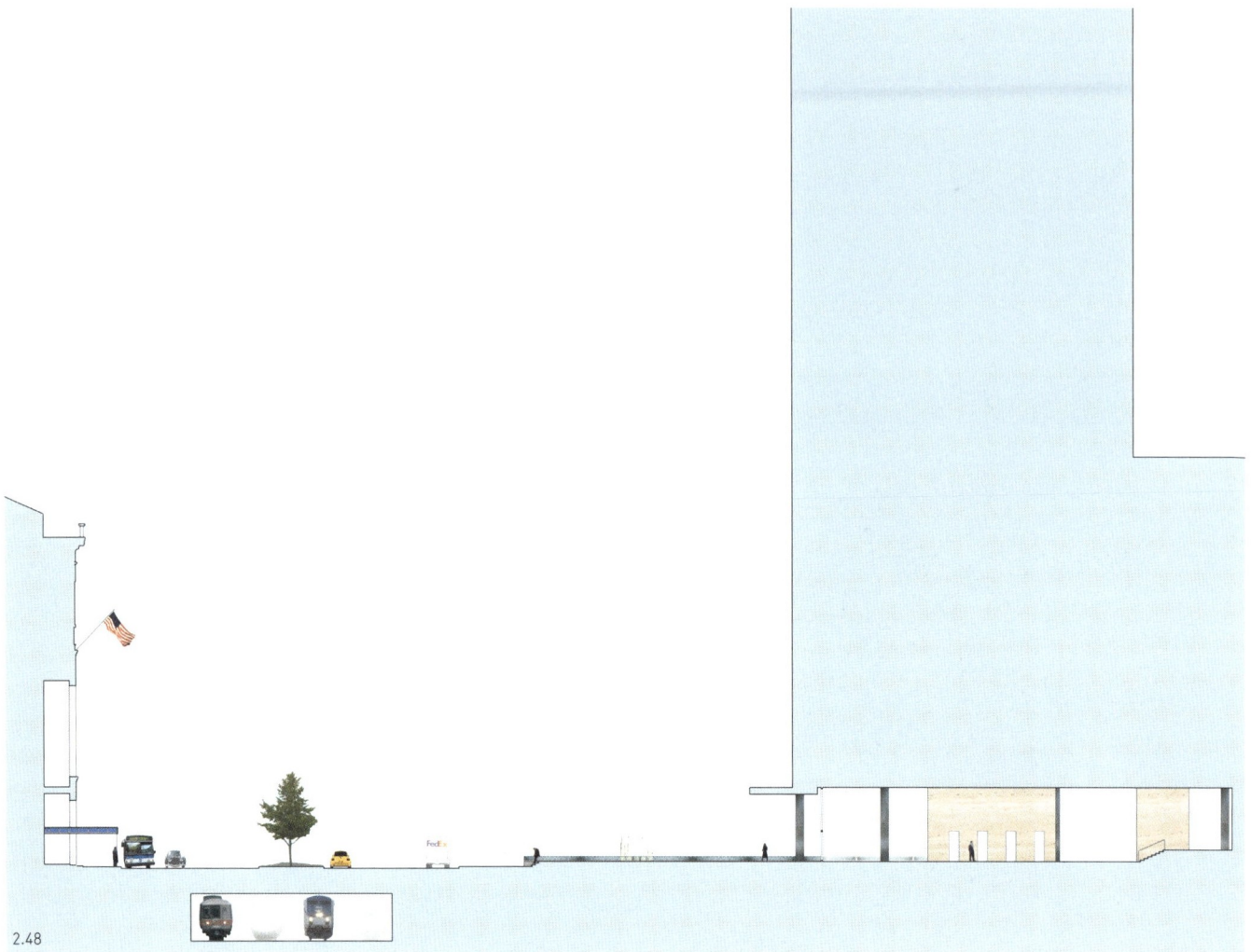

2.48

James Fullton:
2.48 Precedent study drawing through Park Avenue. The New York Athletic Club building is on the left, the Seagram Plaza and the Seagram Building to the right. Park Avenue is similar to Atlantic Avenue in this location, as they both contain a large amount of public transit infrastructure below.

2.49 Aerial view looking down at the arena, entertainment center, public plaza, and three commercial towers.

2.50 Looking down from above the intersection of Flatbush and Atlantic avenues. The pedestrian bridge and commercial tower are in the foreground, with new and existing housing in the back. The pedestrian bridge across Atlantic Avenue connects Atlantic Terminal to the public spaces atop the new housing plinth.

2.51 View of the public plaza and arena, with in-fill townhouses and small residential towers in the foreground.

Keller Easterling: I'm also fascinated with the stadium, but, in America, a firm such as H.O.K. is bargaining on this type of project. We like to regularly blow up our stadiums so we can make them some sort of a

municipal court or a figural space that can be expanded. So the kind of documents I end up thinking about are ones where these things develop in a scenario that happens at the moment where we would ordinarily blow it up.

Anthony Vidler: In Nolli's map of Rome, he depicts the inside and outside of churches, courtyards, etc. There seems to be a need for precisely not treating the arena as a self-imposed wall. If you're going to insert something in an urban area with the kind of understanding we have of what happens when we have gated malls in urban areas like the Beverly Center, in Beverly Hills, then you say to hell with the rest of the city. I think we're looking at something that has that kind of potential. You have a bit

of a footprint and the solid block of the entertainment center, the arena, and the office buildings, with a square line around it. There is a way you move in a little bit, but then you are lost. With a continuous public footprint, how do you get inside to outside and from your block? The block is always a part of something that is another block and another block. It would be nice to see how traffic gets in and out, how people get in and out, and how does public space move into private space and then move into total private space. Footprint plans are terribly important, and I'm so much against gated urban areas. On Sixth Avenue in Manhattan, stores such as Bed Bath & Beyond are placed in great old buildings, but they have ruined small-scale experience on the avenue. It may be economically

2.49

2.50

2.51

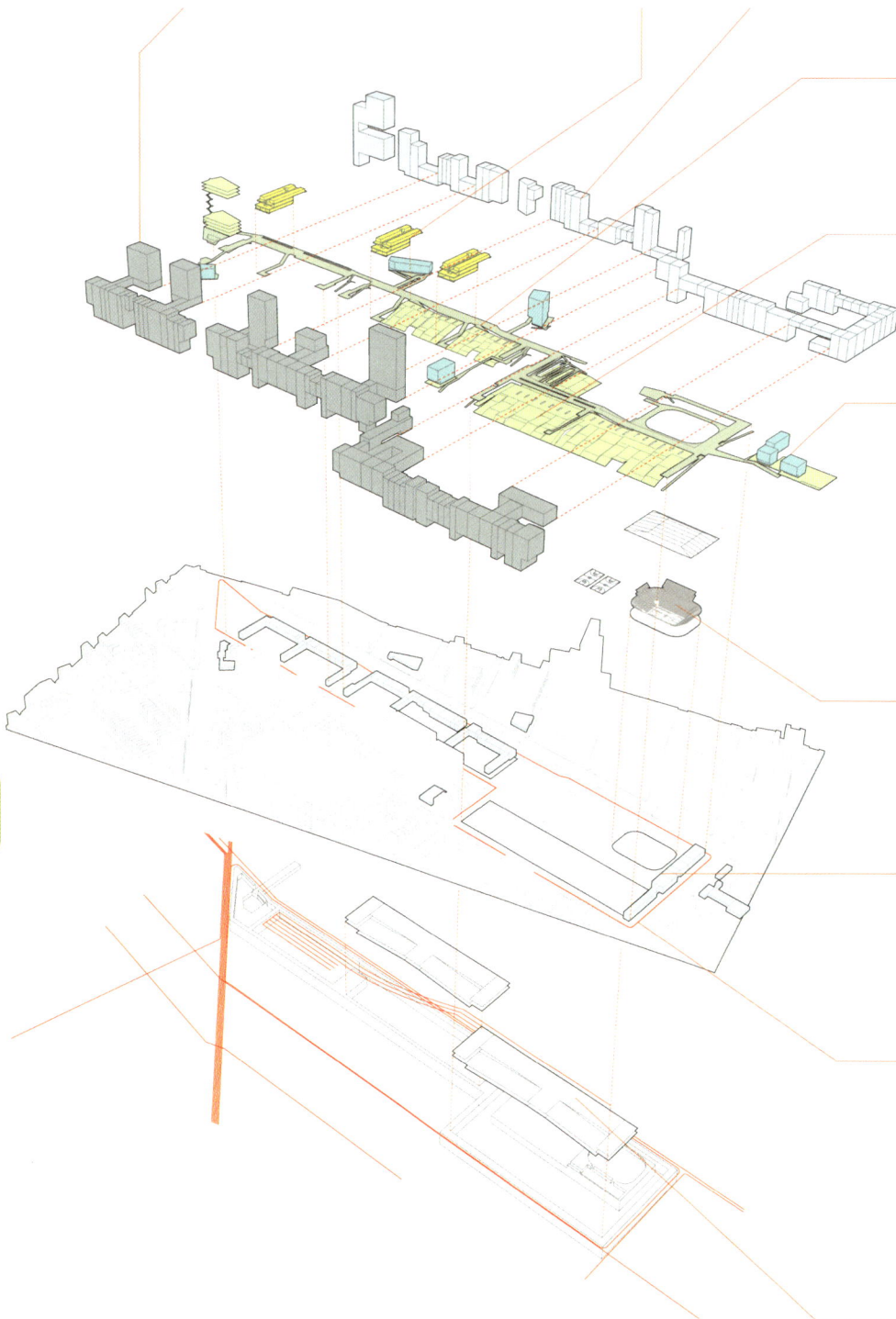

COMMON SURFACE
A publicly accessible level removed from street life below offers a more intimate experience for residents and users

Gives access to different types of amenities other than what are below [seasonal markets, interior parks, views to public arena, etc.]

BLOCK PARKS
Interior parks transition from the common surface down to street level, opening the interior to pedestrians, while covering parking below. The parks protrude through the blocks, inviting passers-by to sit down and chill or pass though.

BONUS HOUSING
Residential Buildings on extensions to the common surface built into fabric adjacent to the proposed site, with access to the parks and other amenities. The extensions also provide easy pedestrian crossing of Atlantic Ave.

150,000-300,000 sf

ARENA
500,000 sf arena built into and surrounded by commercial and residential

Program removed in order to minimize bulk of arena is then dispersed along Atlantic

500,000 sf

STREET LEVEL RETAIL/COMMERCIAL
Retail exists as dispersed elements for the arena, amenities for visitors and locals alike. The nature of these components varies along the site

900,000 sf

OVERALL SITE
Site footprint leaves most exisitng residential intact

600,000 sf

PARKING
Parking below grade between Atlantic/Pacific and Pacific/Dean

Approximately 1500 spaces or 6-8% of the 18,000 seat arena

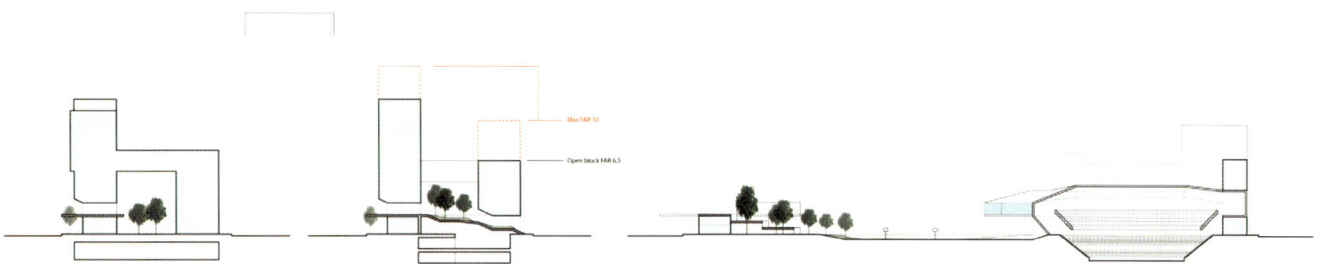

-private block with common surface passing through above street level
-open retail at second floor looks into courtyard but does not access it

-open block with park transitioning from common surface down to street level
-open retail at second floor has access to park

-common surface transitions from elevated state down to the public arena
the multi-use lobby overlooks this park and frames the open space from Atlantic

2.52

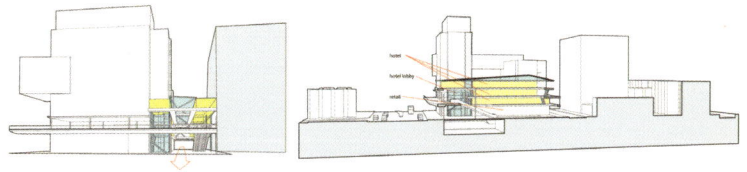

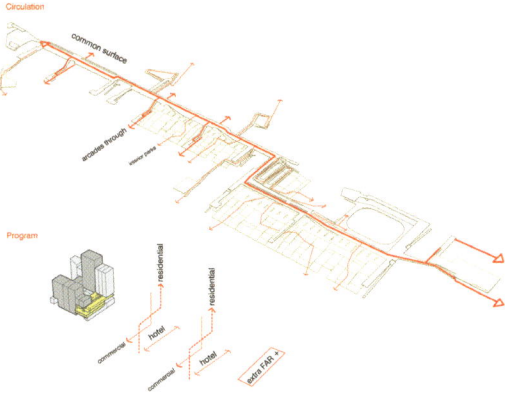

Circulation

common surface

arcades through

interior parks

Program

commercial

residential

hotel

hotel

commercial

residential

extra FAR

The Large Scale:
Moving through the block becomes an engaging experience as one moves along or across the site.

-The hotel mediates between the more commercial Atlantic Ave. and the quieter residential Pacific. Those staying at the hotel are immediate to all amenities, but are removed enough to enjoy the experience of the Brooklyn neighborhood.
-The interior block parks engage pedestrians at street level and extend up to the common surface above the busy Atlantic Ave. They also cover unsightly parking while allowing light through.

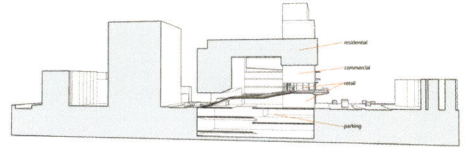

East: the commercial tower at the eastern point of the site contains a vertical extension of the **common surface** that leads to a public lobby [restaurant, health club, etc.] which provides a 360 degree view of New York.

West: a lobby linked to the arena [pre-game, halftime, + post game] looks into the **public arena**. Off-season, the lobby opens to the general public. A terraced extension of the common surface softens the edges of this open public space

The Intimate Scale:
The traditional stoop common all over Brooklyn and New york in general, is replaced by a modified natural version of this classic hang-out.

Existing brownstone stoop   Proposed park surface through block

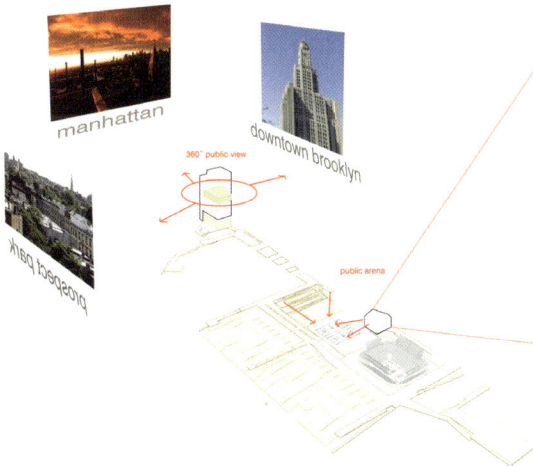

manhattan

downtown brooklyn

prospect park

360° public view

public arena

A view into the public arena from the cantilevered lobby space above with the block park surfaces visible behind.

The interior block parks flow under the residential construction and reach out onto the sidewalk. Views into the block interior invite passers-by to wander in.

2.53

very good for the city but only for parts of city, and it's certainly not economically good for that part of the city where the objects are situated. I think a certain sense of the architectonics of public space is very important.

Matt Hutchinson:
2.52–53 Project diagrams and images. The situation demands that the solution mediate between the intimate scale of existing historical Brooklyn neighborhoods and the larger scale of urban amenities, such as the underground links to the subways and LIRR as well as to the new arena.

By looking to urban situations that successfully combine programmatic elements of disparate scales and overlap the public and private realms, this project aims to provide the required square footage while impacting the surrounding neighborhoods as little as possible, seeking to connect the neighborhood fabric separated by the wide Atlantic Avenue. A common pedestrian path from the transit hub to the arena removes the public from the hostile Atlantic Avenue by elevating to second-level retail. The same path that provides flow along the length of the site also gives access across and through the site and into the block. Opening the blocks through to the street was a major component of the plan, essentially rethinking the nature of the stoop and making it a green version of the classic New York hangout.

BEYOND NOW

The studio looked at the site in its larger socioeconomic context and as a catalyst for redevelopment, not only in form but in kind. The former industrial site has been converted to loft apartments and buildings have been abandoned, signaling a widespread problem: the exodus of industry and quality blue-collar jobs. This problem is not local or singular but global and on a political scale. Addressing the labor issue requires the reinvention of the current ways of production and idealistic solutions that can alter our current habits. One project attempted to restore and modify the former use of the site for current economic conditions. Another project saw the site as a missing link in a chain of local parks; the project became an opportunity to complete the chain using the arena as a public park space as well as a special event venue. Both projects produced not only an architectural proposal but a change in lifestyle.

2.54

subway

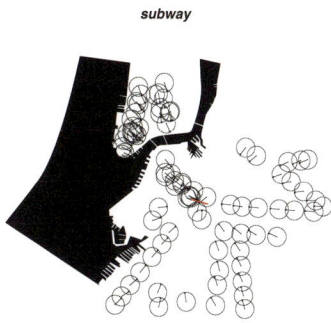

5 min. walking radius from subway stops
subway is most popular of transit options

bus

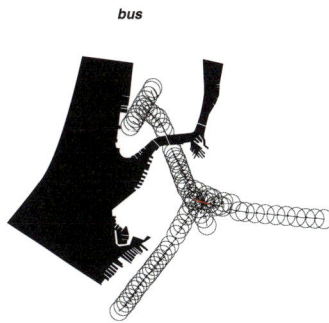

5 min. walking radius from bus stops
bus is slowest of transit options and often used for short distance commutes

cab

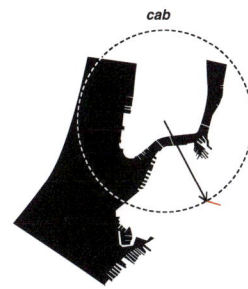

12 min. driving radius from manhattan
based on average cab ride
80% of cab rides in metropolitan nyc are to/from manhattan

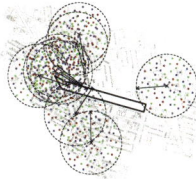

7

subway population
because subway is most popular of transit options, it carries a diverse population of commuters from all five boroughs

4.5 million commuters / day

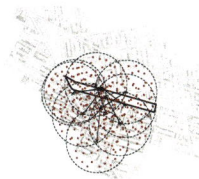

4

bus population
because bus is used for short distance commutes, it carries mostly local commuters

2.5 million commuters / day

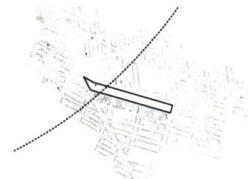

1

cab population
660,000 commuters / day

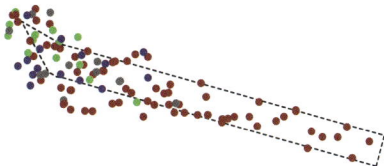

potential access
more potential for cross-borough traffic to access western rather than eastern end of site while local traffic more likely to access entire site equally

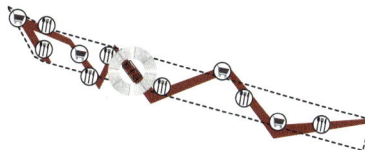

arena location
locate arena at junction of cross-borough and local traffic. distribute concessions and retail. main concourse across length of site

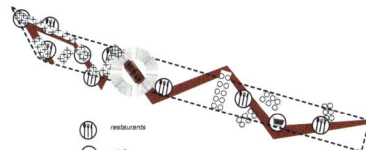

⊗ restaurants
🛒 retail
╫ office
888 community / leisure programs

program distribution
- develop commercial office and retail space above and below main concourse on western end of site.
- develop community related programs on eastern end of site.

2.55

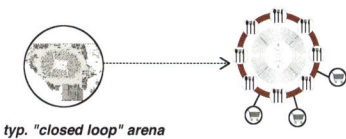

typ. "closed loop" arena

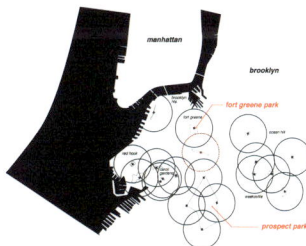

existing park infrastructure - 10 min. walking radius

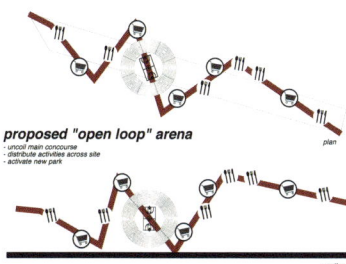

proposed "open loop" arena
- uncoil main concourse
- distribute activities across site
- activate new park

plan

section

proposed residential strategy
use new arena to create open space "disturbances" in housing

elevation

2.56

Aniket Shahane:

2.54 Model view of the intersection of Atlantic and Flatbush avenues, with the arena truss in background.

2.55 This project proposes to "uncoil" the concourse, which typically binds the arena so that programs that would normally stay inside the arena (retail, restaurants, recreation) become public and act as seeds for a new park. The location and volume of these public programs can then be used to determine the envelope for residential development.

2.56 Project diagrams. A site that is contested by two parties, the Brooklyn Yards is one in which both the developer and the community claim the needs of one to be the desires of the other. This project attempts to mediate between the two sides by using the wants of the developer to fulfill a requirement for the community.

2.57 The typical closed-loop arena is opened so amenities that are usually inside the perimeter of the arena (concessions and retail) are brought outside to activate a public park. The event inside the stadium is used to engage the community outside the stadium, economically and socially. Moreover, the park becomes the missing link in an existing ten-minute public park infrastructure. As such, it also becomes an amenity that makes the other, more profitable aspect of the project more feasible: housing.

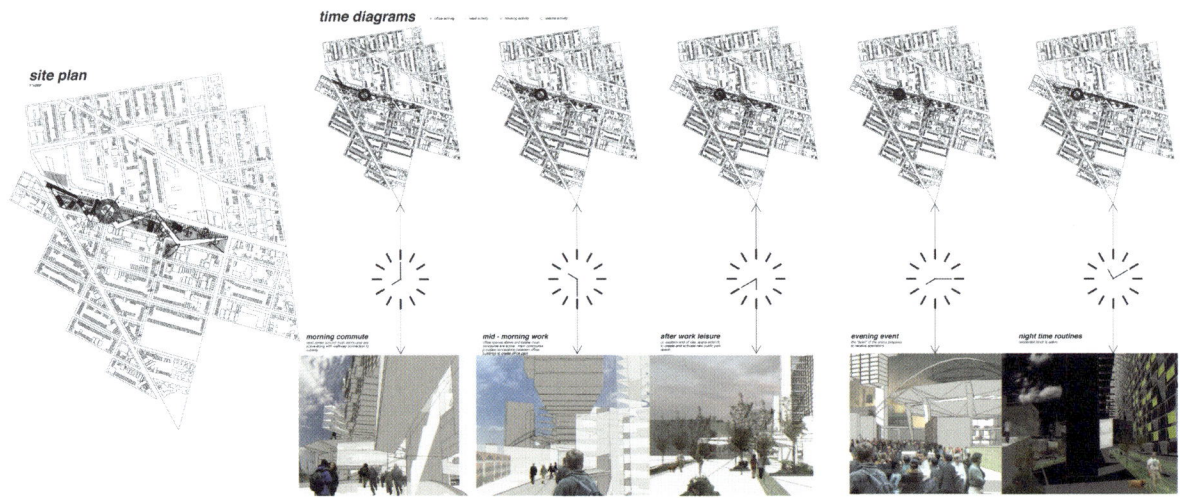

site plan

time diagrams

2.57

2.58

2.59

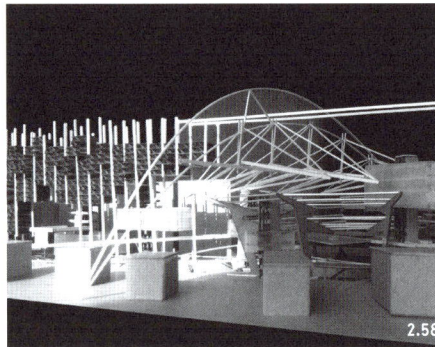

2.58–59 Study models of arena and concourse ideas.

These opportunities can help guide the development that takes place at various points along the site in space as well as in time. The above scenarios are attempts at testing different parts of the site to accept and take advantage of this potential.

Julia Stanat:
2.60 Text and images describing the program that integrates all levels of the community.

Real estate in New York continues to rise in value. The need for more land for high-end housing and manufacturing are at odds. The city is in the process of creating new mixed-use zones where both could potentially exist; however, the manufacturing industry is slowly being moved out as rents are raised and developers move in. This is forcing businesses to redefine their work environment in order to survive. Many businesses are developing cooperative practices in which they share resources and overhead costs with other businesses. I have created a totalizing cooperative that contains small manufacturing, small business, housing, and automobile cooperatives as well as a transportation hub. With a unilateral lack of space in the city, this gives people a place to share their personal, business, and support resources, rather than owning.

2.61 Exploded axon showing program distribution.

Anthony Vidler: The sense of a program, which is not simply a

relationship of FAR to square footage, is in relationship to very broadly classified occupations such as commercial, residential, and so on. Program, to me, is always a kind of utopia. The program has to have built into it an idea of the social politics that surround it. Your program should not impinge on the social realm. This is terribly important as an architect and as a thinker.

If you are working as you are here for huge developers and corporations, your civic responsibility as an architect is to simply follow the outline of the economic productive schemes that the corporations give you. Or it is to say, "I have a responsibility to the neighborhood. I have a responsibility to the city and to the public as an architect, as a thinker, as a planner, not just as a corporate instrument"? I agree with you that this goes a bit further, but I want to see the spirit of some form

of straightforward public politics in the plan: show that you're not just a manipulator of corporate values, but that you understand the nature of the row houses, the nature of the small businesses, the nature of the public parkways, the nature of the shortcuts, the nature of how we live in the city, and the nature of the impact and the power that an object has on a particular neighborhood and what it is giving back to the neighborhood itself.

Marshall Brown: You could be a manipulator of public values, but to what end?

Anthony Vidler: A manipulator, yes; an instrument, no. You can be a manipulator and a fiddler, a subverter, a perverter, absolutely. I think with a plan of this size, social politics is everything for architects, for people who are not simply tools of corporations.

HOUSING CO-OP

The housing cooperative is an old cooperative that exists throughout the city. The city is of course always in the middle of a housing crisis and this would help to solve that.

PARK CO-OP

There would be two types of green spaces. One would be public and open to the neighbor hood and one for private use to the residents of the co-op.

CAR CO-OP

In the car cooperative people would pay a fee to maintain a group of cars that they would have access to at anytime. In addition their would also be regular parking spaces.

TRANSIT HUB

The transportation hub is a program that comes from the circumstance of the site. It simply would provide the cooperative members with easy transportation.

ENERGY CO-OP

The cooperative would also have a biomass and geothermal power producing system that would serve the cooperative itself and the surrounding community if they choose.

BOOK CO-OP

The library is obviously an old type of cooperative where people pay a fee to share books. This would be a private collection.

INDUSTRIAL CO-OP

The industrial cooperative would function in a similar manner to the office cooperative in that companies would share space and resources to have a competitive advantage over their adversaries.

HEALTH CO-OP

The health club cooperative would function in the same manner as most other health clubs. Although being in close proximity with other services would allow them to move freely in-between buildings.

OFFICE CO-OP

Companies would pay for space in certain buildings designed for their needs. This would also allow for like companies to work cooperatively on large projects and share common resources.

CHILDCARE CO-OP

Individuals would pay to have their children watched during the course of the day. They would be able to drop off their child at any time during the day.

ADVERTISING CO-OP

Companies or individuals would pay to have their advertisements on the advertising wall. Their money would go towards their space on the wall, maintenance of the and to the overall cooperative.

2.60

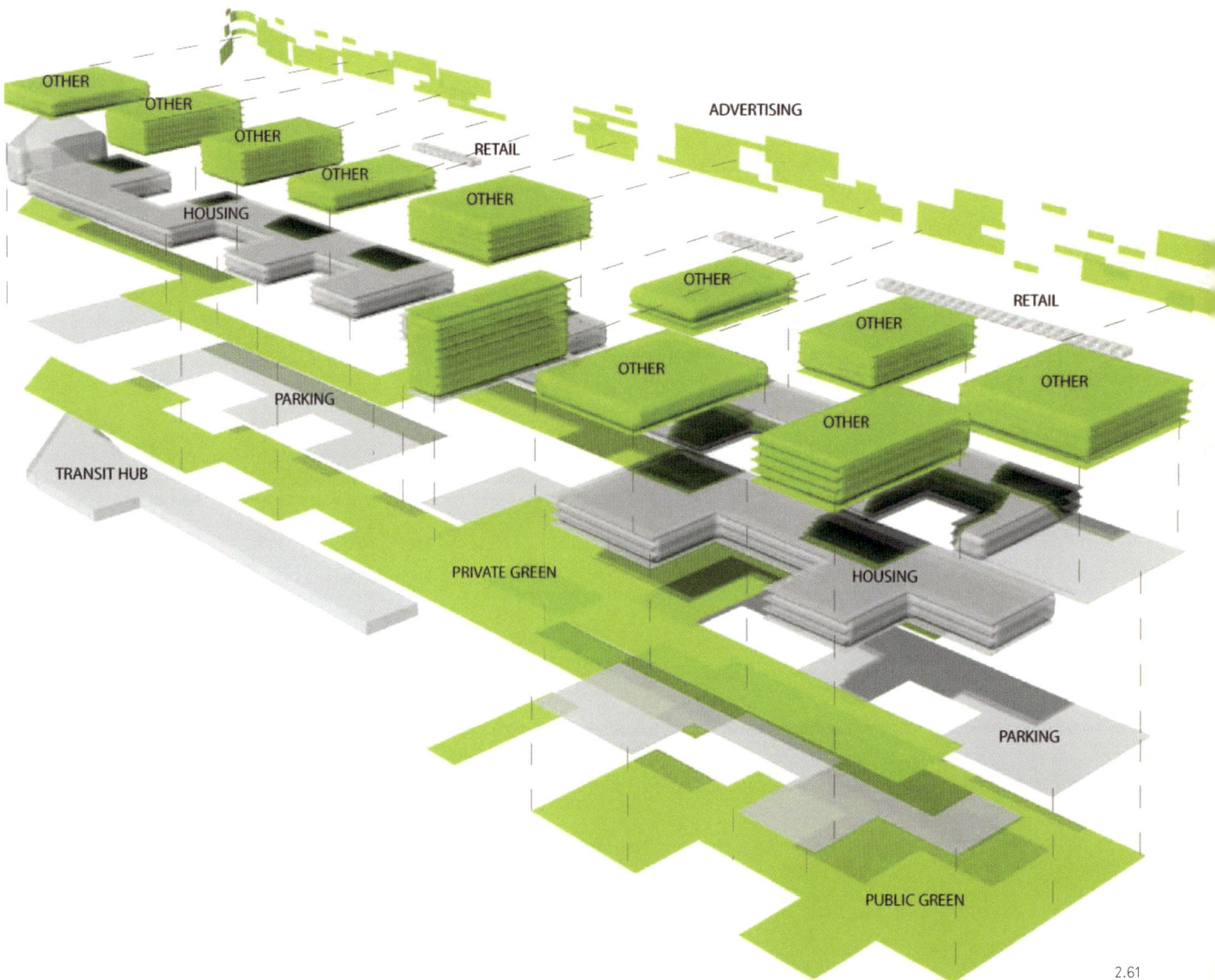

2.61

MARIO
GOODEN

Mario Gooden was the third Louis I. Kahn Visiting Assistant Professor at Yale School of Architecture. He studied at Columbia University and joined in an architectural partnership with Ray Huff, in Charleston, South Carolina, to form Huff + Gooden. He now lives in New York, where Huff + Gooden has opened an office. Huff + Gooden gained recognition when it received an "Emerging Voices" award in 2001 from the Architectural League of New York; that same year the firm was invited to be a competitor in the Brooklyn Public Library International Design Competition, and it has continued to work on many cultural and public projects around the U.S. Gooden discussed his practices and approach to architecture with Laurie Hawkinson of Smith-Miller Hawkinson Architects and Nina Rappaport.

Laurie Hawkinson: As someone who is interested in contemporary culture and not a historicist architect, what is it like to practice in Charleston in terms of dealing with ideas of stereotypes and expectations of a place? How are you thinking about the issues of place?

Mario Gooden: We are trying to make an architecture that is an instrument that reveals the alternate realities of social and cultural conditions. Working in the South, we see a culture that works to deny the projected stereotypes while paradoxically affirming some of those very conditions. In the 1980s there was a rebirth of Southern cities: Charlotte, Charleston, and Atlanta. However, what people see in Charleston is what Charlestonians want them to see, such as the Daughters of the American Revolution buildings, but without the cultural implication of that situation. The Slave Market is just an artifact for them; it is a tourist destination.

LH: I am hesitant to ask you about race and architecture, for the same reasons that I don't like questions about gender. How have you approached the cultural and racial aspects of our society for the project House for the Future President?

MG: The National Building Museum, in Washington, D.C., asked us to do a theoretical project, in conjunction with a celebration of Mount Vernon, for a retreat house for a future president. We thought a future president might be one of the kids we have been designing schools for in the past few years, and his retreat could be in Charleston. Then how would he or she be received in the neighborhood when they returned?

We also looked at the spatial practices in the neighborhood and the way people occupy the corners, streets, and public spaces, and how part of the house and the main façade of the building, which would be ceremonial, would become part of the street, showing the relationship between the individual and community.

LH: Did you incorporate that into the existing fabric?

MG: We pinned it to the traditional houses and sited it near where artist David Hammons did a piece in 1991 for the Spoleto Festival USA's *Places of the Past* site-specific art. One corner of his project was called the "House of the Future"—a version of a Charleston house—and on the other corner he replaced a cigarette ad with images of children looking toward a flagpole with the American flag in the colors of the *African Liberation*. Our project is on the other corner and forms a new communal space; the social space exists on the outside as much as it does on the inside of the house.

LH: It seems that you are trying to come to terms with the local and the global as a spatial condition and as a way to reconstitute day-to-day social life. So when you design institutional buildings, how have you proposed those projects as a thinking architect in considering and opening up the program?

MG: What we attempt to do is look at the circumstances—the physical site and the social and political conditions—and construct a series of strategies that lead to an architectural response that is not directly related to a form. This creates an instrument that forms a new reading of that condition. In a renovation of a 1950s two-story school called the Mary Ford Elementary School, which is adjacent to low-income housing, a cement plant, a railway, and a wetland, we wondered what we could do with the edge between the school and these adjacencies in order to construct a sanctuary for the schoolkids. We came up with the device of an urban hedge that could stabilize the situation in the form of a two-story vegetated screen, which became a landscape piece to provide shade and also gave the kids something to look at outside the window. No one said we couldn't fold the ceiling along the corridor, so we created reveals with moments that interrupted the monotony of the hallways as the light changed throughout the day. It could trigger a different response than what occupants get at home. It needs to be the best kind of place that it can be.

Nina Rappaport: You were also involved in the exhibition sponsored by the Netherlands Architecture Institute, in Rotterdam, which included three Americans and three Dutch and traveled to the National Building Museum and the Venice Biennale. How did you approach development concepts for a new school so soon after Hurricane Katrina's damage, addressing not only an individual building design but issues of urbanism?

MG: We were asked to design a school in a depressed neighborhood. MVRDV was the Dutch counterpart working on the same project. We were not interested in the school as an object but as a catalyst for the urban condition. The site is located where some of the worst flooding occurred, so it was not just about how to replace the school but how to stitch the neighborhood back together. We expanded the program to include housing, festival spaces, and urban gathering spaces to think about space, not so much in a physical sense but in a cultural sense—to recapture the culture of a place when the physical is gone.

NR: When you are looking at the cultural situation and seeing the school as more than just its singular program but as a place that can also serve the community, how do you learn about the place and decide what you think should best go there?

MG: Everyone on our staff has been to New Orleans several times, but it involved quite a bit of research to understand who

lived there, who had to leave, what did they do. In New Orleans, for example, they have a certain practice of eating different foods on specific days, such as po'boys on Mondays, red beans and rice on another, or fish on Fridays. We also researched the businesses that were in or near the neighborhood and what social and cultural organizations were a part of the community. So we did research and found out about cultural life in New Orleans and how social practices translated to spatial practices that affect the urban space.

NR: How do you then include all the conditions around a site?

MG: With each project we try to discover what defines the project, the client, and the cultural sphere. Even with summer houses on the beach for very wealthy clients, we are looking at who these people are and what defines them and how we should think about the space they operate in. What are the invisible dimensions of the *everyday* and domesticity that can be revealed in architecture?

We were asked to curate an exhibition, *Unspoken Spaces*, at a nineteenth-century museum whose collection primarily consists of portraiture and typical Southern plantation imagery. We wanted to shake things up a bit by getting things off the wall and having the museumgoer involved in a different way by seeing things from a different perspective.

We took sixteen works of art and paired them in terms of spatial descriptions such as deep/shallow, interior/exterior, upper/lower, openness/closeness, center/field, public/private, passage/margin, and major/minor, not simply

reading them for architectural features but reading the paintings and photographs with social, political, and cultural emphasis. We enlarged some 200 percent, and some we produced on translucent fabric scrims in the gallery; for others, we fabricated metal stands for display so that people could walk around the object. We created a layering of art and culture, light and dark, shadow and scale, in the installation. As people in Charleston say, "Certain things are not spoken of in pleasant company," and we wanted these issues to be spoken of as they viewed the art in a new way.

NR: As one of the four teams selected to compete in the 2003 Motown Center project, what were some ideas developed for the project, and how did you then use these ideas for later competitions and cultural projects?

MG: The program was a hybrid entertainment venue, museum, education facility, and offices located at an important intersection of Detroit at Woodward and Interstate 75. We approached the project by thinking about the meaning of classic Motown in the early 1960s to the 1980s, before it moved to L.A. One of the first things we did was to map the music as a timeline to determine the significant cultural, political, and cultural events relative to the Motown hits. We started to think of it as a soundtrack to a certain time period. So the parti developed out of intertwining these things to make an architectural promenade through the Motown experience.

Motown wanted visitors to take something away, so our idea was to create glass chambers where

Huff + Gooden, Mary Ford Elementary School, renovation and addition, north Charleston, S.C., 2003.

Huff + Gooden, Early Childhood Development Center, Charleston, S.C., 2005.

Huff + Gooden, Mary Ford Elementary School, view from garden, north Charleston, S.C., 2003.

Huff + Gooden, rendering showing significance of entire site as incorporated into the project for Virginia Key Beach Park Museum, Miami, Florida, 2005.

you record your own piece of Motown music. Our initial strategy was to think of the cultural and historical context as well as the urban context and how it is the final piece for a catalyst of other interventions around it.

NR: Some programs are perhaps more obvious in terms of how they integrate culture, history, race, and place. How did you do this in the California African-American Museum, and your new museum in Miami, for the Virginia Key Beach Park?

MG: For the California African-American Museum, in Los Angeles, where we were asked to do a pre-schematic design, we are looking at the intertwining of history, art, and culture as well as how to reconstruct the existing museum as a cultural medium for expanding the definition of culture and for expanding conceptions of diversity. The existing building is located in Exposition Park, near buildings by Tom Mayne and Frank Gehry. It is also near the behemoth California Science Center. The existing renovation portion is 40,000 square feet, and the expansion is 30,000 to 35,000 square feet. We hope to continue to do projects that ask these kinds of questions. Architecture can help construct awareness and lead to discussion and dialogue. I often tell my students that when you finish a project, there is not going to be a sign that tells you what the architect was thinking. The architecture must communicate at another level and start to beg some questions. In our work we want to think of architecture as being instrumental rather than providing a definitive answer.

We are now working on a museum in Miami; it's a project we won in an invited competition in 2005. It is on the site of the Negro beach in Dade County during the segregation years. Citizens who used to visit this beach as children saved the beach and the island from developers, and they felt it should be something other than a condo development. And as it turns out, it was still on the city books that it was for use as a Negro beach. They organized a charrette and decided that one of the things to do would be to create a commemorative museum and restore the park. That project also required research in terms of understanding South Florida African-American culture, which is different from that in Alabama, Georgia, and other states; there are influences from Cuba, the Caribbean, and Native Americans, and in discovering the identity of the social space of the beach we told stories of how the fishermen would drop people off in the early morning and pick them up late in the day. It became a place of refuge as they took the abject condition of segregation and sublimated it to a position of freedom. And that is what the museum will celebrate.

NR: How do you then translate the ideas and the cultural issues into something physical and or visual as architecture? You can't necessarily write the history on the walls in every case or use vernacular images to then create a recognizable identity to your work.

MG: The project has to move people so that it also becomes about materiality and tectonics. We think about each project in cultural terms but also translate

that into a real tectonic and spatial setting; it is not just projecting an image or cultural reference but how you imbue the space with an almost tactile sense of that translation. Each project is different. While there are ideas that we carry from project to project, there is no signature to our work. We try to not make it about us or about making a form or a fetish but about something beyond ourselves. In our work we start with research, and whatever the form is evolves out of it. Form or image is not the starting point.

NR: How do you integrate ideas of urbanism with individual architectural projects, and how is architecture part of urban design? Do you see a separation between the two, or are they one and the same?

MG: When we research context, whether it is urban or rural, we start out far away and then zoom in to the program with a set of urban programs and strategies. With each of our projects, we begin with looking at the site in an urban context, making a set of hypotheses, and testing the urban condition and how that relates to the surrounding fabric. For example, for the new performing arts theater for the Spoleto Festival USA, in Charleston, we are designing a black-box theater that is in the historic district of Charleston where there is a confluence of urban, cultural, social, and economic issues. The site is at a location where public housing sits next to wealthy homeowners, a public school, and a high-rise building for retirees. Hence, our primary interest is with the exterior space, so we have been working with a group of artists called Places With a Future to design a public garden that will be a new plaza space. For us that is about extending the festival to the people who are not able to afford opera, ballet, or performances, and we are creating fluidity between the urban condition and the built condition. For us, the building became a background piece to the urban setting.

NR: You were also selected as one of the young architecture teams to receive commissions through the First Impressions project of the General Services Administration to reevaluate security and surveillance issues in various federal buildings so that they are less visible and people can enter a space with out fear. How do you design for security and safety?

MG: We have completed the construction documents for improved security for the Gerald Ford Federal Courthouse, in Grand Rapids, Michigan. Security has been imbedded in our lives, and there are large questions not just of how to make it invisible, but how does it affect your awareness and the way you interact with people when security cameras are everywhere.

For our project at the Whipple Federal Building, outside of Minneapolis, it is also about how you think about socialization in this condition of heightened security. Each GSA project is a different situation within the midcentury modern building, and the constituents are all different.

We are now working on a design manual for security in historic buildings that includes the design and reconfiguration of the circulation space, the free zone, the security booths, and the standard items. Every federal building has on display the charters of freedom, and we are looking at how you display that kind of information while integrating good design and the program.

NR: Do you feel the Yale studio about the United Nations addresses the challenge sufficiently?

MG: We are dealing with security issues the same way as the Yale studio, but the actual work is more related to the building rather than the urban fabric. The students solved the issues, but what was important was they could go beyond the scope—they had to explore ideas and test them related not only to the security inside the building but also the urban design of the park, the plaza, and the highway and how reprograming urban space could be both critical and subversive at the same time.

Huff + Gooden, *Unspoken Spaces: Inside + Outside the Boundaries of Race, Class, and Space,* Installation, Gibbes Museum of Art, 2005

Huff + Gooden, Herbert Hassell Aquatic Facility exterior view, 2005.

GLOBA

LOGIES

GLOBALIZATION AND SECURITY

The cultural landscape uses geographic concepts to emphasize where and why people and human activities are located and what significance these observed arrangements represent. That significance reveals relationships of power defined by parameters of technology, race, class, gender, and sexuality. That these sets of relations can be understood as space is to theorize that space is "heterogeneous" and that "we live inside a set of relations that delineate sites, which are irreducible to one another and absolutely not superimposable on one another. One might attempt to describe these different sites by looking for the set of relations by which a given site can be defined."[1]

Michel Foucault challenges modern rationality based on so-called universal, transcendent, disinterested knowledge, arguing instead for situated, interested knowledges that are imbricated with space and power. Hence, cultural theory and the cultural landscape often concern themselves with issues of space and spatial metaphors, fronting concepts such as social space, discursive space, virtual space, city space, and a host of related spaces. By foregrounding spatial concepts, we challenge modernism's focus on time (history) and temporal metaphors. These "new" ways of seeing power/ knowledge structures, hierarchies, boundaries, and borders in our political and socio-economic world (obscured by modernist history) can be revealed through architecture's ability to articulate spatial relationships among people and situations. Furthermore, by expanding the scale of these spa-

tial concepts to the scale of geopolitics, economic power structures, and social and political forms of resistance and conflict, the cultural landscape may include the forces of globalization and strife at hot spots around the globe.

In the aftermath of September 11, the cultural landscape (relationships of space and power) has been reshaped in public spaces as a result of security and the ongoing threat of terrorism having entered into the restructuring of cultural values and everyday life. Changes include new airline screening policies; tightened patrolling of the nation's borders and ports; the fortification of government facilities; ongoing police and National Guard presence at potential "high value" targets; the enactment of new laws and regulations, and the creation of the Department of Homeland Security to oversee and direct these measures. Not only do these changes raise issues of safety but also of civil liberties, national identity, and much larger questions regarding the relationships (cause and effect) between the politics of representation and globalization on the one hand and security and terror on the other. In *The Violence of the Global,* Jean Baudrillard examines the relationship between universalization, globalization, and the singularity of terrorism. He states that terrorism is not the product of a traditional history of anarchism, nihilism, or fanaticism, but it is instead the contemporary partner of the excesses of globalization and the reality of impossible exchanges between global powers and singular forces.

The spring 2005 Louis I. Kahn Distinguished Visiting Assistant

Professorship studio engaged the relationships of space and power, restructured by globalization and security, by investigating proposals for interventions at the United Nations Headquarters, in New York. The studio contemplated a critical architecture that might be deployed as an instrument to construct a discourse regarding the repositioning of the UN in the space between universalism and the reality of globalism, which is a network of information exchange, commercial exchange, technology, political reorganization, instability, tourism, and terrorist acts.

Critical Architecture
The production of architecture can be situated between two (sometimes dialectically opposed) positions. From one view, architecture is born of social or economic need, reflecting the values of a cultural or political situation. From another view, architecture is generated as an ideal of pure conceptualization or with an internal, hermetic logic that is already complete but can be programmed or not. K. Michael Hays in *Critical Architecture: Between Culture and Form* describes critical architecture as "cutting across the dichotomy of, on the one hand, a social/cultural context and, on the other, that of form to occupy a position that is resistant and oppositional. This is an architecture that cannot be reduced either to a conciliatory representation of external forces or to a dogmatic, reproducible formal system. If a critical architecture is to be worldly and self-aware simultaneously, its definitions are in architecture's difference from other cultural manifestations and from a priori categories or methods."[2]

Critical architecture demands architecture that is always already design research; that is, architecture is the diligent and systematic inquiry to discover, uncover, and reveal facts, theories, and applications. Furthermore, in the process of investigation, sets of relationships are constructed between knowledge, social/cultural contexts, and architectural space. Hence, architecture should be deployed as an instrument that enables the conception, perception, and spatial experience of relationships. Toward this end, the studio investigated the means of producing architectural interventions that are critical to the understanding of relationships within contemporary social and cultural contexts set against the iconic formalism of architecture itself.

Universalism
While a convenient handle used by curators of the Museum of Modern Art's *Exhibit "15"* of 1932 to restructure the historical landscape of modern architecture and to declare a new and thoroughly modern architectural movement predicated upon "style and nothing but style,"[3] the International Style with its deceptive homogeneity of planar forms, free plan, and open space nonetheless implied universality adaptable to any climatic or cultural condition. The notion of international and universal architecture implied the end of nationalities and nationalism before World War II and the Cold War. Hence, the United Nations Headquarters was conceived as the architectural apotheosis of modernist universalism in the International Style. The goal of the United Nations design was to aesthetically "supplant national traditions and prejudices with a

universal, progressive design to suit the new organization."[4] The international architects for the UN searched for an appropriate architectural expression for the most important symbolic building constructed in the aftermath of World War II. Upon presenting the final design to the United Nations, chief architect Wallace K. Harrison remarked, "The world hopes for a symbol of peace; we have given them a workshop for peace." Yet upon completion of construction, the reception by the critics and architectural community was lukewarm. There seemed to be some ambivalence about the ability of the International Style to convey the symbolic meaning produced by traditional design. And to politicians, the International Style sounded too much like "internationalism," prompting unease about the growing presence of America's role in the world. Questions continue to remain regarding architecture's ability to convey meaning and engage in discourse related to global affairs, particularly within today's complex socio-political and cultural landscape.

Globalization
At the end of the twentieth century, the universalist ideals of the word *international* (that is, peace, human rights, liberty, culture, and democracy) were supplanted by the forces of globalization, which by contrast is informed by technology, capitalism, tourism, and information and seems to be irreversible. In the Enlightenment, universalization was viewed as unlimited growth and forward progress. Today, by contrast, universalization exists by default and is expressed as a forward escape, which aims to reach the

most minimally common value. The globalization of exchanges puts an end to the universalization of values. What is globalized is first and foremost the market, a profusion of exchanges and all sorts of products, the perpetual flow of money and information. Culturally, globalization gives way to a promiscuity of signs and values. Far from being an uplifting move, it is instead a downward trend toward a zero degree in all values.[5] Globalization's most profound effects are not economic but cultural; indeed, it is reordering societies all over the planet. "The battleground of the twenty-first century will pit fundamentalism against cosmopolitan tolerance. In a globalizing world, where information and images are routinely transmitted across the globe, we are all regularly in contact with others who think differently, and live differently, from ourselves. Cosmopolitans welcome and embrace this cultural complexity. Fundamentalists find it disturbing and dangerous. Whether in the areas of religion, ethnic identity, or nationalism, they take refuge in a renewed and purified tradition and, quite often, violence."[6] Fundamentalism is the other side of the cosmopolitanism of globalization. It's not accidental that fundamentalists make use of mass communications and the modern forms of identity, which they also pretend to condemn. Hence, as globalization, security, and terrorist acts reshape the cultural landscape, what are its effects upon the issues of space and "new" ways of seeing power/knowledge structures, hierarchies, boundaries, and borders in our political and socio-economic world?

3.01

3.02

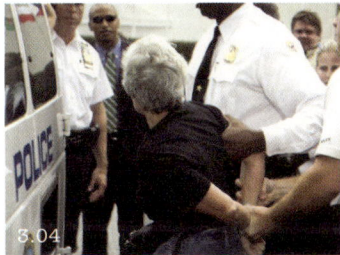

3.03

3.04

3.05

3.01 The United Nations Headquarters, New York, New York. Ezra Stoller, © Esto.

3.02 Members of the Board of Design Consultants appointed to plan the construction of the UN permanent headquarters on Manhattan's East River site. Foreground, left: Liang Ssu-cheng, China; Oscar Niemeyer, Brazil; Nikolai D. Bassov, USSR; and Ernest Cormier, Canada. Second row, from left : Sven Markelius, Sweden; Charles E. Le Corbusier, France; Vladimir Bodiansky, engineer consultant; France,

Wallace K. Harrison, chief architect, USA; G.A. Soilleux, Australia; Max Abramovitz, director of planning; USA, and consultants Ernest Weismann, Yugoslavia; Anthony C. Antoniades, Greece, and Matthew Nowicki, Poland. New York, April 18, 1947.

3.03 The United Nations General Assembly. Ezra Stoller, © Esto, 1953.

3.04–05 Protesters and police at the UN, September 19, 2006.

METHODOLOGY

The studio's overall approach was experimental with regard to both program and design methodology. The assignments were divided into two sections that operated at multiple scales. The first section explored the relationships between the global and the local at the scale of the body through a mapping exercise based on sites of global conflict and the 1:1 tectonic translation of these maps and the spatial conditions they revealed. The mapping exercise entailed a digital "sampling" analysis of data based on a current UN Peacekeeping Mission in order to explicate the infrastructural components and spatial implications of globalization related to conflicts at various sites around the globe. Additional goals of the mapping, or cultural cartography, were to interpret and translate a cultural context as filtered through media and information technology and encourage the subjective exchange between the global and local as well as the emergence of a new form of global urbanism. Mapping as a spatial technique in cultural theory can allow us to rearticulate the world we live in and visualize changing structures and boundaries.

Each student in the studio was asked to select a current United Nations Peacekeeping Mission site as the context for the mapping. In general, UN Peacekeeping Missions are precipitated by actions within a country between opposing forces. Depending on its mandate, the UN Peacekeeping Mission may be required to:
1. Deploy to prevent the outbreak of conflict or the spillover of conflict across borders; stabilize conflict situations after a cease-fire; create an environment for the parties to reach a lasting peace agreement.
2. Assist in implementing comprehensive peace agreements.
3. Lead states or territories through a transition to a stable government, based on democratic principles, good governance, and economic development.

At each UN Peacekeeping Missions site, students were asked to:
1. Map the spatial relationships between opposing forces prior to UN involvement; map the movement patterns, strategies, and actions of these forces.
2. Map the flow of resources that support the opposing forces and/or that precipitated the situation or condition.
3. Diagram the UN involvement or intervention through mapping the structure of its operation in each mission; map the flow of aid and resources from the local headquarters to the UN sections.
4. Map the movement patterns of displaced populations and trace the flows from settlement to settlement in relationship to the actions and reactions of opposing forces.
5. Diagram the UN relief effort to those affected by the instability in the country and map the flow of relief aid to those affected.
6. Map the changes to borders and boundaries and their significance to understanding the dynamics of the situations.
7. Map the flow of information internal to the situation on the ground and to the world at large.

The data for the mapping were sampled from digital maps; Internet web sites dedicated to human-rights monitoring; news web sites and publications; web sites sponsored by individual countries and groups engaged in conflict; nongovernmental agency sources, and United Nations reports, publications, and videos. The studio examined the role of technology in shaping the dissemination of information and perception of cultural geographies at various scales of engagement, from the local scale of the conflict to the global scale of inter-related political structures, as well as the economic effects at home and abroad. Information, media, and technology constantly reframe and filter our perceptions of culture as well as social and political contexts, resulting in a heterotopic landscape that collapses temporal distances, realigns the coordinates of knowledge, and constantly challenges the meanings of representations. Anthony Giddens in *The Consequences of Modernity* provides a means for considering an understanding of the media and everyday life, saying that modernity's new dynamism "derives from the separation of time and space."[7] In the transition from traditional to modern society, human relations have been "lifted" out of situated locales and "stretched" across vast geographical distances. "There is a dramatic 'tearing' of space from place—an accelerating 'time-space distanciation process.' As a result of this historical shift, relationships between 'the local' and 'the global' are constituted in such a way as to reconstitute day-to-day social life, along with our basic senses of self-identity. Place becomes phantasmagoric."[8] The resultant effect upon architecture today flows toward infrastructural systems of interfaces, directing flows, recombinant orders, and iterative processes. Urbanism and

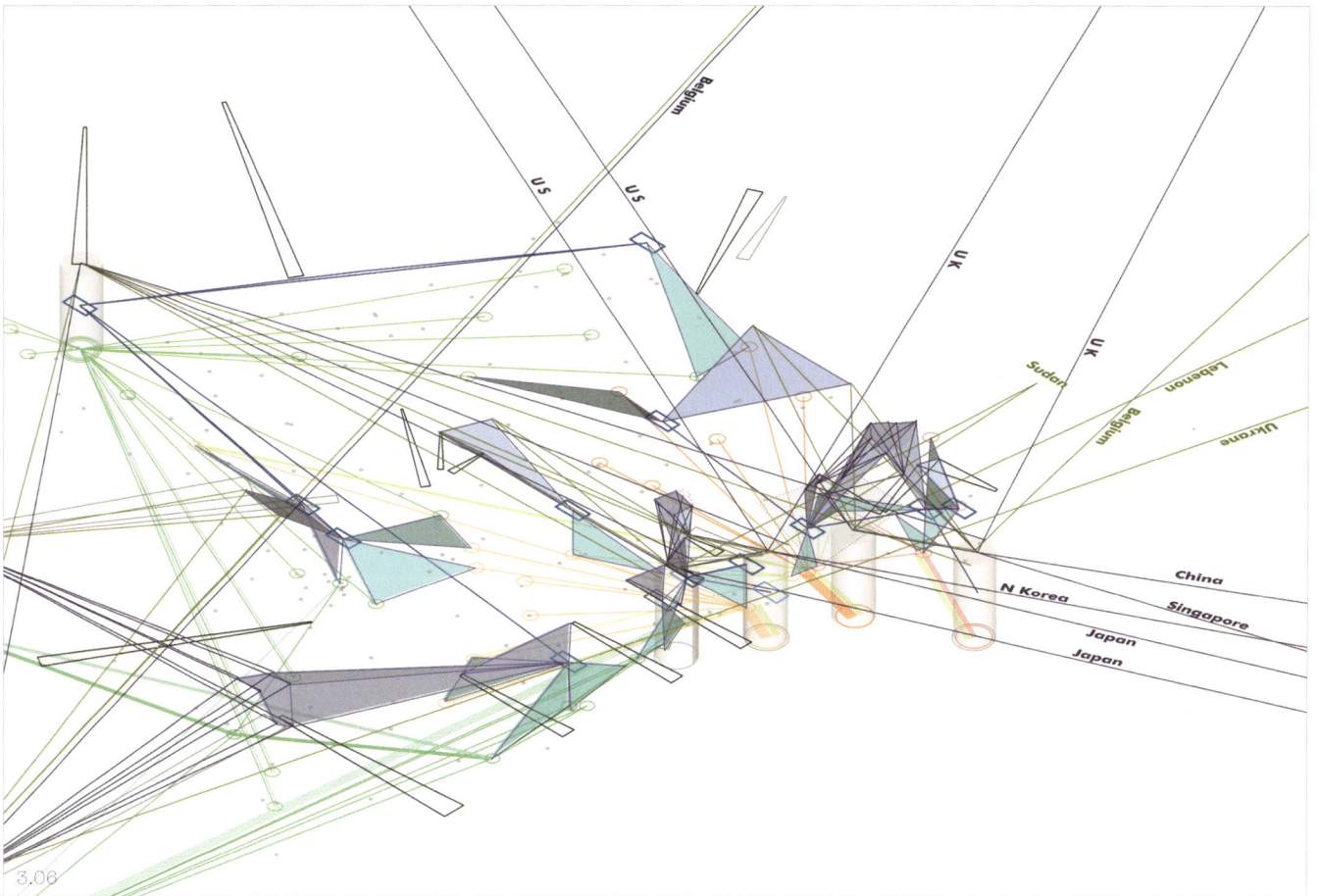

3.06

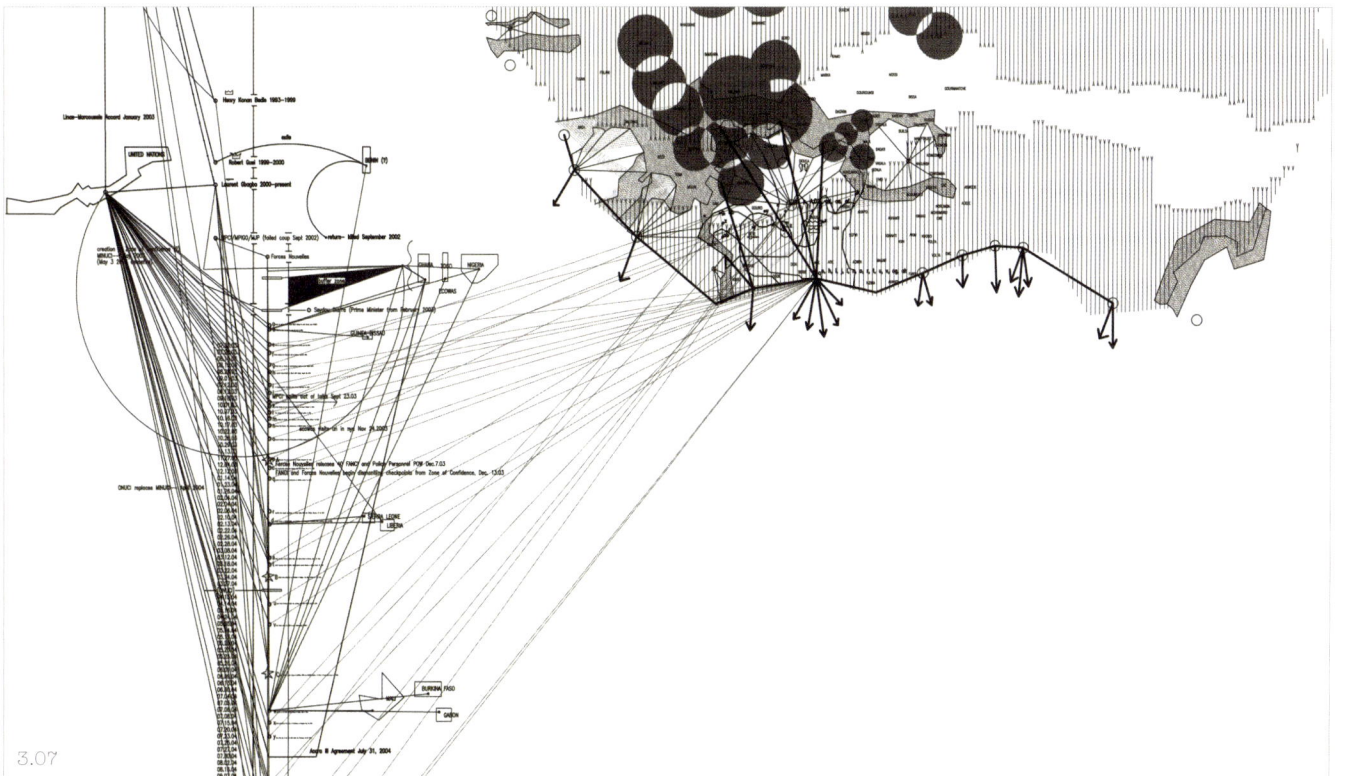

3.07

3.06 Detail of map diagramming the UN
Peacekeeping Mission in the Democratic
Republic of the Congo. (Lee Lim)

3.07 Detail of map diagramming the UN
Peacekeeping Mission in Kashmir.
(Ruth Gyuse)

3.08 Map diagramming the UN
Peacekeeping Mission in Cyprus.
(Derek Hoeferlin)

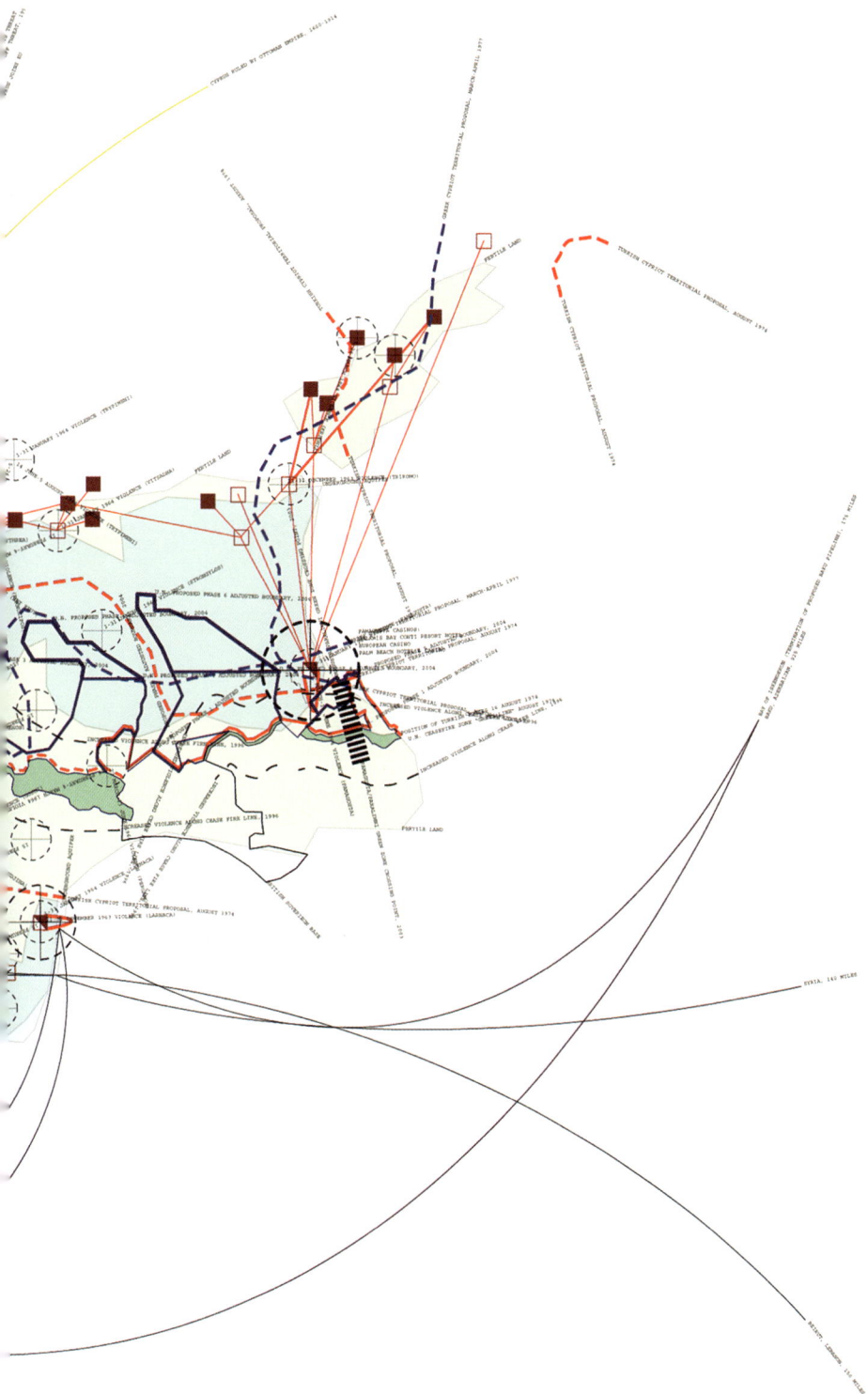

architecture merge in this mediated condition.

The second part of this first section of investigation was the 1:1 tectonic translation from the mapping exercise. The goal of the tectonic translation was to extract from the mappings specific spatial and conditional relationships that might operate at various scales and enable a future architecture to be deployed in a discourse of power and space. As a design exercise, the translation involved the following components: a field of operations with specific physical limitations (site); situations with specific actions as well as motives (program); and three zones for action that were given as Gather, Disperse, and Watch (place). In the translation of their projects from idea to physicality, each student was asked to program a series of related spatial situations within a site that brings the occupants into a "global theater" as a space of exchange.

Catalysts were suggested to the students as a means to engage program and extract spatial and conditional relationships from the mapping.

Catalysts:

ACTIONS	CONDITIONS	MOTIVATIONS
Assemble	Negotiation	Memory
Display	Observation	Contemplation
Exchange	Mediation	Exhibition
Perform	Intervention	Reflection
Project	Intermission	Recollection

Redeploying the UN
In the second section of the studio students were asked to design an intervention at the United Nations Headquarters, in New York. In general, the program for the intervention was a new security sequence for visitors, diplomats,

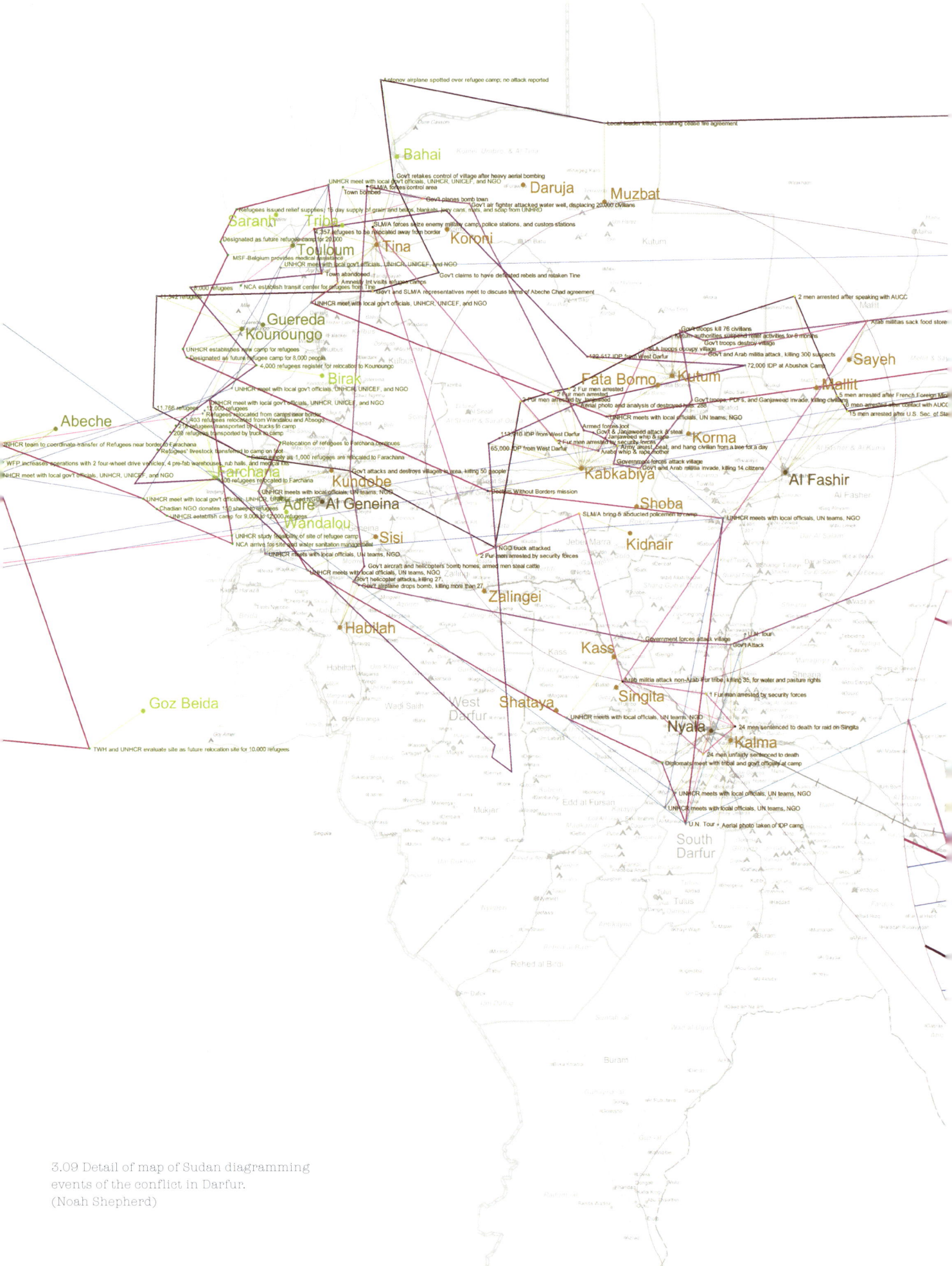

Antonov airplane spotted over refugee camp; no attack reported

Local leader killed, breaking cease fire agreement

Bahai

Gov't retakes control of village after heavy aerial bombing
Daruja   Muzbat
UNHCR meet with local gov't officials, UNHCR, UNICEF, and NGO
SLM/A forces control area
Town bombed
Gov't planes bomb town
Gov't air fighter attacked water well, displacing 20,000 civilians
Saranh   Tribe
Refugees issued relief supplies; 15 day supply of grain and beans, blankets, jerry cans, mats, and soap from UNHRD
Designated as future refugee camp for 20,000   SLM/A forces seize enemy military camp, police stations, and custom stations
Toutoum   Tina   Koroni
MSF-Belgium provides medical assistance   2 men arrested after speaking with AUCC
UNHCR meet with local gov't officials, UNHCR, UNICEF, and NGO
Town abandoned   Amnesty Int'l visits refugee camps   Arab militias sack food store
4,000 refugees NCA establish transit center for refugees from Tine   Gov't claims to have defeated rebels and retaken Tine
11,342 refugees   Gov't and SLM/A representatives meet to discuss terms of Abeche Chad agreement   Gov't troops kill 76 civilians
UNHCR meet with local gov't officials, UNHCR, UNICEF, and NGO   Kutum authorities suspend relief activities for 8 months
Guereda   SLA troops occupy village   Gov't troops destroy village
Kounoungo   122,517 IDP from West Darfur   Sayeh
UNHCR establishes new camp for refugees   Fata Borno   Kutum 72,000 IDP at Abushok Camp Mallit
Designated as future refugee camp for 8,000 people   2 Fur men arrested   Gov't troops, PDF's, and Ganjaweed invade, killing civilians 5 men arrested after French Foreign Mid
4,000 refugees register for relocation to Kounoungo   2 Fur men arrested by Janjaweed   3 men arrested after contact with AUCC
Birak   Aerial photo and analysis of destroyed huts: 288   15 men arrested after U.S. Sec. of Sta
UNHCR meet with local gov't officials, UNHCR, UNICEF, and NGO   Armed forces loot   Korma
11,766 refugees UNHCR meet with local gov't officials, UNHCR, UNICEF, and NGO 113,910 IDP from West Darfur Ganjaweed attack & steal
15,000 refugees   65,000 IDP from West Darfur   Janjaweed whip & rape
1,403 refugees relocated from Wandalou and Absoog   Army arrest, beat, and hang civilian from a tree for a day
Refugees relocated from camps near border   Arabs whip & rape mother
7 refugees transported by 5 trucks to camp   Government forces attack village
208 refugees transported by truck to camp   Relocation of refugees to Farachana continues Gov't and Arab militia invade, killing 14 citizens
UNHCR team to coordinate transfer of Refugees near border to Farachana Kabkabiya   Al Fashir
Refugees' livestock transferred to camp on foot   Gov't attacks and destroys villages in area, killing 50 people
WFP increases operations with 2 four-wheel drive vehicles, 4 pre-fab warehouses, rub halls, and medical kits Doctors Without Borders mission
Abeche   Farachana
UNHCR meet with local gov't officials, UNHCR, UNICEF, and NGO
00 refugees relocated to Farachana   Shoba
Kulbobe   UNHCR meets with local officials, UN teams, NGO
UNHCR meets with local gov't officials, UN teams, NGO   SLM/A bring 5 abducted policemen to camp
Adre   Al Geneina   Kidnair
Chadian NGO donates 150 sheep to refugees
UNHCR establish camp for 9,000 to 12,000 refugees
Wandalou
UNHCR study feasibility of site of refugee camp   Sisi   2 Fur men arrested by security forces
NCA arrive for site and water sanitation management
UNHCR meets with local officials, UN teams, NGO
Gov't aircraft and helicopters bomb homes; armed men steal cattle
UNHCR meets with local officials, UN teams, NGO
Gov't helicopter attacks, killing 27   Zalingei
Gov't airplane drops bomb, killing more than 27

Habilah   Government forces attack village Gov't Attack
                                                                              U.N. Tour
Kass
Arab militia attack non-Arab Fur tribe, killing 35, for water and pasture rights
Singita   1 Fur man arrested by security forces
UNHCR meets with local officials, UN teams, NGO
Goz Beida   West   Shataya   Nyala   24 men sentenced to death for raid on Singita
                    Darfur   Kalma
                                                        24 men unfairly sentenced to death
TWH and UNHCR evaluate site as future relocation site for 10,000 refugees Diplomats meet with tribal and gov't officials at camp

UNHCR meets with local officials, UN teams, NGO
UNHCR meets with local officials, UN teams, NGO
U.N. Tour Aerial photo taken of IDP camp

South
Darfur

3.09 Detail of map of Sudan diagramming
events of the conflict in Darfur.
(Noah Shepherd)

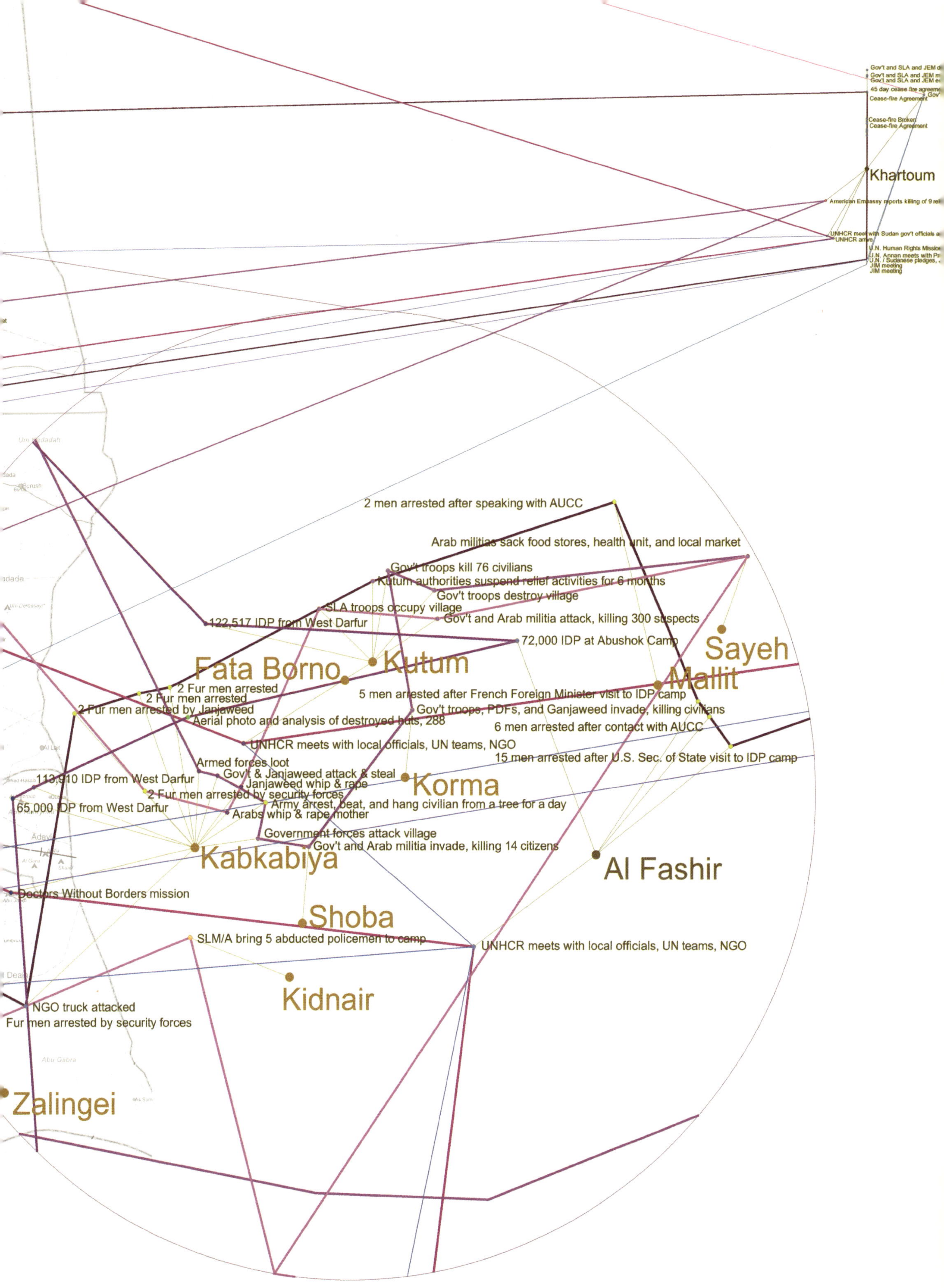

Khartoum

Gov't and SLA and JEM d
Gov't and SLA and JEM m
Gov't and SLA and JEM m
45 day cease-fire agreeme
Gov
Cease-fire Agreement

Cease-fire Broken
Cease-fire Agreement

American Embassy reports killing of 9 reli

UNHCR meets with Sudan gov't officials a
UNHCR arriv
U.N. Human Rights Missio
U.N. Annan meets with Pr
U.N. / Sudanese pledges,
JIM meeting
JIM meeting

Um Buradah

2 men arrested after speaking with AUCC

Arab militias sack food stores, health unit, and local market

Gov't troops kill 76 civilians
Kutum authorities suspend relief activities for 6 months
Gov't troops destroy village
SLA troops occupy village
122,517 IDP from West Darfur
Gov't and Arab militia attack, killing 300 suspects
72,000 IDP at Abushok Camp

Sayeh

Fata Borno • Kutum
Mallit

2 Fur men arrested
2 Fur men arrested
2 Fur men arrested by Janjaweed
Aerial photo and analysis of destroyed huts, 288

5 men arrested after French Foreign Minister visit to IDP camp
Gov't troops, PDFs, and Ganjaweed invade, killing civilians
6 men arrested after contact with AUCC
UNHCR meets with local officials, UN teams, NGO
15 men arrested after U.S. Sec. of State visit to IDP camp

Armed forces loot
113,910 IDP from West Darfur
Gov't & Janjaweed attack & steal
Janjaweed whip & rape
2 Fur men arrested by security forces

Korma

65,000 IDP from West Darfur
Arabs whip & rape mother
Army arrest, beat, and hang civilian from a tree for a day

Government forces attack village
Gov't and Arab militia invade, killing 14 citizens

Kabkabiya

Al Fashir

Doctors Without Borders mission

Shoba

SLM/A bring 5 abducted policemen to camp

UNHCR meets with local officials, UN teams, NGO

NGO truck attacked
Fur men arrested by security forces

Kidnair

Zalingei

113

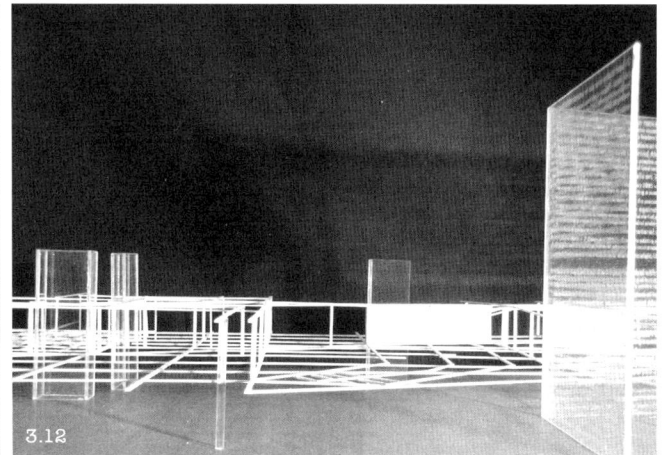

3.10-11 View of a model translating a
cartographic investigation of the UN
Peacekeeping Mission in Kosovo.
(Sal Wilson)

3.12 Views of a model translating
a cartographic investigation of the UN
Peacekeeping Mission in Georgia.
(Christopher Yost)

and journalists. This site was extremely appropriate given that the UN has been an arbiter between the forces of globalization, geopolitics, and indigenous cultures; it was under barricaded protection in the days following September 11, and it remains a target as high-profile leaders from around the world routinely visit the headquarters to carry out diplomatic business.

In December 1946, John D. Rockefeller, Jr., offered the United Nations a gift of $8.5 million to acquire the present site on the East River. At the time, this area, known as Turtle Bay, consisted mainly of slums, slaughterhouses, and breweries. The construction program, costing over $67 million, was financed in large part by the United States, which made available an interest-free loan of $64 million that was entirely reimbursed by annual payments; the balance was paid from the United Nations budget. The Secretariat Building opened in 1950, and two years later the first meetings of the Security Council and the General Assembly were held at the permanent site. The Dag Hammarskjöld Memorial Library was completed in 1962. More than forty years later, as the United Nations Headquarters prepares to undergo a major renovation, two key components will be security screening and the reengagement of the visitor with the mission of the UN. Even though, in the aftermath of September 11, the UN is no longer the open symbol of international extraterritoriality, an average of 3,000 people a day visit the UN as a tourist destination for those who honor and respect its mission.

Program

While the issue of security reflects the current state of world events, the security screening process serves as a metaphor for the complex relationship between globalization and violence (conflict, ethnic violence, and wars in various locales around the globe) and between fear and the possibility of terrorism (the complex "blowback" of political, military, and economic policies that retaliates against the imposition of globalization and superpower desires upon cultures that have been undervalued).

In general, the program for the UN intervention can best be understood as being similar to a visitors-center experience. The security procedures for the studio were guided by the U.S. government's *Design Notebook for Federal Building Lobby Security*, which specified: a Free Zone, to include an information desk and concierge; a Security Zone, to accommodate six visitor security stations and two UN-staff screening posts; a Temporary Gallery, for changing UN exhibits; a Permanent Gallery, for installations dedicated to the architecture of the United Nations Headquarters; the Global Theater, with seating for 250 people for thirty-minute digital media presentations, twelve times a day; a UN Tour staging area; circulation; public amenities, and service. In order to develop the intervention, students were asked to filter the program through the research developed during the first half of the semester; diagram, draw, and construct each component of the program given an action, condition, and motivation, and develop a set of event spaces

(program) in relation to an occupant (visitor) or occupants (tour group). Each student developed an overall conceptual strategy guided by specific urban design intentions, as well as site, spatial, and programmatic strategies. Prior to the deployment of the set of event spaces, a clear tectonic strategy was articulated to translate concepts and ideas (the guiding forces of actions, conditions, and motivations) to all scales of detail.

—Mario Gooden

Endnotes
1. Foucault, Michel. "Of Other Spaces," *Architecture /Mouvement/ Continuité*, October, 1984.
2. K. Michael Hays, "Critical Architecture: Between Culture and Form," *Perspecta 21*, The Yale Architectural Journal. Cambridge: MIT Press, 1984.
3. Terrence Riley, *The International Style: Exhibition "15" and the Museum of Modern Art*, New York: Rizzoli, 1992, p. 15.
4. Peter Reed, associate curator, Department of Architecture and Design, *The United Nations in Perspective*, New York: Museum of Modern Art, 1995.
5. Jean Baudrillard, "The Violence of the Global," Trans. by Francois Debrix, Ctheory.net, Arthur and Marilouise Kroker, editors, May 20, 2003, www. ctheory.net/.
6. Giddens, Anthony, *Runaway World*. London: Profile Books, 1999.
7. Anthony Giddens, *The Consequences of Modernity*, Cambridge, UK: Polity Press, 1990, p. 16-19.
8. Ibid.

PROJEC

MEDIATION

The intervention by a third party between two sides in a dispute in an attempt to help them reach an agreement.

The United Nations mediator engages in a process as a third party when those in conflict either seek or accept the assistance of the United Nations with the aim to prevent, manage, or resolve a conflict. Mediation skills, therefore, could be employed in all of the following contexts: prior to conflict through diplomacy; during a conflict through peacemaking activities; after a conflict to promote agreements and their implementation; during peace-building efforts to consolidate peace and lay the foundation for sustainable development.

Source: The Beyond Intractability Knowledge Base Project (formerly the Conflict Research Consortium), University of Colorado.

Correlational Application
The threats implicit in today's cultural landscape have forced rapid developments in the technology and techniques of security and surveillance. These new security protocols, typically shoe-horned awkwardly into existing architecture, were brought to the foreground in student projects that sought to explore the threshold between "free" and "secure" space. Here, architectural strategies emerge from the technology and organization of defense to sponsor event spaces that redefine the public and private zones of the UN as based upon temporal conditions.

3.13

Aniket Shahane and Christopher Yost:
3.13 Scenario: Tour (May). Nearly a half-million visitors tour the United Nations every year. The tour begins at the open-air Global Theater on the park grounds, includes a visit to the chambers of the Security Council, the Trusteeship Council, and the Economic and Social Council, and ends at the bookstore and library at the north end of the site. (Free Zone: 220,000 square feet; crowd capacity: 20,000).

3.14 Scenario: Protest (February). A crowd of thousands marches in front of the United Nations in protest of the impending war. The perimeter of the UN is reinforced along First Avenue. Crowd estimates vary from 100,000 to 500,000 people. (Free Zone: 20,000 square feet; crowd capacity: negligible).

3.15–16 The site and its infrastructure are reconfigured to create several "hot spots," locations where a fixed and adaptable architecture is wired to serve as both event space and security hub. Multiple perimeters can be achieved when this permanent condition is used in conjunction with lighter, more agile tools—metal barricades, chairs, fountains, police tape, etc.—to fine-tune the line between free and secure zones to respond to any number of scenarios. While capable of facilitating certain kinds of events, these tools also provide a subtle means of crowd control by subtracting occupiable space and modulating access.

3.17 The calendar of events serves as an urban infrastructure, a rhythm of spikes in economic, social, and spatial normality. The risks implicit in these occasions demand a comparable counterspike of security and supervision. Whether for a parade, protest, marathon, rally, or street fair, a perimeter is designed and implemented to anticipate and control that event. Permanent structures (buildings, curbs, landscaping, street furniture) are used in conjunction with temporary devices (barriers, fencing, tape, automobiles) to demarcate space, manage access, and control crowds. The calendar illustrates the intensity of several New York City events as measured by the crowd in attendance (in black) and the estimated security force required (in red). The United Nations calendar is superimposed (in blue) as evidence of the UN's inaccessibility and the opportunities missed by the organization's public-outreach engine.

Yen-Rong Chen:
3.18–19 The security pavilion and procession toward the UN complex is the primary focus for this project. The sequence of event spaces in the procession is much like the UN guided tour, an orchestrated experience that presumably opens the UN and its missions to the public. The project examines this procession and its role in offering the public glimpses of the work of the delegates, revealing what is needed to support the UN's mission and conveying it to the public.

Diala Hanna:
3.20 The project introduces a raised platform to host protests and other media-dependent events to replace the

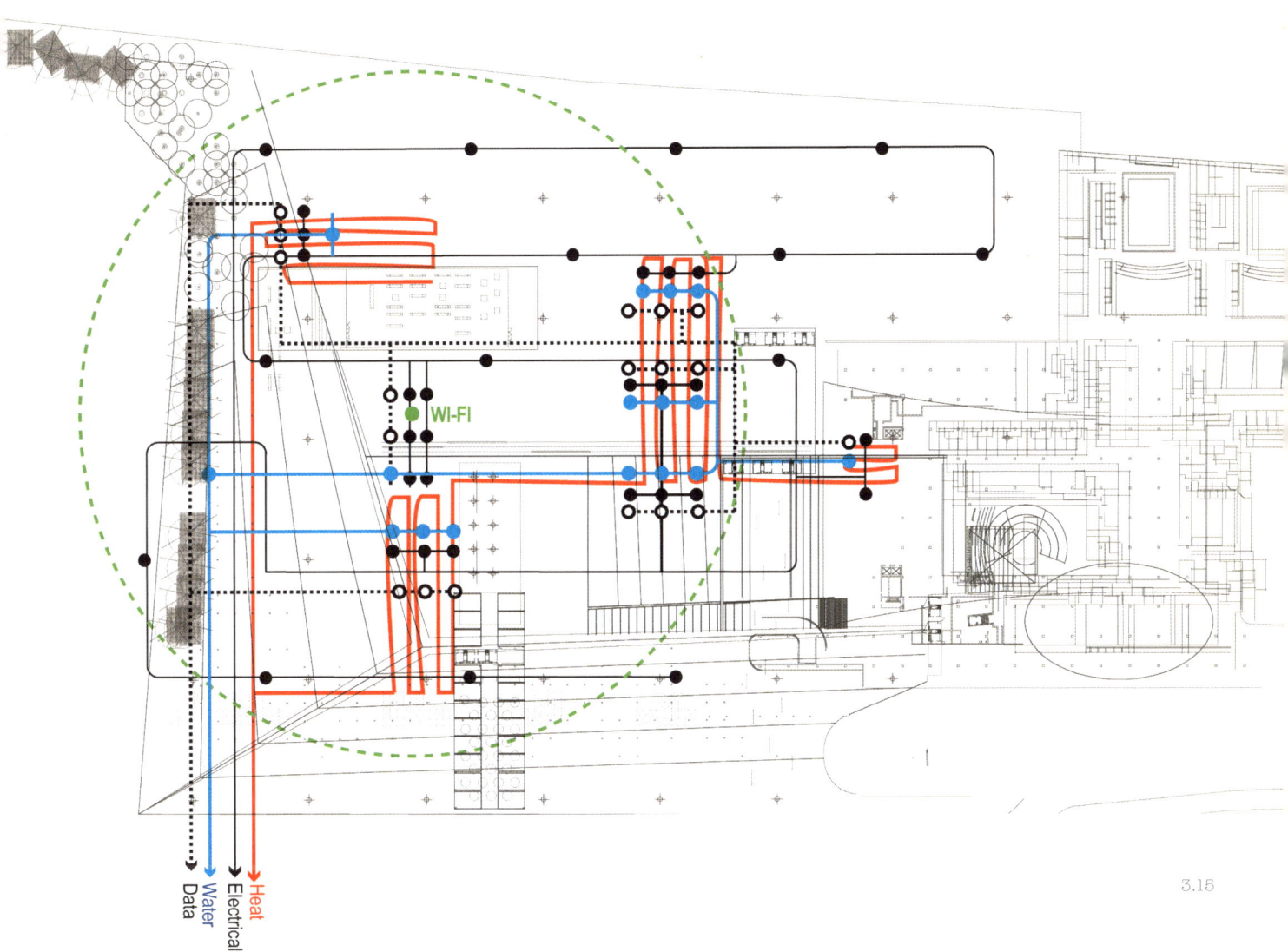

WI-FI

Data
Water
Electrical
Heat

3.15

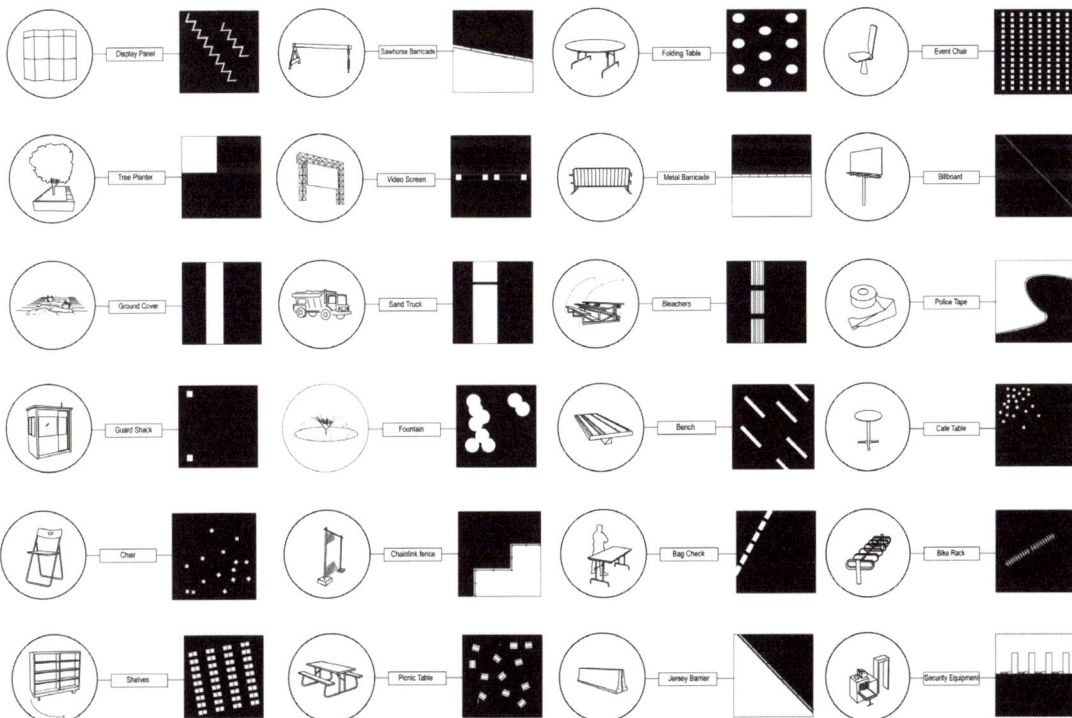

Display Panel

Sawhorse Barricade

Folding Table

Event Chair

Tree Planter

Video Screen

Metal Barricade

Billboard

Ground Cover

Sand Truck

Bleachers

Police Tape

Guard Shack

Fountain

Bench

Cafe Table

Chair

Chainlink fence

Bag Check

Bike Rack

Shelves

Picnic Table

Jersey Barrier

Security Equipment

3.16

119

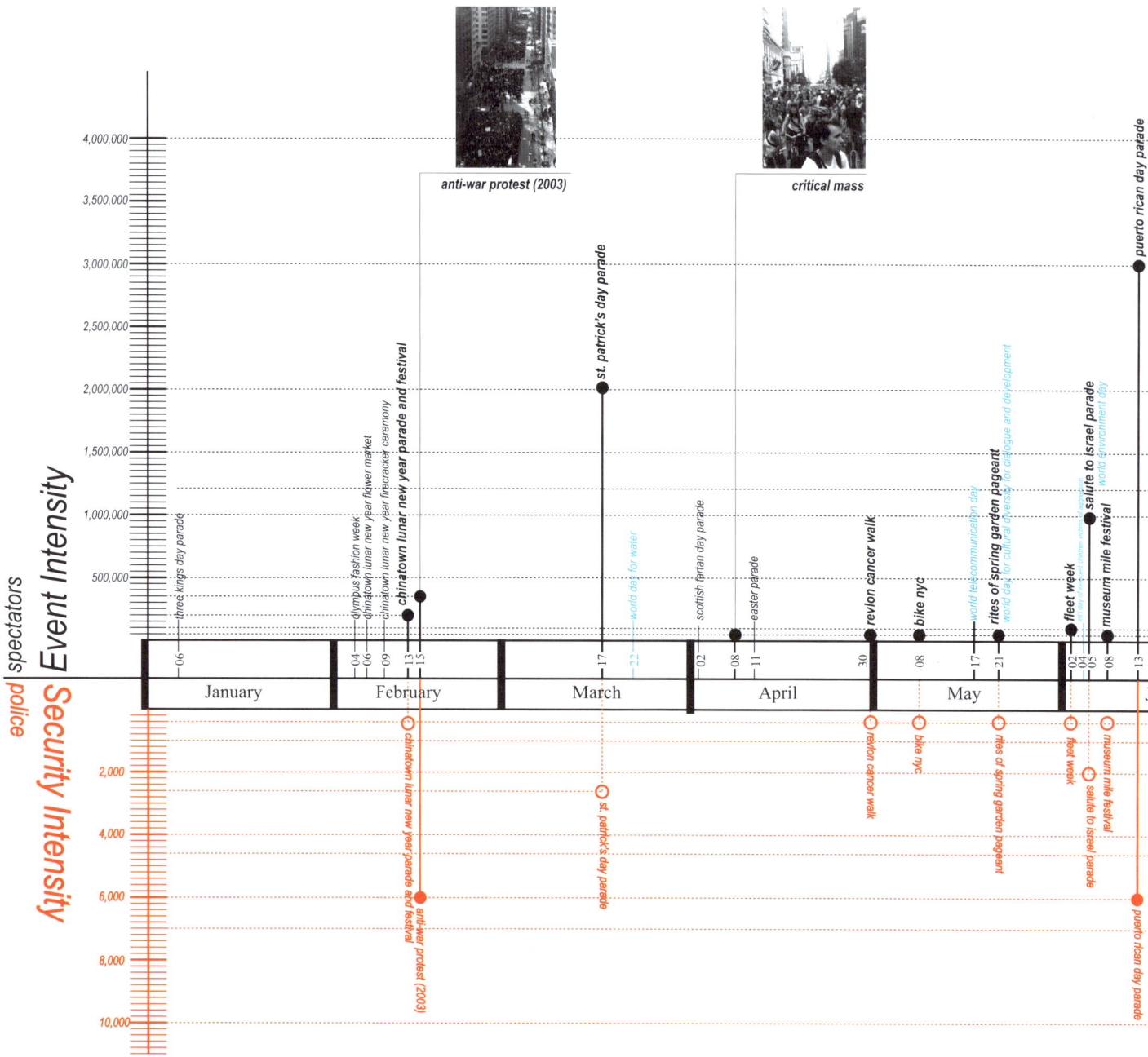

anti-war protest (2003)

critical mass

spectators

Event Intensity

police

Security Intensity

4,000,000
3,500,000
3,000,000
2,500,000
2,000,000
1,500,000
1,000,000
500,000

2,000
4,000
6,000
8,000
10,000

January — February — March — April — May

three kings day parade —06

olympus fashion week —04
chinatown lunar new year flower market —06
chinatown lunar new year firecracker ceremony —09
chinatown lunar new year parade and festival —13 —15

st. patrick's day parade —17
world day for water —22

scottish tartan day parade —02
easter parade —11

revlon cancer walk —30

bike nyc —08

world telecommunication day —17
rites of spring garden pageant —21
world day for cultural diversity for dialogue and development

fleet week —02 —04
salute to israel parade —05
world environment day
museum mile festival —08

puerto rican day parade —13

chinatown lunar new year parade and festival
anti-war protest (2003)

st. patrick's day parade

revlon cancer walk

bike nyc

rites of spring garden pageant

fleet week
museum mile festival
salute to israel parade

puerto rican day parade

3.17

120

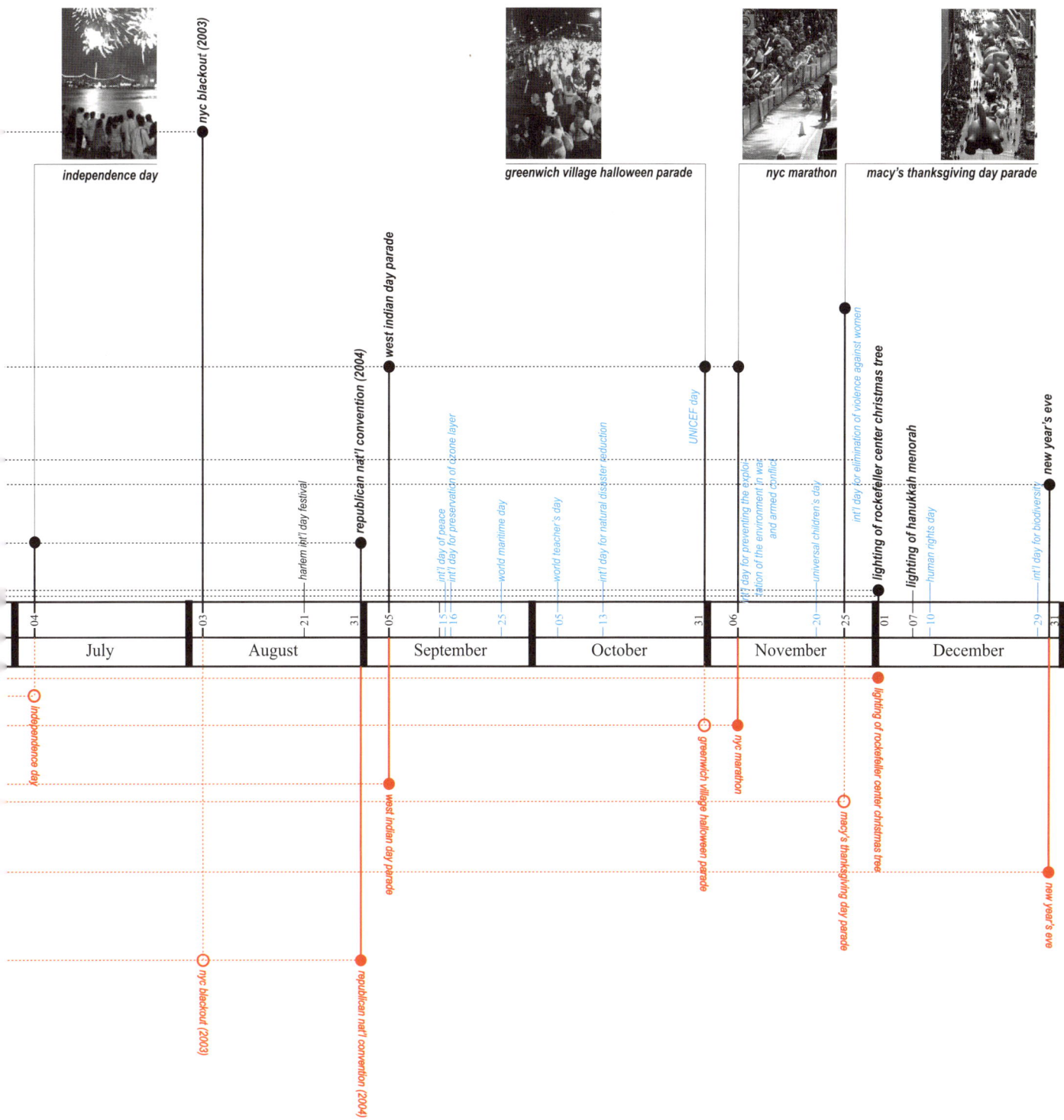

independence day

nyc blackout (2003)

greenwich village halloween parade

nyc marathon

macy's thanksgiving day parade

west indian day parade

harlem int'l day festival

republican nat'l convention (2004)

int'l day of peace
int'l day for preservation of ozone layer

world maritime day

world teacher's day

int'l day for natural disaster reduction

UNICEF day

int'l day for preventing the exploitation of the environment in war and armed conflict

universal children's day

int'l day for elimination of violence against women

lighting of rockefeller center christmas tree

lighting of hanukkah menorah

human rights day

new year's eve

int'l day for biodiversity

04		03	21	31	05	15 16	25	05	13	31	06	20	25	01	07	10	29	31

July	August	September	October	November	December

Independence day

nyc blackout (2003)

republican nat'l convention (2004)

west indian day parade

greenwich village halloween parade

nyc marathon

macy's thanksgiving day parade

lighting of rockefeller center christmas tree

new year's eve

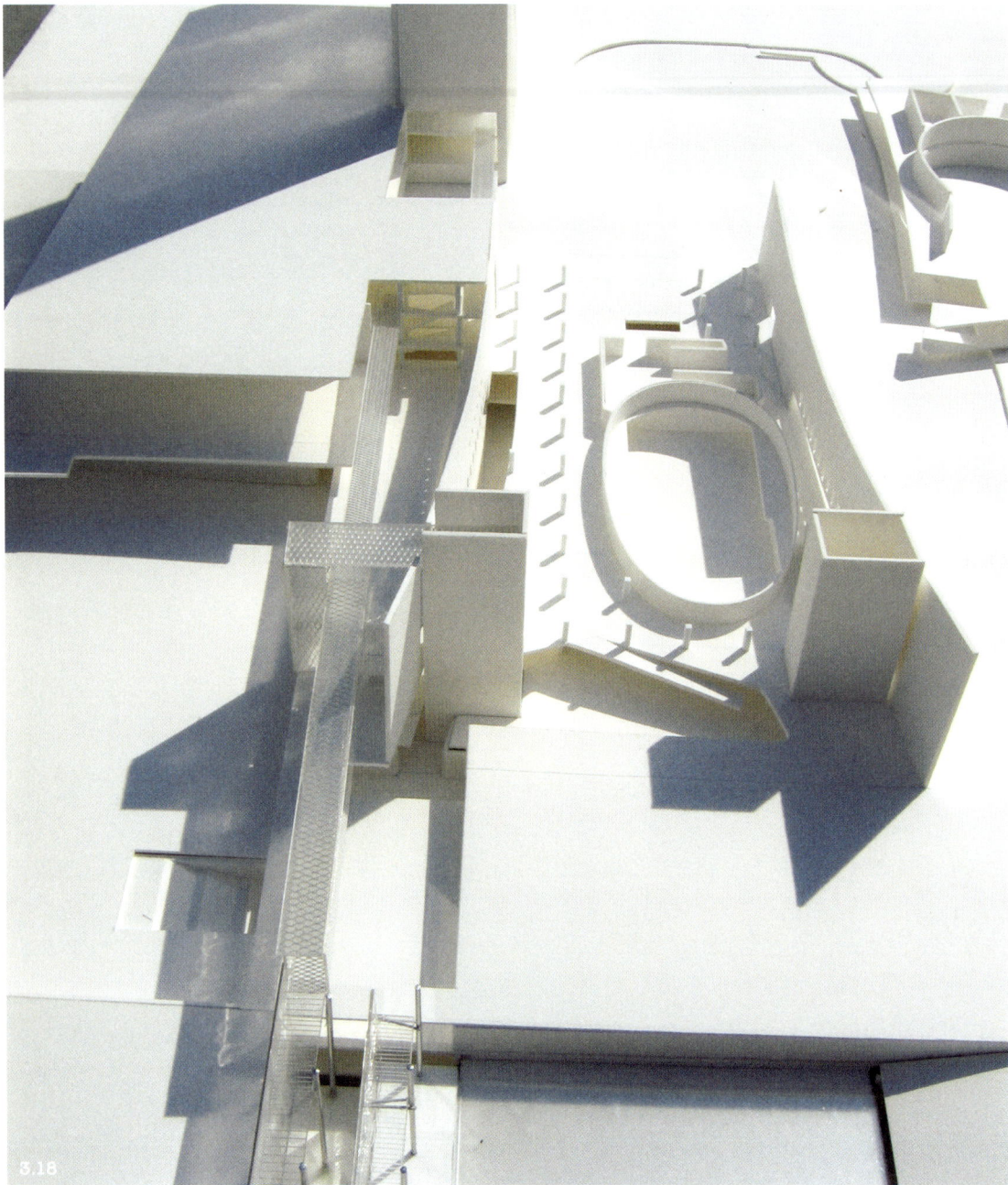

3.18

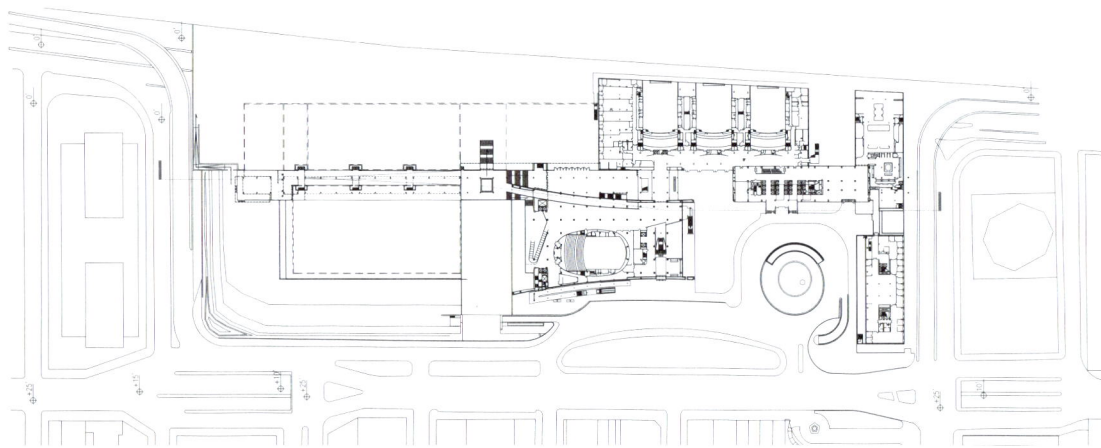

3.19

3.20

current location, a small plaza on the opposite side of First Avenue, for public rallies at the United Nations Headquarters. The platform extends across the site as a field for open expression, elevating the activity of the street.

Doris Sung: There is actually irony in this project. In some ways, you make this huge ramp or stepping system that makes a very magnificent entry. How much more inviting can grand steps be? But then you have pointed the cameras right in your face, saying, "We're going to watch you very carefully." You form a herding technique, where the people move up, but you could almost lock everybody in. You can control how they move by this gesture of beckoning. I actually find a little humor in how it's presented.

Deborah Berke: The greatest insight here is that the only way that protest really registers is when it is covered by the media. A million people marching doesn't mean much unless it's covered by every satellite in the world. You can't have twelve TV-camera trucks parked on First Avenue during a New York City rush hour. What you really want to do is recognize the moment of setting up protesters in order to be filmed for television. News around the world really requires that the zone of the media not just be the sidewalk. If this pretty little park at the side of the river is left untouched, so what? You should shift the whole thing over and make the statement that you are making about protests very visible architecturally.

Diala Hanna:
3.21 View of protest platform from 46th Street.

3.22 The platform can rotate to become a security wall or a projection screen for public events.

3.21

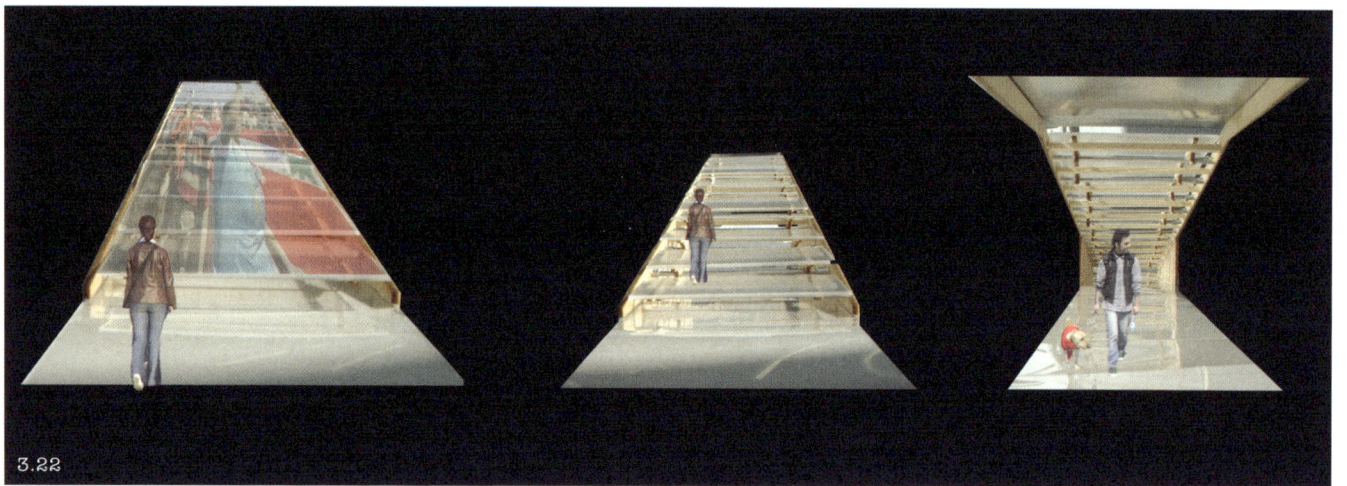

3.22

SUBVERSION

...An action, plan, or activity intended to undermine or overthrow a government or other institution.

Insurgency is an organized movement comprising a minority of the population with the goal of mobilizing a mass political base and toppling the government. Typically the weaker power, insurgents use guerilla tactics, subversion, psychological warfare, and asymmetric violence in a protracted conflict to wear down the will of the opponent, the population, and the international community.

Source: The Beyond Intractability Knowledge Base Project (formerly the Conflict Research Consortium), University of Colorado.

Correlational Application
The modern, iconic figure of the General Assembly Building is confronted and ultimately transformed by projects that aim to reposition the United Nations within new social, cultural, or political contexts through methods of exposure that lead to ambiguities; recontextualizing the UN's network of flows and challenging relationships between above/below and inside/outside. The status of the original complex is updated through critical interventions that challenge its presumed neutrality or reorder its programmatic relationships.

3.23

Lee Lim:
3.23 Studies of the sectional relationships across the site. The ground plane folds to weave together free and secure zones of space.

3.24 The façade of the General Assembly distorts to accommodate new subterranean spaces.

Vanessa Ruff:
3.25 Program is calibrated by analyzing the UN as a conglomeration of information generators.

3.26 Patterns of circulation allow architecture and exhibition to blur while security is maintained. These circulatory paths become the infrastructure for the flow of both information and people at the scale of the site and the city.

Derek Hoeferlin:
3.27 In early explorations, a large "scanning" bar is proposed for the north side of the General Assembly to both screen and expose the various programmatic elements within it and around it. The nature of this static bar reinforces the flattened condition created by scanning technologies. In final investigations, I stretched the bar in multiple ways across the site and homed in on specific areas to further exaggerate this notion of scanning, exposure, and spatial distancing, most specifically at the juncture between the new intervention and the General Assembly visitors lobby.

The spaces on either side expose the landscape and the spaces in between the buildings as they get flattened, exposed, and distributed on either side.

3.28 Biometric and X-ray scanning, in their myriad applications, render an opaque object transparent. Something protected and impenetrable immediately becomes exposed. What is whole and volumetric becomes flattened onto a single plane, and everything is seen at once. Certain types of objects, such as organic ones that tend to be more dangerous, are further articulated. When everything is flattened onto one picture plane, aspects overlap. This imbricated condition becomes one of interest because it may not just add a sense of clarity but also a new type of spatial condition, where ambiguities arise among the overlaps. My intention is to critique this flattening and respatialize it in three dimensions.

3.29 Model.

Emmanuel Petit: You use the X-ray scanning technique and compact the depth of the space into one surface to then redeploy that surface. What you had in the beginning was not a flattening out of different aspects but a separating; you were putting spaces

3.24

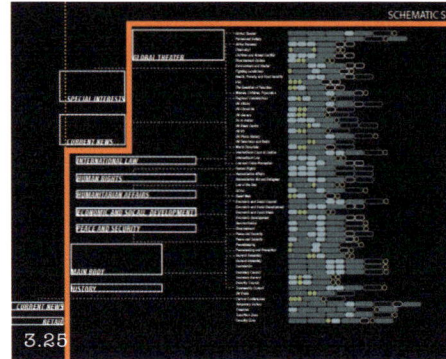
3.25

3.26

3.27

3.28

3.29

in between different forces. This is a spacing technique, not a flattening technique. Going back to that spacing technique would help you to tear that building apart again and make it more complex, as opposed to reducing it to one bar.

Billie Tsien: In your analysis of the Cyprus Peacekeeping Mission, the shifting of boundaries and the blue line that becomes a concession were interesting. Your building starts to look at making concessions, changing the boundary line, because now the boundary lines of the UN are very clear. This idea of a shifting line—what gets conceded to a general public versus what's held as a more secure space—seems to be something of depth, to think about changing the perception of that part of the UN, this broad, open plaza and what is claimed and what is left for other people. The concessions can be more bold in terms of what you take back, what you add.

Emmanuel Petit: One would have to understand on what level this mapping has an influence on the building. There are two possibilities: either you use it symbolically, or you use it as an analog. If you use it symbolically, you would transform your building into a sign that talks symbolically. If you use it as an analog, you would have to first show what kind of boundaries are being negotiated at this place. We would then have to see how you contextualize that boundary, and then one would be able to understand that your project is a way of mediating between the inside of the UN island and the outside, Manhattan.

NEGOTIATION

The reaching of an agreement through discussion and compromise.

When parties negotiate, they give and take. While they have interlocking goals that they cannot accomplish independently, they do not want or need exactly the same thing. This interdependence can be either win-lose or win-win in nature, and the type of negotiation that is appropriate will vary accordingly. The disputants will either attempt to force the other side to comply with their demands, modify the opposing position and move toward compromise, or invent a solution that meets the objectives of all sides. The nature of their interdependence will have a major impact on the nature of their relationship, the way negotiations are conducted, and the outcomes of these negotiations.

Source: The Beyond Intractability Knowledge Base Project (formerly the Conflict Research Consortium), University of Colorado.

Correlational application

In early mapping exercises, students explored the shifting relationships and disputed territories of United Nations Peacekeeping Missions. This analysis translated, in some instances, into an investigation of boundaries and edges at the project site. The United Nations Headquarters, an island of extraterritoriality in the middle of New York City, inspired explorations of the relationship between the local and the global, the tourist and the delegate, and the city and the UN. This was manifest in landscape strategies that sought to reconfigure the site as a field of overlapping boundaries, jurisdictions, agendas, subverted identities, or in architectural interventions that alternately defined and blurred edges.

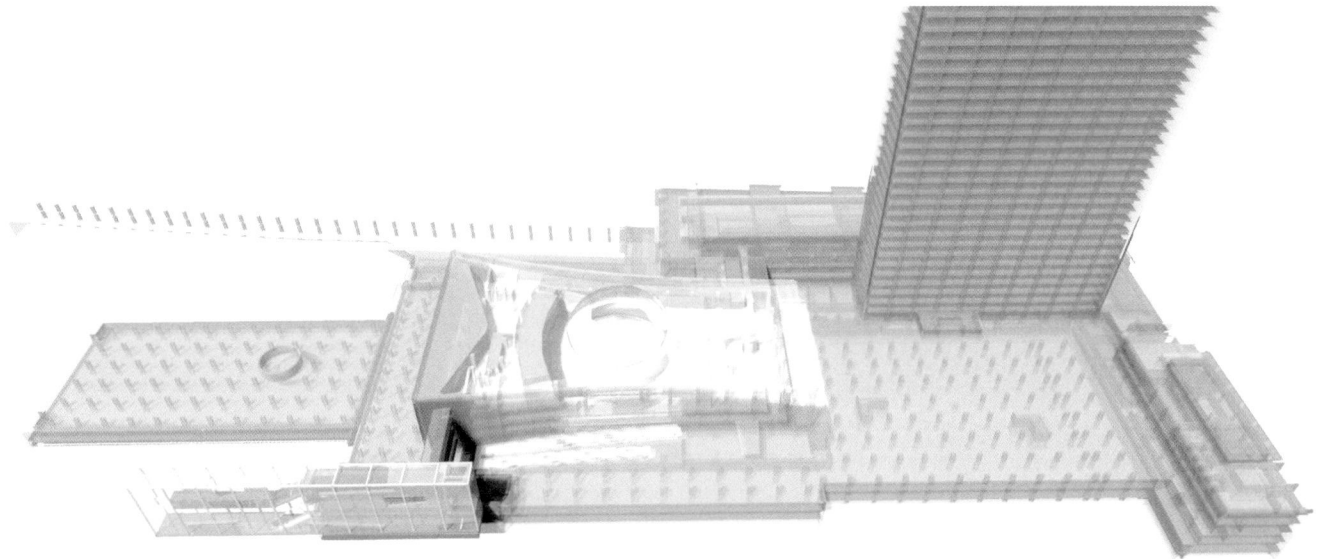

3.30

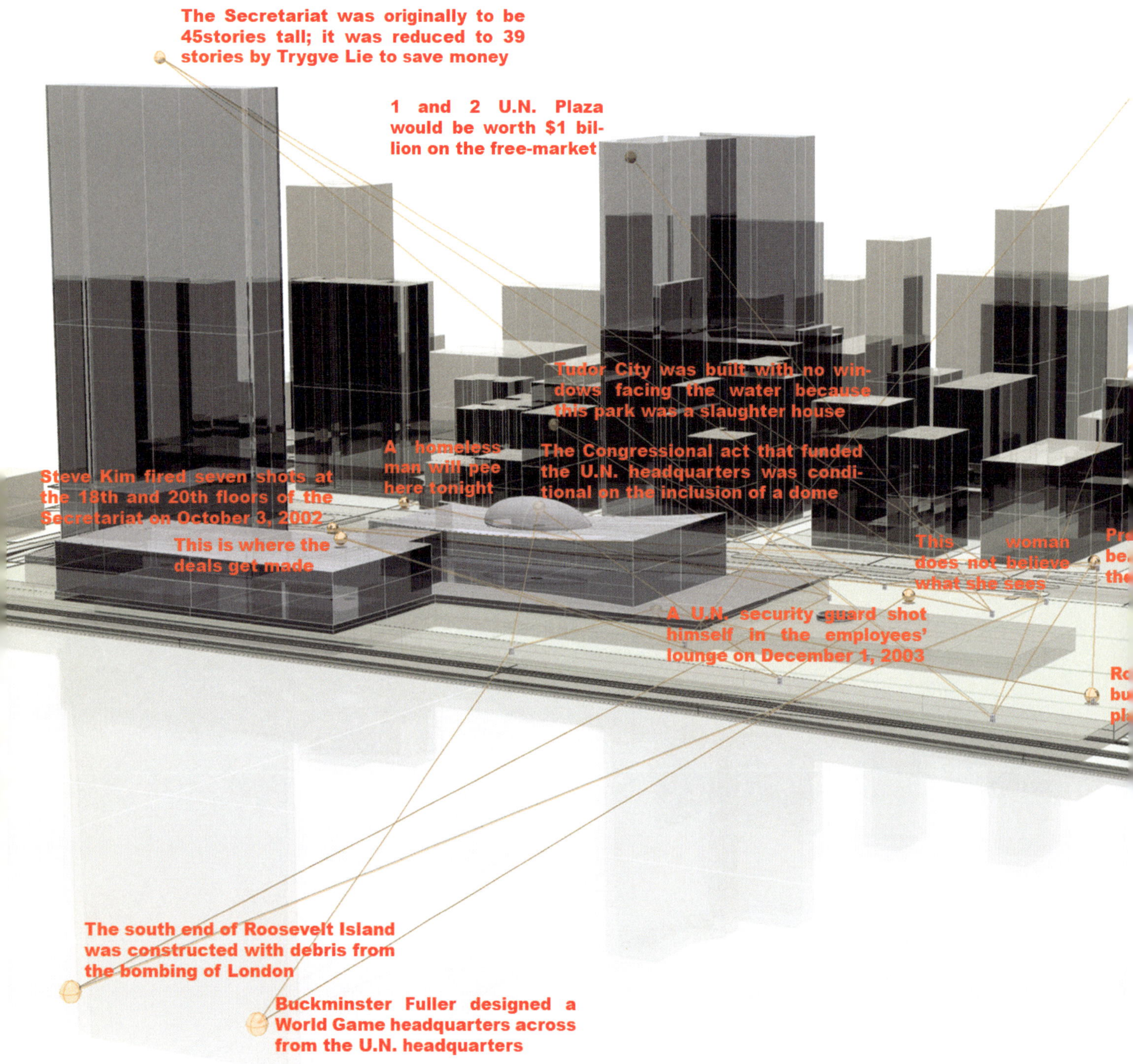

The Secretariat was originally to be 45stories tall; it was reduced to 39 stories by Trygve Lie to save money

1 and 2 U.N. Plaza would be worth $1 billion on the free-market

Tudor City was built with no windows facing the water because this park was a slaughter house

Steve Kim fired seven shots at the 18th and 20th floors of the Secretariat on October 3, 2002

A homeless man will pee here tonight

The Congressional act that funded the U.N. headquarters was conditional on the inclusion of a dome

This is where the deals get made

This woman does not believe what she sees

Pre be the

A U.N. security guard shot himself in the employees' lounge on December 1, 2003

Ro bu pla

The south end of Roosevelt Island was constructed with debris from the bombing of London

Buckminster Fuller designed a World Game headquarters across from the U.N. headquarters

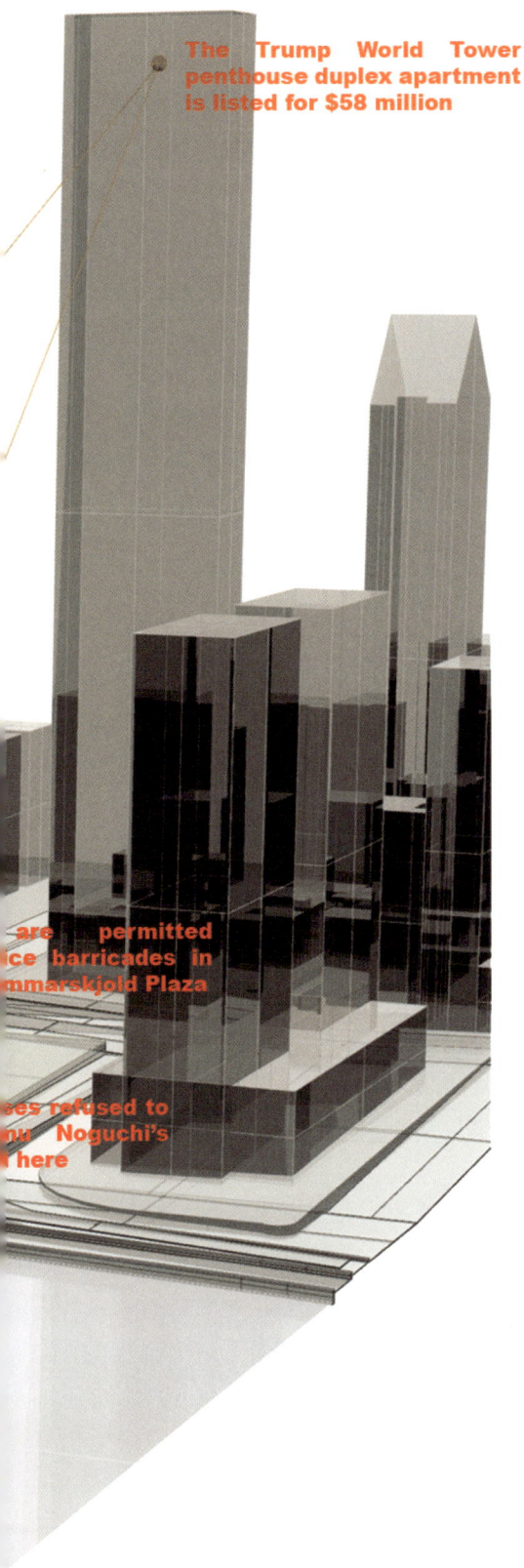

The Trump World Tower penthouse duplex apartment is listed for $58 million

are permitted ice barricades in mmarskjold Plaza

es refused to nu Noguchi's here

3.31

Noah Shepherd:
3.30 From the street, the United Nations appears to be a collection of individual buildings, but, below grade, the buildings are connected in a series of levels containing printing and television production facilities, loading areas, utilities, storage, and parking. The Security Building marks an edge along First Avenue, connecting both the upper and lower United Nations buildings and creating a continuous circuit throughout the complex.

The UN's proclaimed openness and inclusiveness is undermined by the need for control and separation. Rather than continuing this contradiction architecturally, the Security Building accepts and makes legible the division and separation of the complex. In this acceptance, the building permits the reopening of the north park—currently closed for security reasons—to the public again.

3.31 A "map" of events related to the United Nations and the project site.

Doris Sung: At what point does this boundary need to be friendly to the city? At what point does the boundary allow free movement through, or does it become a Checkpoint Charlie? You have consolidated access to the building, not only single-point access but you can manifest it in a building. The other thing is the façade value and the iconography that comes from it; how is that associated with the idea of the UN historically, relative to these very modern structures? How do you value the iconography, freedom, liberty, and peace of all these missions of the UN? That question is brought to the forefront in your project.

Deborah Berke: Although the UN is in New York, it is virtually invisible from New York. There is almost nowhere, except a stretch on First Avenue, where you can see it. You can't look down the canyons of the city blocks to see it. You are making a billboard, something that allows the TV camera or the tourist to catch the UN from the streets of Manhattan. You are willing to make a building this long and this skinny and a little improbable, so why not make it a little longer, a little taller, and a little bit more improbable? Let it replace the Secretariat Building that you see on postcards but never see in real life.

Ruth Gyuse:
2.32–33 The site is a third thing, the in-between. For example, to enter and leave the U.S. through the airports, you are really in a no-man's land. Having investigated the history behind how the buildings were built, I propose that the UN is physically and politically linked to the United States. My intervention starts to celebrate that link. This evolved as I moved through programming, so that as the link became stronger the question became whether to put up taller fences to highlight that difference or start to blur the boundaries.

Sunil Bald: Your intervention may be read so that the UN behaves as a third-party mediator, or it may behave between conflicts or in the conflict between the United States and the UN. Do you see this as a part of United States, the UN, or another entity?

Deborah Berke: The UN is so clearly physically bounded that it is possible to think of it as extraterritorial. It has edges in relation to the city that cannot be breached, and it's bounded by the river. You are trying to expand the size of the territory, not blur the territory, in fact, take over First Avenue. The gesture of taking more is interesting to me. As New Yorkers, we often don't feel part of the United States; we, too, are bounded and separated. I think the UN wants to be clearly bound to and separate from New York. Through creating this landscape you could make security, by starting with these dramatic lines, that is both landscape and yet clearly defines the territoriality of that which should be outside of the United States. It makes the landscape more complex and clearly reinforces the boundary.

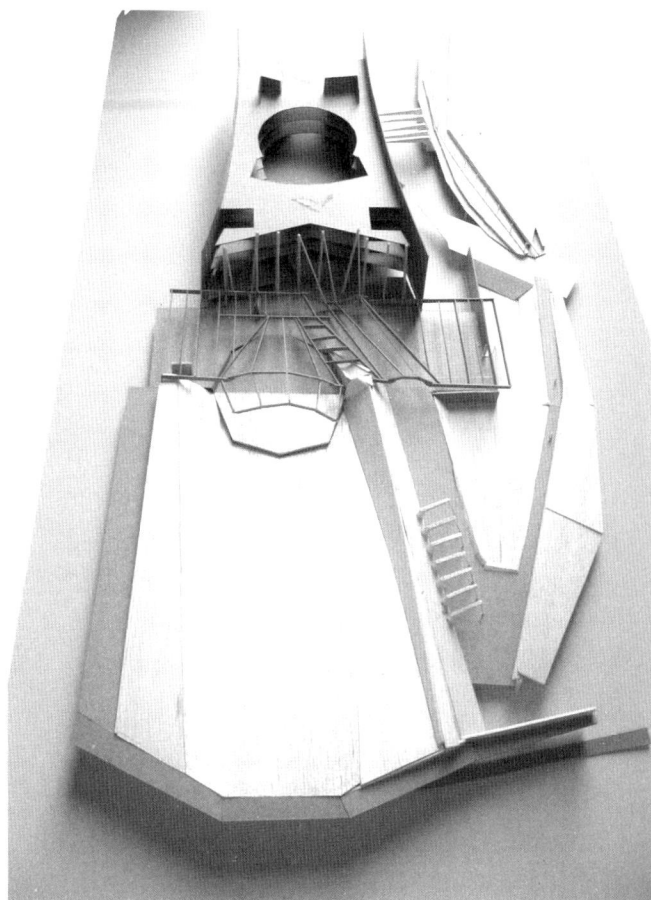

3.32

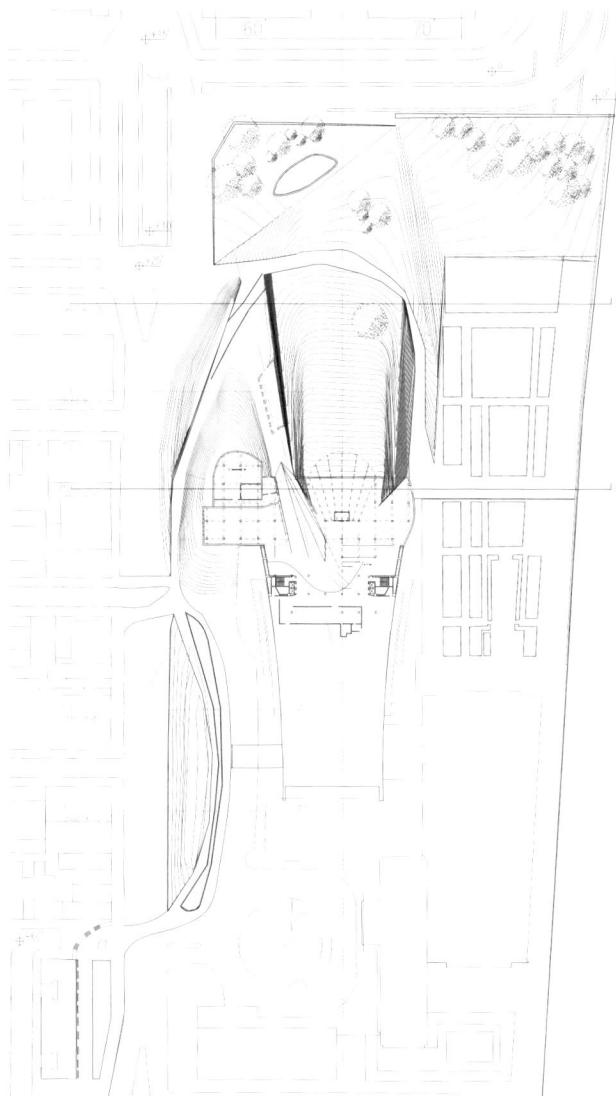

3.33

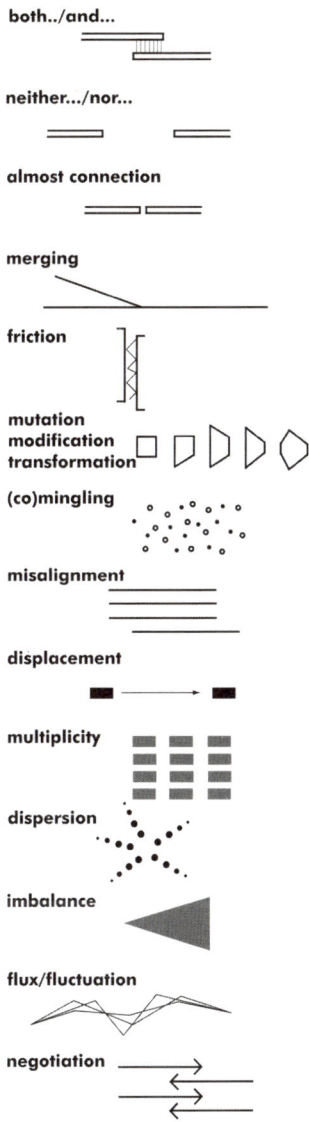

both../and...

neither.../nor...

almost connection

merging

friction

mutation
modification
transformation

(co)mingling

misalignment

displacement

multiplicity

dispersion

imbalance

flux/fluctuation

negotiation

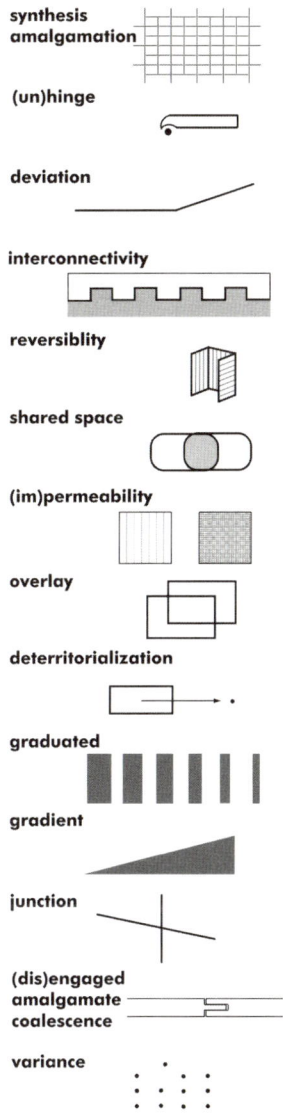

synthesis
amalgamation

(un)hinge

deviation

interconnectivity

reversiblity

shared space

(im)permeability

overlay

deterritorialization

graduated

gradient

junction

(dis)engaged
amalgamate
coalescence

variance

3.34

3.35

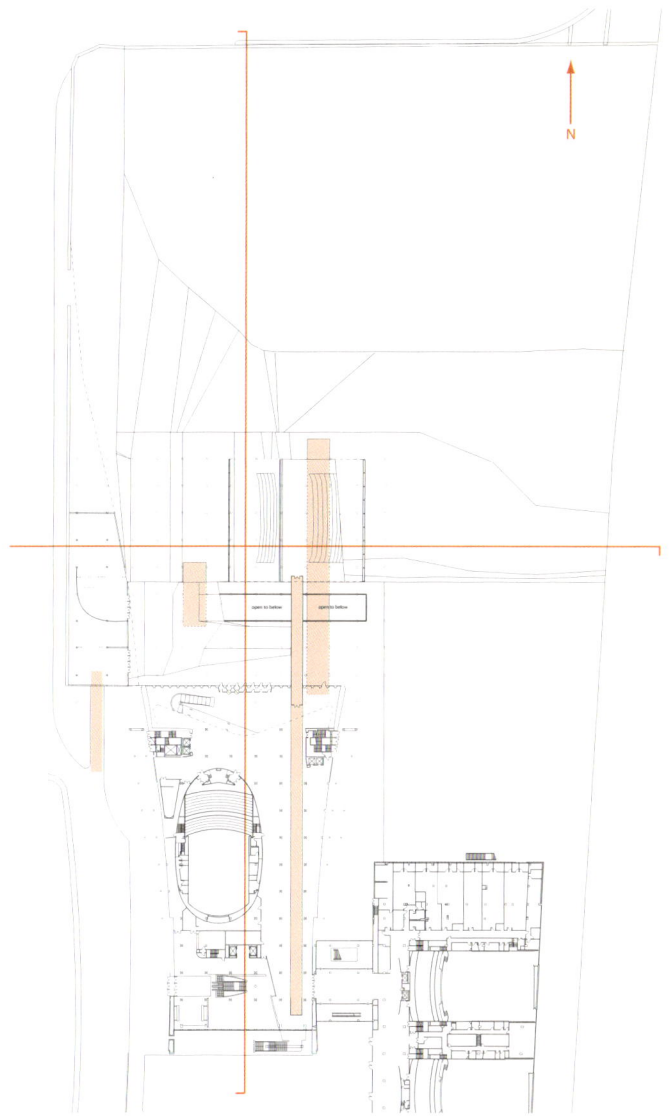

N

3.36

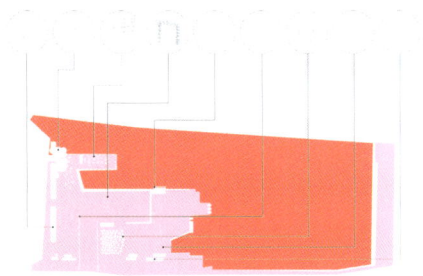

Low Security

Free Zone
290,000sf
Crowd Capacity
19,000

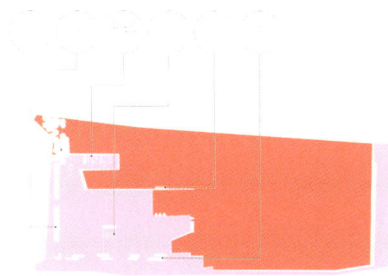

Medium Security

Free Zone
123,000sf
Crowd Capacity
21,000

High Security

Free Zone
59,000sf
Crowd Capacity
negligible

Proposed Security

Variable Perimeter

UNHQ

SECURITY   OUTREACH

3.37

3.38

3.39

Sal Wilson:
3.34 The mapping exercise provided a starting point from which to seek out form-driving spatial relationships. Initial studies sought to convert spatial translations from the political concepts uncovered in the map into a future architecture.

3.35 First-floor plan. An interactive public landscape weaves between direct, secured connections into the UN.

Aniket Shahane and Christopher Yost:
3.36 A collage study of one of the infrastructure hubs that facilitate both event and security.

3.37 Among the recommendations made by the NYPD's counterterrorism division is the technique of "hardening," in which existing buildings, gates, fences, and perimeters are reinforced. By contrast, this project proposes an architecture that privileges performance and adaptability over the fixed and hardened. Much like the crowd-control strategies, multiple security strategies could be developed by the UN to permit a variable perimeter responsive to the cyclical as well as spontaneous bursts of activity that make a city vibrant. Here, the boundary between the Free Zone and the Secure Zone changes with new opportunities, and threats.

3.38–39 Scenario: November Marathon. On the eve of the New York City Marathon, the United Nations sponsors the International Friendship Run, drawing some 10,000 runners from more than 100 different countries. Pre-race ceremonies include speeches, performances, and a runners' breakfast. (Free Zone: 290,000 square feet; crowd capacity: 35,000)

OBSERVATION

An act or instance of viewing or noting a fact or occurrence.

The role of the United Nations Observation Missions is strictly limited to observation. The task of the Observation Missions is not to mediate, arbitrate, or forcefully prohibit illegal infiltration, although it is hoped that its very presence on the borders would deter any such traffic. The military observers may conduct regular and frequent patrols of all accessible roads from dawn to dusk, primarily in border districts and the areas adjacent to the zones held by the opposition forces. A system of permanent observation posts may be established and manned by military observers. The observers check all reported infiltration in their areas and observe any suspicious development. An emergency reserve of military observers may be stationed at headquarters as well as main observation posts for the purpose of making inquiries on short notice or investigating alleged instances of smuggling. Aerial reconnaissance may be conducted by light airplanes and helicopters, the former being equipped for aerial photography.

Source: *Peace and Security Section*, United Nations Department of Public Information. The United Nations Observation Group in Lebanon was set up by Security Council Resolution 128 in June 1958.

Correlational application

Primary among the tasks required of the UN for each of its many mandates is the collection and dissemination of data. Additionally, the organization employs Internet resources, print media, radio, and on-site exhibitions and events to advance awareness of certain international issues, as well as its own general mission. Indeed, the consequences of an increasingly connected global culture, whether benign or violent, are entirely enabled by media and information technology. Some student projects thrust media into the foreground of architectural processes, aiming to challenge the opacity and introversion of the United Nations complex. Others wove moments of virtual and physical interaction into new circulation systems for both the public and the UN delegates. Still others saw opportunities to merge the technology and infrastructure of both the city and the UN to maximize the possibilities inherent in their adjacency.

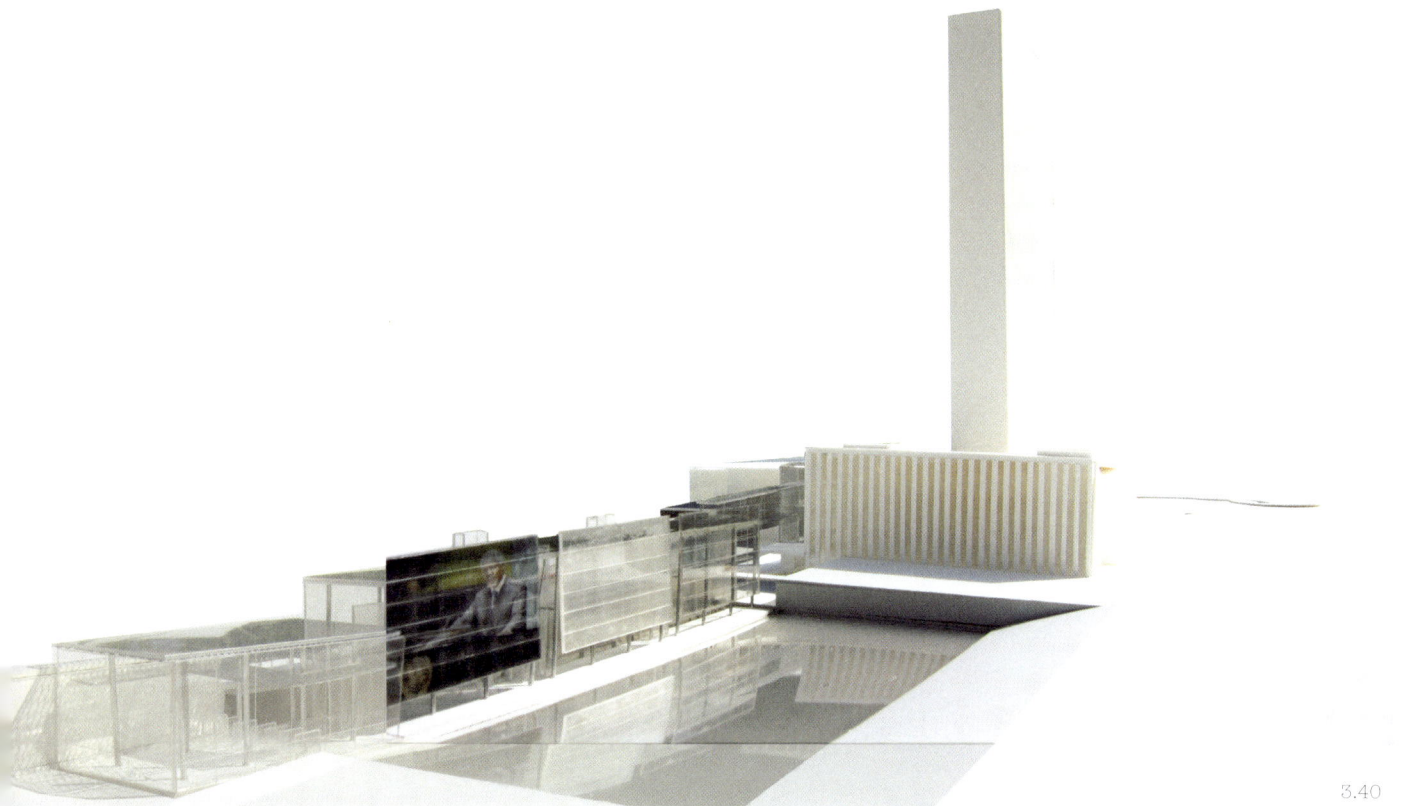

3.40

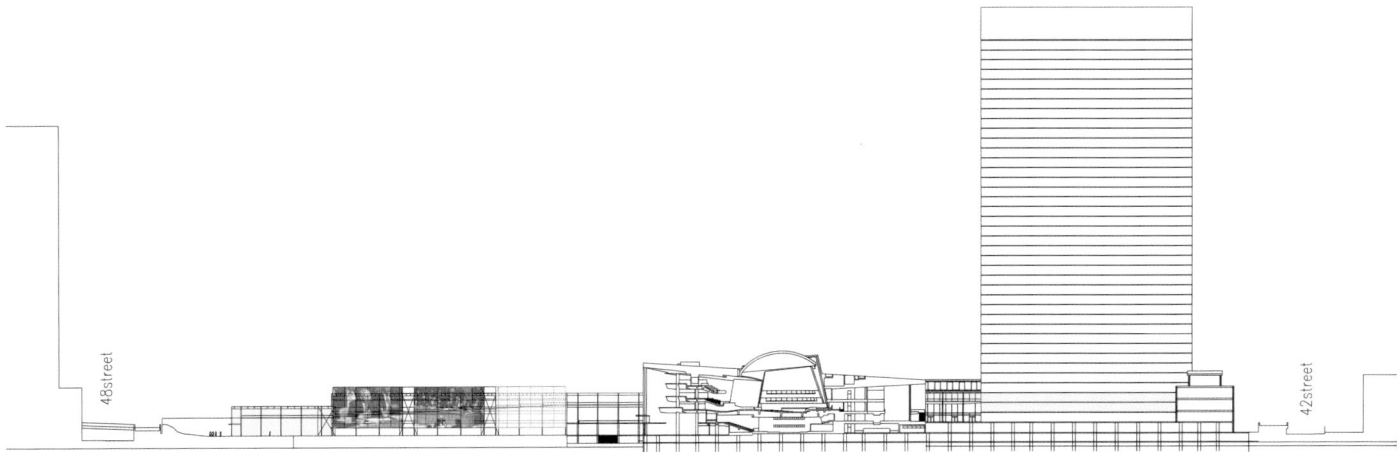

3.41

Yen-Rong Chen:
3.40 The media bar is a way of addressing image. With the media bar and its projections to the public, the UN is appropriating instruments of globalism for disseminating its own workings or propaganda in addressing issues around the world. The UN has an instrument to critically position and assert itself.

3.41 The emphasis on landscape and the subterranean reinforces the concept of the UN's operation at a seemingly neutral physical and political ground. At the same time, the intervention seeks to blur the distinction between "insiders" and "outsiders" by revealing those spaces typically closed to public observation. Looking at the moment in the circulation when the delegates and the public would intersect could have increased experiences.

Ray Huff: This is a remarkably clear, straightforward scheme in terms of how the security elements work. The introduction of the water element makes even more sense. Let me pose a question to you, which is this question of the brief: "How can critical architecture be deployed as an instrument to construct a discourse regarding a repositioning of the United Nations in the space between universalism and the reality of globalism?" In examining the existing building critically, it shows the opportunities the existing building has to offer relative to how it could be exploited in the project.

Sunil Bald: It is both examining the building and examining the examination of the building. We have talked about security but not so much about control. Security and control actually go hand in hand in this situation. Here, there is a semblance of authenticity you encounter when you go into this working institution. And it's not just you in front of something else but, supposedly, you in front of something in process. How do you maintain control of the visitors in that environment? There is a clear environmental threshold outside of the building, but what are the threshold conditions from the inside?

Doris Sung: This idea of spying on the weaving of the visitor gives the project more complexity.

Mario Gooden: With the idea of spying you have examined the guided UN tour, you have examined the *promenade architecturale*. You have made a tube, which collapses and weaves the tour back through. And now it's about taking the *promenade architecturale*, about taking certain prescribed points of view, and reordering those points so that the visitors can see things they are not supposed to see, allowing them close-up views of delegates or staff, which they don't show you on the existing tour but you know are there.

Vanessa Ruff:
3.42 A collage perspective of the intertwining circulation streams that provide moments of exchange between the public, delegates, and the media.

Noah Shepherd:
3.43 I was interested in the distance between leaving the city and entering the UN. The project hovers as much as possible in that distance. In looking at the UN in the early design sketches and the language that the team of architects used, it was conceived as an open field within which the UN sits. The reality of its execution has been noted: it is severely bounded on all four sides either in section by the FDR Drive or at the edge by the fence; this is the edge that I investigated. Additionally, I wanted to explore the physical relationship of a person moving through security and investigated those opportunities. On First Avenue, the Security Building is open to the street, providing physical and visual access to the United Nations and to the park at the north end of the site. In contrast to the language of opposing transparent and solid walls that characterizes the headquarters, the Security Building is both open and closed on all sides, reflecting the uneasy conflation of access and limitation inherent in the United Nations mission.

Charles Eldred: There is a boundary, but what if I thicken that line? Is it really just a single, thick line? In doing so you are making this manifold. It raises a few questions: What is it made out of? What does it mean to have this thing be consistent as an object in character from one side to the other? Or should it be different on either side? There's a kind of simplicity and directness to the proposal. It takes guts to put a building next to these icons. You can tell that there's an instinct for everybody to dive down low and get out of the way.

Ray Huff: It is a credible gesture in terms of security. But how does it work as an urban device? How does it work the tension with the city? As we drive by, it is such a striking piece on the river—extraordinary. You don't see it close up. Now that you have made the gesture, how do you make the architecture? Cutting into it is completely gratuitous. Because it's removed,

theoretically, it provides a buffer, so maybe it's all glass. That begins to address and reveal the security condition rather than this heavy-laden, seemingly cast concrete. Also, the scale of the movement can somehow be underwhelming with a narrow escalator and the elevation of the security to the third level. It's a shame that it's an escalator, rather than a ramp. The story of the UN could be told as you migrate toward the security. It should be about fineness and delicacy and how you connect the two pieces as a finely tuned gesture.

Sal Wilson:
3.44 An enormous screen anchors the Global Theater, which functions at a number of different scales, oriented both toward the city and, internally, toward delegates and the visiting public. Even those who have not been through security can read and post stories onto the central screen. An idea of a public forum is latent within the original concept of the UN, and this project attempts to find a way to reinstate that notion.

The extrusion of the structural grid of the existing UN generates the placement of the theater. This is a conceptual connection between the media center belowground, the public-accessible landscape, and the path by which the delegates bypass it.

Charles Eldred: I like the gesture of the theater expressed as a theater out in a park because of the relationship to the General Assembly itself that is embedded in there, and now you are going to build this public General Assembly. This is beyond just symbolic—it's critical. On the one side of it, you are embedded, and what's supposed to be transparent is behind the doors. But we are going to build here a much more permeable public assembly hall. Even in the placement, as one looks forward or back, there is significance. These are all things that could become much more loaded. It could be a more critical element.

3.42

3.43

3.44

Charles Eldred: That area in front engages with the city, so it need not be conceived in the same way as the General Assembly, with its classic dome where people meet in the center. You could make yours different and become part of the critique of that domed center.

Sunil Bald: You show an interest in the mechanism of the UN, looking at the underlying layer of what exists there. You are choreographing the experience. Through the extension you start to integrate a kind of interrogation of what you are about to see, or what you are seeing and what you are about to go through, which goes back to your initial analysis of this mediation, with global media and theater. With that, I would question why the theater should be embedded, rather than that which allows you to interrogate the points along the journey.

Derek Hoeferlin:
3.45 The project challenges the General Assembly's political and physical opacity with an intervention that deconstructs the building and foregrounds the theater of its operations.

3.46 The security entry, Global Theater, and exhibition space are stretched like an accordion in plan and section. The public can occupy the existing lobby of the General Assembly in the entire vertical dimension. Exhibitions and other public spaces wrap and ramp around the Global Theater, similar to the translator booths circumscribing the existing General Assembly Hall.

3.47 View of the Global Theater from the lobby of the General Assembly.

3.48 View of the north façade.

Evan Douglis: The UN is, in many cases, a reactive system. In other words, it recognizes what the current structure is, the performing logic of those events, and seeks to intervene in such way that it can mediate. Whether it can resolve it or not, one doesn't know, but there's a relational link. The same question can be asked here:

3.45

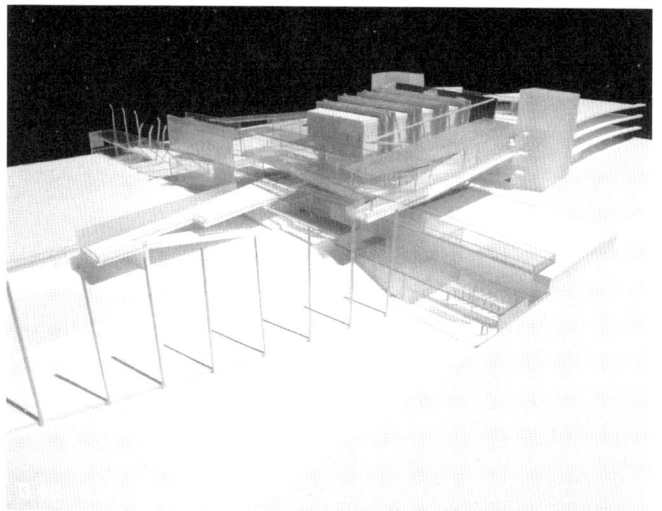

3.47

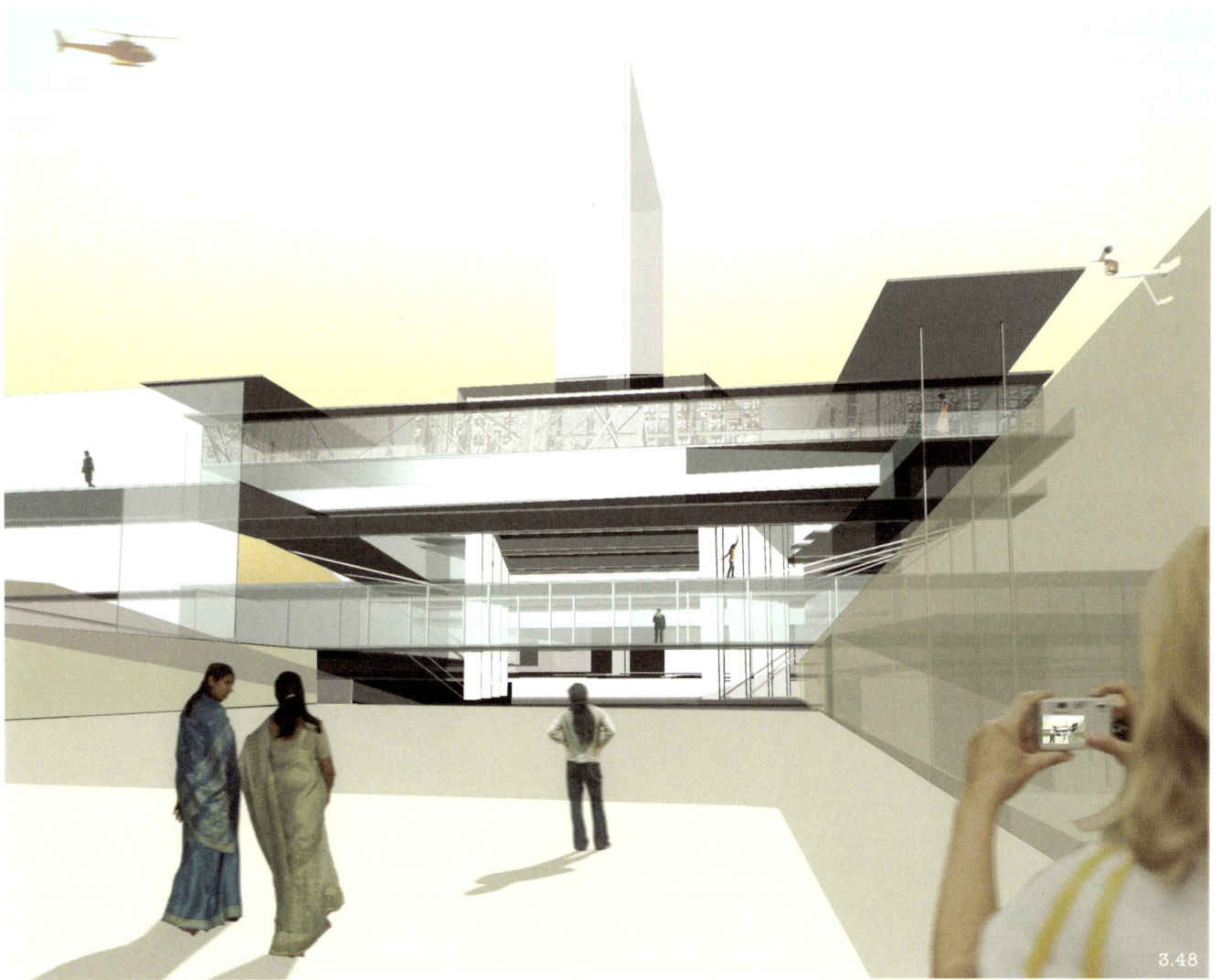

3.48

To what extent can you modify the current performance of that site with as little architecture as possible? And at what moment is it proper to reveal a new architecture as an authority that is working both on the level of intervention, in terms of some kind of collaborative relationship, and at the same time is willing to present itself as a discrete and autonomous addition to this historical legacy? I suppose my question to you would be, how is that new architecture beginning to change, modify, and challenge the current system? What ultimately is the criticism? It is going to come down as a critique.

Sunil Bald, the spring 2006 Louis I. Kahn Visiting Assistant Professor at Yale, is a partner in Studio SUMO, a New York-based architecture collaborative he co-founded with Yolande Daniels. Previously, he worked for Antoine Predock Architect. Recent SUMO projects include a temporary space for the Museum of African Art in Long Island City; MoCADA, a museum of contemporary art in Brooklyn, and the Josai University New School of Management, in Sakado, Japan. SUMO's work has been widely published and exhibited. Bald has received a Young Architects award from the Architectural League of New York, a Graham Foundation fellowship, a NYFA fellowship, and a Fulbright fellowship, and he was a finalist in MoMA's Young Architects program. On receiving his M.Arch from Columbia, he was awarded the AIA medal. Over the last decade, Bald has taught design and theory at Cornell, Columbia, University of Michigan, and Parsons and is a critic in architecture at Yale. He also has conducted research in modernism, popular culture, and nation-making in Brazil.

Deborah Berke is an adjunct professor at the Yale School of Architecture and is principal of Deborah Berke and Partners. She has also taught at the University of Maryland, the University of Miami, the Rhode Island School of Design, and the Institute for Architecture and Urban Studies, as well as serving as a jurist and guest lecturer at many venues. She has won numerous design awards for her work, which includes the Holcombe T. Green Jr. Hall for the Yale School of Art. Berke's work has been widely published in magazines such as *Architecture, Architectural Review, Architectural Record, Newsweek,* and *Vogue.* She was the co-editor with Stephen Harris of a collection of essays, *Architecture of the Everyday* (Princeton Architectural Press, 1998).

Marshall Brown is an assistant professor of architecture at the University of Cincinnati College of Design, Art, Architecture, and Planning. Brown holds a master's degree in architecture and urban design from Harvard University, where he was awarded the 2000 Harvard Druker Fellowship and traveled to Morocco. His research focused on the historical transformation of Moroccan cities under the influence of French Colonial urbanism. He was also director and co-founder of the Atlantic Yards Development WorkShop, in Brooklyn, New York; the project's purpose was to create a cooperative development model for the air rights of the MTA Atlantic Avenue Rail Yards. In partnership with New York City Councilwoman Letitia James, the WorkShop developed a community-based development plan for the 11-acre site in the heart of downtown Brooklyn that received widespread support among local community organizations.

Evan Douglis is the chairman of the department of architecture at Pratt Institute, in Brooklyn, New York. He is principal of Evan Douglis Studio, an architecture and interdisciplinary design firm committed to innovative design. Established in 1990, the firm investigates self-generative systems, membrane technology, contemporary fabrication techniques, and multimedia installations as applied to a range of diverse projects. Previously he ran the first-year studio at Columbia University School of Architecture and was the director of exhibitions.

Winka Dubbledam is an associate professor of architecture at the University of Pennsylvania. She holds an M.Arch from the Institute of Higher Professional Architectural Education, in Rotterdam, and an M.Arch and an AAD from Columbia University. She teaches advanced architectural design studios and is director of the post-professional program at the University of Pennsylvania. Dubbledam has taught at Columbia and Harvard and is principal of Archi-Tectonics, in New York. She has been a juror and lecturer at Cornell University, the Architectural Association in London, and Yale. Her monograph, *Winka Dubbeldam, Architect,* features the range of her projects.

Keller Easterling is a professor at the Yale School of Architecture, an urbanist, and writer. Her book *Enduring Innocence: Global Architecture and Its Political Masquerades* (MIT Press, 2006) researches familiar spatial products in difficult or hyperbolic political situations around the world. Easterling is also the author of *Organization Space: Landscapes, Highways, and Houses in America,* a book that applies network theory to a discussion of American infrastructure and development formats; *Call It Home,* a laser-disc history of suburbia, and *American Town Plans.* Professor Easterling has been widely published in journals such as *Grey Room, Assemblage, Praxis, Harvard Design Magazine, Perspecta, Cabinet, Metalocus, ANY,* and *JAE.* She has received Graham Foundation grants, National Endowment of the Arts fellowships, MacDowell fellowships, Whitney Humanities Center grants, a New York Foundation for the Arts fellowship, and a Design Trust for Public Space fellowship. She received a B.A. and a M.Arch from Princeton University.

Charles Eldred is an adjunct assistant professor at Columbia University and holds a B.Arch. from Cornell University and an M.Arch. from the University of California at Berkeley. He received the Eidlitz fellowship while at Cornell.

Ray Huff is a principal and partner in the firm Huff + Gooden Architects LLC. Huff teaches graduate design at the Clemson University School of Architecture, in Charleston, South Carolina, where he received his B.Arch. Huff has lectured at Yale University, Savannah College of Art and Design, and at the Tuskegee Institute and has had his work published in *Architectural Record, Southern Education Foundation Magazine,* and *Built Environment Education Quarterly.* He received the Emerging Voices award from the Architectural League of New York in 2001 and has received Merit and Honor awards from the AIA.

Jeffrey Kipnis is an architectural critic, urban designer, filmmaker, theorist, and professor of architecture at Ohio State University, where he is also curator of architecture and design at the Wexner Center for the Arts. From 1992 to 1995, Kipnis taught at the Architectural Association School of Architecture, London, where he ran the graduate design program. In 2006 he was a visiting professor at Harvard University. As a critic he has written for many different periodicals, such as *Assemblage* and *El Croquis.* As a designer Kipnis has collaborated with architects Reiser and Umemoto on projects such as the Water Garden, in Columbus, Ohio. Kipnis received a master's degree in physics from Georgia State University. In 2006 Kipnis was awarded an honorary diploma by the Architectural Association School of Architecture, London, in recognition of his contributions to the discipline of architecture as a teacher, critic, and theorist.

Keith Krumwiede is assistant dean and assistant professor at the Yale School of Architecture. Prior to teaching at Yale, Krumwiede taught at the Otis College of Art and Design, in Los Angeles, the Konstfack University College of Arts, Crafts, and Design, in Stockholm, Sweden, and at Rice University. He received a B.A. from the University of California at Berkeley and an M.Arch from the Southern California Institute of Architecture.

Ed Mitchell is an assistant professor at the Yale School of Architecture and an architect and writer. Prior to teaching at Yale he taught at Columbia University, Pratt Institute, and the Illinois Institute of Technology. His work has received awards in competitions such as the Atlanta Olympics and UCLA's "New Public Space," which work has been featured in *Alphabet City* and *A+U.* His work has also been exhibited at the Rome Academy's exhibition Architecture on the Edge. In 1999, Mitchell received a Young Architects award by the New York Architectural League. He holds a B.A. from Brown University and an M.Arch from Princeton University.

Enrique Norten is principal of TEN Arquitectos (Taller de Enrique Norten Arquitectos, SC), New York and Mexico City. He holds the Miller chair at the University of Pennsylvania. He has held the O'Neal Ford chair in architecture at the University of Texas, at Austin, the Lorch Professor of Architecture chair at the University of Michigan, and was the Elliot Noyes Visiting Design Critic at Harvard University. He was professor of architecture at the Universidad Iberoamericana, in Mexico City, and has served as a visiting professor at Cornell University, Parsons School of Design, Pratt Institute, SciArc, Rice University, and Columbia University and as a Eero Saarinen Visiting Professor at Yale. Norten has received the Mies van der Rohe Award for Latin American Architecture, a Gold Medal from the Society of American Registered Architects, the Certificate of Merit from the Municipal Arts Society of New York, and the Leonardo Da Vinci World Award of Arts by the World Cultural Council and is an honorary fellow of the American Institute of Architects, the National Creator System Grant; in 2006, TEN Arquitectos received a project citation for the design of the Guggenheim Museum in Guadalajara by the AIA NY Chapter.

Emmanuel Petit is an assistant professor at the Yale School of Architecture, where he teaches design studios and twentieth-century architectural history and theory. His work focuses on architecture's diverse epistemological models since the mid-Sixties in the intersection of architectural theory with philosophy, literary theory, and poetry. His essays on formalism, criticism, virtuality, and architectural body metaphors appeared in *Log, Thesis* (Bauhaus), *Trans* (ETH), *Perspecta* and *Constructs* (Yale), and *Thresholds* (MIT). From 1999 to 2004, he assisted Peter Eisenman in advanced-studio teaching at Princeton University and Yale. He was co-curator for Peter Eisenman's exhibition *Barefoot on White-Hot Walls* at the Museum for Applied Art, in Vienna. He holds a master's of architecture from the Swiss Federal Institute of Technology (ETH) in Zurich, and he received his Ph.D. in the history and theory of architecture at Princeton University. His dissertation, *Irony in Metaphysics's Gravity: Iconoclasm and Imagination in Architecture, 1960s to 1980s,* analyzes the role of irony in the construction of the alternative postmodernisms of Venturi, Tigerman, Isozaki, Eisenman, and Koolhaas.

Chris Sharples received his master's of architecture from Columbia University, graduating with honors for excellence in design. He was employed at Richard Meier and Partners and Aoshima Sekkei, Nagoya, Japan, where he worked as a project designer for three years prior to establishing SHoP Architects PC with his four partners in New York City. He has taught at Parsons School of Design, City College, City University of New York, the Graduate School of Architecture, Planning and Preservation Columbia University, and at the University of Virginia as Shure Professor of Architecture. In spring 2008, he will be a Louis I. Kahn Assistant Visiting Professor at Yale.

William Sharples holds a bachelor's of architectural engineering (a five-year professional degree) from Pennsylvania State University, and a master's of architecture from Columbia University (1994), where he graduated with honors for excellence in design, and was the recipient of the Lucille Smyser Lowenfish Memorial Prize and the William Kinne Fellowship for postgraduate travel and research. Prior to enrolling at Columbia University, Sharples worked as structural and project engineer for George Hyman Construction, in Bethesda, Maryland, where he was involved in the project management of a new hanger for Air Force One, The National Law Memorial, and the Washington Design Center, after which he formed SHoP Architects. Sharples has taught design studios and construction technology at the Parsons School of Design.

Billie Tsien is a painter and architect and a partner at Tod Williams/Billie Tsien Architects (TWBTA). She received her undergraduate degree in fine arts from Yale and her M.Arch. from UCLA. She has taught at the Southern California Institute of Architecture, Parsons, Yale, Harvard GSD, and the University of Texas at Austin. Tsien has served on various panels for the National Endowment for the Arts and the Percent for Art Jury for the cities of New York and Seattle; she also is on the board of the Public Art Fund, the Architectural League, and the Municipal Art Society in New York, With Tod Williams, she is the recipient of the Brunner Award from the American Academy of Arts and Letters, the Medal of Honor from the New York City AIA, and the Chrysler Award for Design Innovation. The firm's widely published projects include the Spiegel Pool House, Feinberg Hall at Princeton University, the Neurosciences Institute, in La Jolla, California, and the Whitney Museum of American Art downtown branch and the Museum of Folk Art, both in New York City.

Anthony Vidler is dean of the Irwin S. Chanin School of Architecture at the Cooper Union. He received his B.A. in architecture and fine arts, his diploma in architecture from Cambridge University, England, and his Ph.D. from Delft University of Technology, the Netherlands. Dean Vidler was a member of the Princeton University School of Architecture faculty from 1965 to 1993, during which time he served as the chairman of the Ph.D. committee and director of the program in European cultural studies. He was appointed the William R. Kenan, Jr., Chairman of Architecture in 1990. In 1993 he was professor and chairman of the department of art history at UCLA, with a joint appointment in the School of Architecture from 1997. He is a historian and critic of modern and contemporary architecture, specializing in French architecture from the Enlightenment to the present. He has received awards from the Guggenheim Foundation and the National Endowment for the Humanities; he was a Getty scholar at the Getty Center for the History of Art and the Humanities from 1992 to 1993. His

books include *The Writing on the Walls: Architectural Theory in the Late Enlightenment, Claude-Nicolas Ledoux: Architecture and Social Reform at the End of the Ancien Regime; The Architectural Uncanny: Essays in the Modern Unhomely*, and *Warped Space: Architecture and Anxiety in Modern Culture*.

IMAGE CREDITS

Every effort has been made to acknowledge
rights holders. We sincerely regret any mistakes
or omissions.

Numbers indicate page number; t = top, b = bottom,
c = center, l = left, r = right.

Esto, 107t, 107b; Develop Don't Destroy Brooklyn,
71b; Frank O. Gehry Architects, 70b; Google Maps,
70–71; Huff + Gooden Architects, 101b; David
Josef, 63t; John Jacobson 11t; Seong Kwon, 15t; 17t;
Catherine Menard, 23; Robert Mikrut, p. 101l, 101c,
103r; Milton Morris 11b; Stanley Rogouski, 107r;
SHoP Architects, 15b, 17b; Solomonoff Architecture
Studio, 61, 63b; William Struhs, 101r, 103l; United
Nations Archives, 107c.